HISTORIES AND STORIES FROM CHIAPAS

HISTORIES AND STORIES FROM CHIAPAS

BORDER IDENTITIES IN SOUTHERN MEXICO

BY R. AÍDA HERNÁNDEZ CASTILLO
Translated by Martha Pou
Foreword by Renato Rosaldo

University of Texas Press, *Austin*

Frontispiece: Monument at the Mexico-Guatemala border
Copyright © 2001 by the University of Texas Press

First edition, 2001

Requests for permission to reproduce material from this work should
be sent to Permissions, University of Texas Press, P.O. Box 7819,
Austin, TX 78713-7819.
utpress.utexas.edu/index.php/rp-form
⊗ The paper used in this book meets the minimum requirements
of ANSI/NISO Z39.48-1992 (R1997) (Permanence of Paper).

Library of Congress Cataloging-in-Publication Data

Hernández Castillo, Rosalva Aída.
Histories and stories from Chiapas : border identities in Southern
Mexico / by R. Aída Hernández Castillo ; translated by Martha Pou ;
foreword by Renato Rosaldo.— 1st ed.
        p.   cm.
Includes bibliographical references and index.
ISBN 978-0-292-73149-3

1. Mam Indians—Mexico—Ethnic identity.   2. Indians of Mexico—
Mexico—Chiapas—Ethnic identity.   I. Title.
F1465.2.M3 H47   2001
972'.7500497—dc21

00-011976

Para Alejandro y Rodrigo
Por el nuevo sentido que le han dado a mi vida

CONTENTS

FOREWORD

BY RENATO ROSALDO

R. Aída Hernández Castillo's *Histories and Stories from Chiapas* traces the historical vicissitudes of Mexican Mam identity, showing how these people have both disappeared from official view and continued to exist as a self-conscious group. In other words, her innovative study explores the dilemmas of an ethnic group whose very existence has been called into question. The Mexican Mam disappeared from view because of the changes that they underwent in language, dress, religion, and subsistence. These changes made them appear to have vanished as an indigenous minority and to have assimilated into the mestizo majority, thereby losing their collective identity. Official discourse used a rather quaint and folkloric schema to determine whether or not people belonged to an indigenous ethnic group; it made judgments as to the existence or nonexistence of indigenous groups in accord with such criteria as speaking an indigenous language, wearing distinctive costumes, practicing an indigenous or folk Catholic form of religion, and doing subsistence agriculture (preferably cultivating maize, beans, and squash) in a well-defined territory.

The Mexican Mames fell outside official definitions of the indigenous when most of them became monolingual speakers of Spanish, stopped wearing their "native" dress, became members of the National Presbyterian Church (and later became Jehovah's Witnesses), and worked for wages on coffee plantations. Each of the above changes would have seemed a sign of absorption into the national mestizo identity, a process which was regarded a one-way street and irreversible. Hernández herself once

held precisely the view that there were no Mexican Mames, as she recorded
in her field diary and in her Honors Thesis during the late 1980s. Thus
her book is at once a personal and more general theoretical reconception
of what it is to be a member of an indigenous ethnic group in Mexico.
Perhaps where the author most vividly brings home the dilemma of the
Mexican Mames is in one of her "Border Crossings," vivid biographical
portraits that deepen her analysis. A Mam man named Pedro brings home
the issues that animate Hernández's study in the following poignant and
ingenious observation about the limits of using language as a criterion for
determining indigenous ethnic identity: "I am also Mam, even if I do not
speak the language. Because, after all, what is language? I speak English,
and I am not gringo, right?"

Histories and Stories from Chiapas shows that official discourse about
what defines an Indian in Mexico has undergone major transformations
through time. The appearance and disappearance of the Mames results
from the interaction between this shifting official discourse and changes
undergone by the Mexican Mames themselves. The shifts in official discourse with regard to indigenous ethnic identity fall into roughly four
periods from 1935 to the present. First, the period of 1935–1950 was
marked by a policy of forced acculturation and the imposition of Mexican
national (mestizo) identity. The Mexican Mames remember it as the time
of "the burning of the costumes," as people were coerced to abandon their
"native" garb and dress like mestizos. Second, the period of 1950–1970 was
defined by a modernization project that included road construction and
the technological development of agriculture. For the Mames this was the
time of "purple disease" (onchocercosis), which assumed epidemic pro-
portions among Mam workers on coffee plantations. It was also the period
of the first ethnographic field trips through the region inhabited by the
Mames. Third, the period of 1970–1989 involved an ideological shift from
conceiving of Mexico as a mestizo nation to regarding it as a multicultural
nation. Fourth, the Zapatista uprising of January 1, 1994, brought a new
definition of what it meant to be Indian in Mexico, whether or not people
actively supported the EZLN.

If the Mames, to invoke Marx, make their own history, they do so under
conditions not of their own choosing. Their identity is formed and reinvented over and over in a field of power relations in which they occupy
a subordinate position. If at one phase of history the Mexican Mames become invisible as an ethnic group, at other phases they reinvent themselves through ethnic dance groups and through agro-ecological cooperative societies. The border crossings they negotiate in their lives are at times

peaceful and at times violent. These border crossings variously include being Mexican/being Guatemalan, being Indian/being mestizo, a mountain habitat/a rain forest habitat, traditional Catholicism/Liberation Theology Catholicism, Presbyterianism/Jehovah's Witnesses, subsistence agriculture/wage labor, and speaking Mam/speaking only Spanish. Both the conditions imposed by state ideologies and the self-defining actions of the Mexican Mames change through history; they are not static.

The richness and complexity of Hernández's analysis is evident in the range of material the reader is asked to integrate. *Histories and Stories from Chiapas* encompasses not only different analytical points of view but also different sources of evidence. At times the analysis assumes the perspective of official discourse; at other times it focuses on the viewpoint of the Mames. The sources of evidence include Mexican national histories, indigenous oral testimonies, documents written by previous ethnographers, and records of "indigenista" officials. The complexity of the Mam case is indicated by the period of the 1970s when they were in Las Margaritas, a settlement in the rain forest, and many became Jehovah's Witnesses. This period was marked by the reinvention of their indigenous identity through the revival of Mam dances and, from 1985, by agricultural and ecological cooperatives. Throughout the analysis Hernández reminds the reader of the impact of the shift in national policy from the ideology of a mestizo nation to that of a multicultural nation as well as the impact of policies promoted during the era of the Salinas Presidency. Thus the work succeeds in anchoring its concepts in local situations at the same time that it incorporates national and global factors.

I wholeheartedly recommend *Histories and Stories from Chiapas* to readers concerned with indigenous ethnic identity in Mexico and conceptual issues on culture and power, border theory, and the integration of the local, the national, and the global in ethnographic history. The book is vivid in its ethnography and sophisticated in its theory and method. It will prove to be a pioneering work in the study of indigenous peoples of Mexico, whether they elaborate artistic and intellectual self-definitions from urban contexts or work as wage-laborers either inside Mexico or beyond its borders. It will also provide a model for future work in ethnographic history.

PREFACE

The last part of the research that gave birth to this book took place in the midst of a political event that shook the Mexican state and brought into question a national project in which indigenous peoples were still second-class citizens.

On January 1 a group of Mayan indigenous people in the state of Chiapas, in the southeast of the Mexican republic, took up arms against *neoliberalismo*,[1] the neoliberal policies promoted by President Carlos Salinas de Gortari (1988–1994). On the day that the North American Free Trade Agreement (NAFTA) between Mexico, the United States, and Canada[2] went into effect, Chiapas's indigenous peoples showed the world the failure of the new economic model. Their reality clashed with the official version promoted by Salinismo,[3] in the sense that poverty and marginalization were over and Mexico had become a "first world country."

Organized under the name National Liberation Zapatista Army (Ejército Zapatista de Liberación Nacional, or EZLN), Tzotzil, Tzeltal, Chol, and Tojolabal indigenous peoples declared war on "the illegal dictatorship" of Carlos Salinas de Gortari and his official party (PRI). In their political discourse, Zapatistas talked about the immediate causes of their uprising, referring to the effect of neoliberal policies on the lives of thousands of indigenous peasants in Mexico and at the same time linking their struggle to the five hundred years of colonial and postcolonial indigenous resistance against racism and economic oppression.

The movement was immediately dismissed by intellectuals linked to the state, and two weeks after the beginning of the movement Arturo Warman said about the EZLN: "It is not a spontaneous movement, or a popular outbreak, but rather a carefully planned action after years of preparation. . . . Not an indigenous or peasant ancestral riot or uprising, but undoubtedly the product of a political-military strategy of the second half of our century, although it may now be outdated."[4]

This denial of the indigenous origin of the rebellion and the constant search for "authenticity" are products of an ahistoric vision of Chiapas's indigenous peoples, which does not acknowledge their organizational experiences and the hybrid character of their cultural identities. That an indigenous movement should take up arms to reject the terms of NAFTA showed the world a different face of the indigenous population of Chiapas, a face that has little to do with the folkloric and traditional image promoted in the official discourse.

Zapatista indigenous demands are closer to the global village than to the corporate community described by culturalist ethnographies. During the last twenty years, Chiapas's indigenous people have been involved in organizational processes of a political and productive character that have led to the establishment of communication and solidarity links with indigenous and peasant peoples from other regions of Mexico and beyond its national borders. These experiences have had a great influence on their cultural practices and discourses and on the specific ways in which they imagine themselves as indigenous and as Mexicans.

When the Zapatista uprising began, I was trying to understand the emergence of these new collective identities and the reinvention of cultural traditions in response to state policies and global processes among the Mam, an indigenous Maya group in Chiapas's Sierra Madre. Mam peasants, with whom I lived from 1988 to 1990 and from 1993 to mid-1995, have not directly participated in the EZLN armed movement, but they follow the struggle with great interest, and many Mam have supported its demands through so-called peaceful civil resistance. The history of indigenist policies in Chiapas helps us to understand the moment in which the Zapatista uprising broke out and the form it took.

The analysis of the relationship between Mam peasants and the Mexican state from 1934 onward shows at close range how indigenous peoples have rejected, accepted, or negotiated the official discourse on "being Mexican" and their participation in the construction of a national project. There is no single answer from indigenous peasants to state policies and Zapatista proposals. The regional history as well as religious and organizational differences have influenced the different ways of being *Indian* in

Chiapas. The voices and experiences of Mam peasants help us to problematize the view of the state as an exclusive space of domination and control and the perspectives that represent indigenous cultures as homogeneous and harmonious.

This book confronts the dichotomic visions both of those who see the Zapatistas as "manipulated" by left-wing radical groups and of those who represent *PRIista* peasants as state puppets. These Manichaean visions do not allow us to understand the complexity of Chiapas's contemporary political panorama. The search for a peaceful outcome to the conflict has to start from an acknowledgment of Chiapas's indigenous peoples as the social actors in their own history. Turning back to the past and accepting the mistakes of indigenist and developmental policies can open the way for a new relationship between the state and indigenous peoples under new terms.

When this book was being finished in 1999, five years after the beginning of the Zapatista conflict, the Mam zone as well as the rest of the state of Chiapas were completely militarized. More than sixty thousand Federal Army troops were sent there and placed in thirty large military centers. The annual military expenditure in Chiapas was reckoned at $200 million (García de León 1996:51). At the same time, both national and international organizations denounced the approximately thirty-one paramilitary groups that operated freely in various regions in the state.

Militarization and paramilitarization have upset everyday life in communities and have exacerbated the differences that already exist among social groups. The social and cultural impact that such processes may have on Chiapas's indigenous peoples in the long term is still unpredictable. Academic research has much to contribute to the construction of peace by analyzing past mistakes and placing at the center the voices that have been systematically silenced, such as those of Mesoamerican indigenous peoples. This book is an effort to describe the complexity and richness of their experiences.

ACKNOWLEDGMENTS

Finishing this book represents the conclusion of a journey that began in 1985, when I visited for the first time the southern Mexican border. It was my first fieldwork project as a student at the National School of Anthropology and History, and I knew at once that my commitment to the south of Mexico would be a long one. During this journey I have had the support and love of teachers, friends, and relatives. These pages give me the opportunity to acknowledge publicly all those who made this book possible.

My very sincere thanks to Juan Balboa Cuesta and Andrés Fábregas Puig, Chiapas men whose hearts are in the right place and who supported me during my first years in the southern lands and made my stay in Chiapas possible; to Jorge Ramón González Ponciano, who taught me to turn my eyes to the "other border"; to Carlos Saldívar, Carlos Gutiérrez, Mario Ruz, Rafael Ojira Jan, and Ronald Nigh, with whom in different periods I traveled the roads of the rain forest and the Sierra; to Mauricio Rosas, David Velasco, Arturo Lomelí, Otto Schumann, Armando Becerril, Father Jorge Aguilar Reyna, and Andrés Medina, for sharing with me their experiences working among the Mam peasants.

I also wish to extend my gratitude to my companions at Stanford University: Stefan Helmreich, Francisca James-Hernández, Bill Maurer, Heather Paxson, Helen Gremillon, Nikolai Ssorin-Chaikov, Mukund Subramanian, Suzanne Thomas, Federico Besserer, and, especially, my sister and friend Liliana Suárez-Navaz. The intensity of the academic life that we shared and our long discussions on the complexities of culture and power marked my perspectives on the southern lands.

I thank Shannan Mattiace, Jan Rus, Neil Harvey, and especially my professors, colleagues, and unconditional friends George and Jane Collier, with whom I share my love for Chiapas and who read previous drafts of the manuscript and gave me valuable suggestions. I also received thoughtful comments from Rodolfo Stavenhagen, Akhil Gupta, and Renato Rosaldo. The critical intellectual feedback of all of them helped me to improve this book.

I am grateful to my workmates at CIESAS-Sureste, Gabriela Vargas, Xochitl Leyva, Ronald Nigh, Graciela Freyermuth, Igor Ayora, Lourdes de León, John Haviland, and Witold Jacorzynski, with whom I discussed some of the ideas presented here. Sharing a space of intellectual dialogue in a politically divided academic community was a privilege for me.

Thanks to Dr. Kevin Middlebrook and Graciela Platero of the Center for U.S.-Mexican Studies of the University of California at San Diego, for granting me the space and the necessary means to write a previous version of this work; and to the Center's Research Fellows during 1996, David Myhre, Heather Williams, Steve Lewis, and Ligia Tavera, for their support and friendship and for the richness of interdisciplinary exchange.

The members of the San Cristóbal de las Casas Women's Group (COLEM), especially Lupita Cárdenas, helped me to develop my gender perspectives and gave me their friendship and support during the difficult times.

Marta Pou and my brother-in-law and true brother, Ruben Quintero, supported me in my struggle with the English language.

My "support staff," Laura del Cid, Blanca Meléndres, and Gloria Pérez, and my beautiful nieces, Samantha and Casandra Rodríguez de la Gala, helped me with transcriptions of interviews and other secretarial work.

Richard Cisneros y María Teresa Saénz allowed me to use their photographs and share the beauties of southern Mexico's borderlands. Ana Alvarez Velasco was both patient and a constant support in the printing of the photographs that illustrate this book.

The Wenner-Gren Foundation, the Mellon Foundation, the Consejo Nacional de Ciencia y Tecnología (CONACYT), and the Centro de Investigaciones y Estudios Superiores en Antropología Social (CIESAS) generously supported my fieldwork and the writing of this book.

I wish to thank as well the anonymous reviewers for the University of Texas Press for their careful comments and suggestions.

A very special thanks to my mother, Rosalva Castillo Vda. de Hernández, and to my brothers and sisters, Mario, Alma, Evelia, Efrén, Angélica, and Alina. Having such a family made a great difference in my life.

And a very special thanks to my partner, Alejandro Alvarez Bejar, and my son, Rodrigo, without whose love and encouragement I could not have finished this book.

Finally, but very specially, I wish to thank Don Eugenio Roblero, Doña Eduvina de López, Doña Cedema Morales, Don Gregorio Morales Constantino, Don Heriberto López, Don Petronilo Morales, Don Ciro Pérez, Don Leocadio Velázquez (Rest in Peace), Don Bernardino Velázquez, Don Artemio Salas, Don Andrés Morales, Don Walter Escobar, and all Mam peasant men and women who granted me their hospitality during the years I spent traveling in the Sierra and the rain forest and shared with me the memories and hopes I am presenting here. I hope that these histories will contribute to the knowledge of their reality and struggles.

HISTORIES AND STORIES FROM CHIAPAS

INTRODUCTION

In the southeastern Sierra Madre of Chiapas, an extension of the Rocky Mountains that encompasses lowlands at an altitude of about 3,600 feet and highlands at 12,000 feet, live some eight thousand peasants who identify themselves as Mam.[1] The Mam first came to the border region between Chiapas and Guatemala at the end of the nineteenth century and established scattered settlements there. In the 1960s a small group of some three hundred emigrated to the Lacandon rain forest, on the other side of the border (see Map 1).

It was in these rain forest communities, in a small *ejido*[2] on the banks of some nameless waterfalls that mark the confluence of the Santo Domingo and Jataté Rivers, that I first heard of the Mexican "Mam." Contrary to the terms "Tojolabal," "Chamula," "Zinacanteco," and other self-ascriptions used by Chiapas indigenous peoples, the term "Mam" or "Mame" was almost always accompanied by the adjective "Mexican" when used by the local people. I saw this national claim as a wish to differentiate themselves from the Guatemalan Mames,[3] who were refugees in the region. Years later, I would understand that the claim for a "Mexican Mam" identity was the result of a longer, more complex and painful history that began well before their recent encounter with Guatemalan refugees, of which this book gives an account.

I came to this region in 1986, as a member of one of many interdisciplinary teams that, associated with nongovernmental organizations (NGOs) or with the United Nations High Commissioner for Refugees

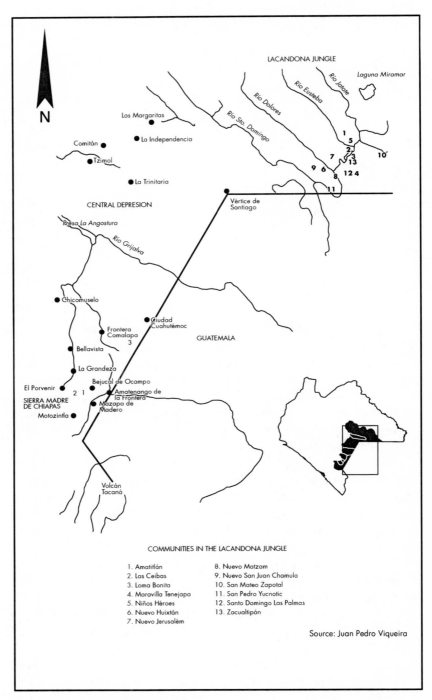

LACANDONA JUNGLE

Laguna Miramar

Río Jatate

Río Eusteba

Río Dolores

Río Sto. Domingo

Las Margaritas

La Independencia

Comitán

Tzimol

La Trinitaria

CENTRAL DEPRESION

Presa La Angostura

Río Grijalva

Vértice de
Santiago

1
5
2
3
13
7
9 6
8 12 4
11

10'

Chicomuselo

Ciudad
Cuahutémoc

Frontera
Comalapa
3

GUATEMALA

Bellavista

La Grandeza

Bejucal de Ocampo

El Porvenir
2 1

SIERRA MADRE
DE CHIAPAS

Amatenango de
la Frontera
Mazapa de
Madero

Motozintla

Volcán
Tacaná

COMMUNITIES IN THE LACANDONA JUNGLE

1. Amatitlán
2. Las Ceibas
3. Loma Bonita
4. Maravilla Tenejapa
5. Niños Héroes
6. Nuevo Huixtán
7. Nuevo Jerusalém

8. Nuevo Matzam
9. Nuevo San Juan Chamula
10. San Mateo Zapotal
11. San Pedro Yucnotic
12. Santo Domingo Las Palmas
13. Zacualtipán

Source: Juan Pedro Viqueira

Map 1. Borderland Mexico-Guatemala

(UNHCR), offered their support to the Guatemalan peasants who had been crossing the border since 1982 in an effort to flee political violence in their country. It was my interest in K'anjobal refugees that first took me to Las Ceibas,[4] one of several border ejidos that welcomed their "Guatemalan brothers." Las Ceibas was classified by the National Indigenist Institute (Instituto Nacional Indigenista [INI]) as a mestizo[5] community and attracted attention because it was the only local settlement in which most houses were made of brick and painted in pastel colors.

My training in anthropology led me to view culture conceptually as synonymous with difference. For this reason Mexican mestizos did not at first attract my attention: they were culturally invisible. My later recognition of all social practices as cultural products, however, helped me to situate my own practices as cultural and to see other elements of the mestizo communities that my previous limited conception of culture did not allow me to perceive.[6] The women in their brightly colored satin dresses and the men in their black trousers, and sometimes wearing a tie, were foreign to the rain forest landscape in which they lived but too much like any poor inhabitants of urban zones to awaken my anthropological curiosity. My initial research interest was in K'anjobal refugees, mostly bilingual, survivors of a low-intensity war, and carriers of a "millenarian culture," with whom I worked for several months for my honors thesis on cultural resistance of refugees (Hernández Castillo 1987). Their hosts, Las Ceibas peasants, considered my work with some curiosity but remained distant; over time, however, something akin to jealousy began to emerge, over what they saw as excessive attention to Guatemalan refugees.[7]

The first of these local people to approach me were attracted by my books and my tape recorder; they told me that they too had some books and some tapes with the "Word of God," and they suggested we make a temporary exchange. It was then that I started to understand the strangeness of the local people and their settlement, for it was, I discovered, a community of Jehovah's Witnesses. At the time influenced by the Marxist nationalism prevailing at the National School of Anthropology and History (Escuela Nacional de Antropología e Historia [ENAH]), I deplored the way in which "American imperialism" had managed to penetrate even this isolated place in the rain forest. This group of "cultureless people," I then believed, was once more the result of the "ethnocidal force" of Protestant "sects." This "discovery" was worth only one or two short paragraphs in my field notes, followed by some anti-imperialist thoughts. My interest remained focused on "K'anjobal resistance."

In rereading my field diary of that time and the thesis written afterward, I have come to recognize the invisibility of Mexican peasants. Refugees settled in the same ejido seemed to be resisting in the middle of the rain forest, in a cultural island where they reproduced their "millenarian knowledge." I spent hour after hour trying to reconstruct elaborate kinship charts, entangled with K'anjobal last names, made up of what I saw as first names used in a haphazard fashion, Pascual Miguel, Miguel Pascual, Francisco Marco, Marco Francisco . . . I was especially enthusiastic about the use among some elders of the ritual calendar of pre-Hispanic origin known as Tzolkin, for the "true religion of the Mayans had survived exile" (Hernández Castillo 1987:15). It was during one of these rainy afternoons, when a K'anjobal elder was repeating to me for the nth time the names of the Tzolkin months, that a Mexican peasant who was paying him a visit told me, "I am an *idiomista*[8] too. I do not know the Tzolkin, but I know stories of the *antiguos*.[9] My parents were Mexican Mam." Other ejido inhabitants confirmed with a shy smile what the old man was saying but told me that these were things "of the past." The last idiomistas were dying, and the Mam language had remained in the Sierra, from whence they had come almost ten years before. The "lost identity" of the Mexican Mam became just one of the footnotes in my honors thesis.

Two years later, in 1988, I returned to Las Ceibas, now as part of a wider project comprising five border states in which I intended to analyze "Protestant penetration" at the southern border. Most of the Guatemalan refugees had been relocated in Campeche and Quintana Roo, and the rest had left Las Ceibas to join other local camps. Free to choose my case study, I decided to return to that strange and paradisiacal place on the Jataté River.

Although I was conducting academic research, under the then head of CIESAS-Sureste, Dr. Andrés Fábregas Puig, financing institutions had a political interest in it. The project was promoted by the Cultural Program of the Borders (Programa Cultural de las Fronteras), an institution linked to the Ministry of Education (Secretaría de Educación Pública [SEP]) and concerned about the antinationalist impact Protestant sects might have on border regions. Thus I unwittingly participated indirectly in still one more effort of the Mexican state to maintain the Mexicanidad of its borders—a political preoccupation that, as I would later understand, had left a painful mark on the historic memory of indigenous people of the borderlands (Hernández Castillo 1989, 1994).

Born along La Frontera, as the northern border is usually called in Mexico, I was accustomed to seeing U.S. Marines who were stationed in San Diego walking along Ensenada streets every weekend. After getting drunk at Hussong's Cantina, the oldest business in town, the Marines would urinate in public and do everything that decorum and law did not permit in their own country. My father would proudly tell us that living an hour and a half away from La Frontera, he had been forty years without "crossing the line" into the United States and owed nothing to "the gringos." For many Mexicans along the northern border, being a nationalist almost necessarily meant being an anti-imperialist. Equally proudly, Mexican social scientists have concluded in their investigations that, contrary to what is believed in the central part of the country, we northerners are more nationalistic than other Mexicans (Bustamante 1992).

It was with this border experience that I came to study anthropology in Mexico City in 1982 and later, as an anthropologist, would migrate to the other border. The debate in the ENAH was then centered on the different possibilities for constructing "the nation." The Ethno-national Question was then one of the required courses of the bachelor's degree program (*licenciatura*) in social anthropology. The so-called Indianists defended the existence of a "Profound Mexico," composed of indigenous peoples who were descended directly from the great Mesoamerican civilizations, opposing an "Imaginary Mexico" that had no authentic identity (Bonfil 1987); Marxists talked about the need to proletarianize Indians so that they could become a real political avant-garde; *indigenistas* talked about the need to integrate them into the nation by means of acculturation (Aguirre Beltrán 1970); *campesinistas* responded by defending Mao Tse-tung; and *descampesinistas* questioned the peasant utopia.[10]

It was a hybrid mixture of northern nationalism and faith in the possibilities of a peasant utopia that colored the way I first approached southern realities. Nevertheless, my first encounters with the darkest face of Mexican nationalism, through my contact with Guatemalan refugees, made me question many of the premises concerning that imagined community we call Mexico. The history of mistreatment by immigration officers, racism, foul play by *coyotes*,[11] lack of rights in "nobody's land"—all these stories told about Mexicans crossing the northern border are not very different from the reality Guatemalan peasants face along "the other border." Even after the third generation born in Mexico, many southern border peasants are afraid of speaking their indigenous language of "Guatemalan origin," or laying claim to their family roots in the Tacaná (a Guatemalan volcano) for fear of losing their ejidal rights or being deported to the neighboring country.

Along the southern border, my northern nationalism had another connotation, for a very thin line separated my "Mexican pride" from the official discourse through which border peasants of Guatemalan origin were denied their cultural rights. Questioning my own nationalism led me to recognize in southern border voices a criticism of cultural purity and ethnic absolutism, as well as homogenizing and excluding discourses and practices.

Following in the footsteps of rain forest–colonizing Mames, I came to the Sierra Madre in 1990 and remained for several months. I returned in September 1993 and this time stayed until June 1995, living mainly in Mazapa de Madero, Motozintla de Mendoza, and El Porvenir, in the region commonly known as Mariscal. During these two years, I visited a number of Mam communities and traveled throughout the southwestern region of the Chiapas Sierra Madre (see Map 2). The Mames' land is now marked by small clusters of pines and oaks that hint at the vegetation that once covered this mountain chain, before timber companies and their slash-and-burn practices gave the landscape a new topography. It was in the middle of this deforested Sierra that I again met with Mexican Mames, seven years after my first contact.

The border became for me no longer a boundary line between two countries but rather a space of identity, a way of being. I refer to this as "la otra frontera," the other border, in a sense recovering the popular language of central and northern Mexico, which opposes La Frontera (the [Northern] Border) to La Otra Frontera (the Other Border, the southern one). But the Other Border is also a way of being and in this sense recovers the theoretical proposal of those who refer to borderlands as hybridizing social spaces, where traditions remain by changing and change by remaining (Anzaldúa 1987; Rosaldo 1989; Lowenhaupt Tsing 1993). Border experiences are of the kind that "undermine the safe ground of cultural certainty and essential identity" (Lowenhaupt Tsing 1993:225). Such border identities challenge any criterion of authenticity and cultural purity and remind us that nothing is static, that even "millenarian traditions" become "millenarian" when someone resignifies and claims them as such. Borderlands are spaces for encounter and contradiction, for multiple identity formation. Gloria Anzaldúa, a Chicana writer, describes what she defines as a struggle of borders, pointing out, "Because I am in all cultures at the same time, alma entre dos mundos, tres cuatro, me zumba la cabeza con lo contradictorio. Estoy norteada por las voces que me hablan simultáneamente" (1987:77).[12] Border identities confront not only cultural traditions but also the way "the tradition" itself is defined:

> Soy un amasamiento, I am an act of kneading, of uniting and joining that not only has produced both a creature of darkness and a

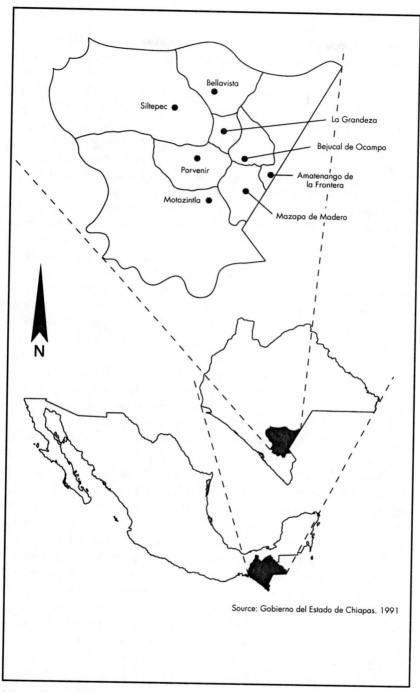

Bellavista

Siltepec

La Grandeza

Bejucal de Ocampo

Porvenir

Amatenango de
la Frontera

Motozintla

Mazapa de Madero

N

Source: Gobierno del Estado de Chiapas. 1991

Map 2. The municipalities of the Mam region in the context of Chiapas and Mexico

creature of light, but also a creature that questions the definitions of light and dark and gives them new meanings. (Anzaldúa 1987:81)

Mam peasants have crossed national borders when moving between Guatemala and Chiapas; geographic borders when moving from the Sierra to the rain forest; religious borders when converting from traditional Catholicism to the theology of liberation, from Presbyterianism to Jehovah's Witnesses; and cultural borders, by acknowledging themselves as mestizos or as Indians in different contexts. They are what Renato Rosaldo (1989:196–217) would define as "border crossers" par excellence.

"Cultural purity" hunters came to the Chiapas Sierra Madre and saw nothing but "some merchants who sold radios and cloths for urban suits." [13] The "cultural invisibility" of the Mexican Mam had left them off the official census on several occasions, and they decided to again wear colorful suits, play marimbas brought from Guatemala, name Supreme Indigenous Councils (Consejos Supremos Indígenas), and cross anew the border of Indian identity. This constant crossing of borders has not been without violence, for the crossings have often been difficult processes, always marked by power relations. This book offers different versions of these border crossings. Many of the stories compiled here refer to encounters and disencounters with the nation-state, in part because the limitations of my research forced me to focus on one of the many "dialogues" Mam peasants have established with institutions or social subjects. I do not mean to imply, however, that their lives are bound up in a constant dialogue with the state. Other conversations appear between the lines of the testimonies included here.

Chapter 1 covers the period from 1934 to 1950, the "time of the burning of the costumes," when the forced acculturation policies for the southern border region were developed. During these two decades, the state through its institutions imposed a Mexican identity, which until then had been alien to the lives of those in the Sierra. I also explore the role played by the National Presbyterian church in the reinvention of Mam identity.

Chapter 2 covers the period between 1950 and 1970, during which the so-called Mexican modernizing project took place, with road construction and land technification. In the Sierra this period is remembered as the "time of purple disease," when onchocercosis reached epidemic levels among *finca* laborers.[14] It was also during this period that the first ethnographers reached the region, and after having disappeared for a while from governmental records, the Mam "entered national history" by being included in the ethnographic hall of the National Anthropology Museum.

The third chapter addresses the experience of a segment of the Mam population that immigrated to the rain forest of Las Margaritas in the late 1970s and became Jehovah's Witnesses. I explore the emergence of new religious identities among the Mam colonizers and analyze the new antigovernment and antinationalist discourses that the converts have developed within their new religious community.

The fourth chapter encompasses the period between 1970 and 1989 from the standpoint of governmental policies toward the Mam population. This period is characterized by a change in the official discourse on "the Mexican": from Mestizo Mexico to Multicultural Mexico. In the Sierra the Indigenist Coordinator Center (CCI) Mam-Mocho-Cakchiquel was founded, establishing a new relationship between the Mames and the state. Chapter 5 covers the same historical period, but this time from the point of view of Mam peasants, starting from the specific experience of the Mam dance groups, called Danzas Mames, that emerged as linked to *indigenismo*[15] but in many ways challenged the official ideology that promoted their formation.

In Chapter 6 I explore the experience of agro-ecological cooperative societies, which have developed an alternative discourse on "Mam culture" that questions many of the premises of national indigenism concerning "the" tradition.

In Chapter 7 I analyze the Salinista economic and cultural project (1989–1994) and its impact on Mam peasants. I also explore the implications of the uprising led by the EZLN for the lives of different segments of the Mam population (1994–2000). The political options for the Mam before the armed movement that erupted in Chiapas on January 1, 1994, had been marked by the historical relations they established with the state, by their organizational experiences, by their religious ideologies, and by their regional location, among many other factors.

In the conclusion I offer some final thoughts on the "different ways of being Mam" and on the way in which the dialogues established with the state and diverse religious organizations have influenced the construction of several collective identities. Finally, I pose some questions about the future of the nation before the rebirth of political movements claiming the need for greater regional and municipal autonomy.

This history has been woven with several voices: written and oral testimonies of Mam peasants, anthropologists, indigenista officials, and local politicians. But, of course, it is my own voice that is the main thread, for it places in one space and one time people who may never have met or known of one another's existence. Don Angel Albino Corzo, secretary of education of the state of Chiapas in 1934, tells his own version of history at the same time that Don Gregorio Morales, a Mazapa de Madero peasant, relates how he lived through the educational policies promoted by Corzo. In my effort to weave together these different voices, I have selectively edited testimonies, leaving out stories of love, jealousy, political struggles, and family conflicts, which were shared with me but were not directly a part of the "dialogue" that interested me.

I focus in this book on how the nation was constructed in the southern border region and on the emergence of new collective, unachieved, changing, and contextual identities. I examine the economic integration of Mam peasants on coffee plantations, the incorporation of organic growers into the global market, and the impact of Protestantism. These "social processes" materialize in the everyday life narratives of Pedro, Don Gregorio, Doña Pina, Don Eugenio, Don Roberto, Doña Luz, and hundreds more who shared their experiences with me. My position as scholar and author privileges me to edit, trim, and paste these voices, to tell the story presented here. Of course, it would be impossible to retell all the stories I was fortunate to hear since I first came to the border in 1986. History is inescapably a reduction, a compressive reshaping into form. Nevertheless, through four interchapters that I have titled Border Crossings, I reconstruct the local history of these cultural encounters from the perspective of different settlers of the southern border region, who, despite their different social, political, and religious spaces, all define themselves as Mexicans and as Mames. These narratives help us to understand the complexity of the processes of identity construction that I describe in the following chapters.

The four Border Crossings, while intended to bring us nearer to the everyday life of social subjects, are a reminder that political and economic structures, historic processes, and social forces are finally but metaphors to organize and represent a reality of concrete lives, otherwise difficult to homogenize in the concept "Mam culture." These personal narratives are not intended to be representative of "the life of the Mames." They are the experiences of four borderlanders who either have shifted from one identity to another or claim several identities at once. Anna L. (Lowenhaupt) Tsing has analyzed the experience of the Dayak and Meratus women of Indonesia, who by linking themselves emotionally to strangers alter temporarily or definitively their cultural identity. She points out the importance, as well as the liabilities, of such personal narratives of border crossers in contrast to those "life stories" that attempt to represent a specific culture:

Even those authors who present individual narratives are more anxious about whether their informants are representative of a culture than they are about situated positionings . . . [avoiding] unusual stories and personal experience in favor of structure. Indeed, [those authors] overstate stability and homogeneity and create clear boundaries around cultural systems. (Lowenhaupt Tsing 1993:223)

The testimonies presented in the interchapters also tell us about transcultural experiences, for some of the narrators have traveled to other countries and made contact with members of political or religious organizations outside the "community." Their lives challenge any definition of "the culture" as an integral, unified, and homogeneous whole.

Mam identity, more than a "political strategy" used by Sierra peasants to resist different forms of domination, is rather a historic construction marked by power relations. Don Roberto, Pedro, Don Eugenio, and Doña Luz are not "free" individuals who have used their identities as "maximizing strategies," the way some identity approaches have stated it (Glazer and Moynihan 1975; Varese 1989), but social agents whose options have been defined by the history where chance placed them. This book intends to reconstruct part of this history.

First Border Crossing

DON ROBERTO

WORKING FOR CHANGE IN THE SIERRA

As I reconstructed the history of forced Hispanicizing campaigns that some elder Mames had told me about, I found in several testimonies references to the National Presbyterian church as one of the few places in which the Mam language could be spoken during the 1930s.[1] These testimonies, together with the Mam-language Bible that circulated in several communities in the Sierra, awakened my interest in the history of this denomination as well as its role in the lives of Mam peasants. I was advised to speak to Roberto Hernández, a schoolteacher and a governor of the Presbyterian church, who knew well the history of Presbyterianism in the region, was an idiomista, and knew many stories about the ancestors.

One October morning in 1993 I left Motozintla for the Sierra communities in search of Don Roberto. Hours later I was knocking at the metal door to a small concrete house near one of the many Presbyterian churches in the Sierra. Don Roberto was a tall man for the Sierra Mam, about sixty years old, wearing an impeccable white shirt and black polyester twill trousers. His appearance made me think of the words in some of the testimonies I recorded: "whiter children born to Mam women who went down to the fincas." It turns out that this man, with his calm speech, had already caught my attention in one of the regional meetings of the leftist Party of the Democratic Revolution (Partido de la Revolución Democrática [PRD]), at which I was present a few months before by invitation of some Motozintla friends. His age and size aroused my curiosity at the meeting, which was attended mainly by young peasants. It never crossed my mind that the "ancient governor" for whom I was looking was the same PRDist who had urged young people not to accept the 300 pesos (about US$31) that the government currently offered through its PROCAMPO program (a state subsidy for small agricultural producers), as a way to gain sympathy for the official party. On that occasion opinions were divided between those who thought that PROCAMPO money should be accepted without committing one's vote and others, like Don Roberto, who said that accepting the money was a way of selling one's dignity—"We may be poor, but we accept no bribes"—a view that won my admiration.

Don Roberto was highly respected by both Catholics and Protestants, as well as by members of different political parties, despite his membership in the leftist PRD in a region where the official—and center right—PRI was very influential and his being a Protestant in a Catholic country. He was seen as a just person, and the importance of his work as a rural teacher in several local communities was generally acknowledged. However, because of his "reputation as a womanizer" during his youth, some Catholics doubted Don Roberto's "Presbyterian rectitude," and there were rumors that he was a *chiman* (sorcerer) who on several occasions had made use of "the ancients' knowledge" to seduce a married woman. In spite of these stories, Catholics, as well as Presbyterians, acknowledged that Don Roberto was a "man of knowledge."

Don Roberto did not seem to be interested in my project of writing a regional history. Although he treated me with respect and listened carefully during my first visit with him, he remained silent and aloof. He gave me an appointment for another day and explained that I would have to spend several afternoons talking with him about the Bible, about my interest in religion, and about my family before he agreed to tell me more about the local National Presbyterian church. It was two months before he began to tell me about his life.

With time, he revealed a mistrust of my interest in Presbyterianism. He knew the governmental discourse on "Protestant sects," which bundled together Protestant denominations with new religious movements, such as the Pentecostals and Jehovah's Witnesses, and he was afraid that my research was part of some "witch-hunt" against Protestants. During one afternoon, in which he reverted to his old mistrust, we talked at length about Mexican nationalism. He told me about the special role played by Benito Juárez and Mexican Presbyterianism and how the support Juárez gave to that denomination was a significant part of his liberal policies challenging the broad authority of the Catholic church. He then took me to the church so that I could see the Mexican flag hanging from a pole at the right of the pulpit. He wanted to make it very clear that one could simultaneously be Mam, Presbyterian, and Mexican.

Don Roberto's testimony, which was videotaped several months after we first met, still expressed his will to defend the Presbyterian church as nationalistic and respectful of cultural traditions:

I was born in 1919 here in the middle of this Sierra. It was in this same house that my mother bore me. The *chuj* [steambath] you can see outside is older than me. It is the same one my mother used to heal herself after she bore me. I repaired it for the first time about ten years ago, but it is the very same that witnessed my birth.

My mother and father spoke Mam. He wore the split breeches, and she wore the wrapped cloth. They came as unmarried young people from a village right on the border called Tacaná, on the skirt of the volcano. My five siblings and I were, then, born in Mexico, and we grew up in this very Sierra.

Of the five children, I was the only one who studied. The others only learned to work the land, and Francisco, the elder, who is now dead, was a "copalero" like my father. In this Sierra there are many copal trees. My father scraped the tree and extracted the resin and then mixed this resin with *ocote* [pine pitch]. He made a mixture, and then with this mixture he made pellets. When we were children we had to make the pellets. I remember the days when we made the copal pellets to sell. It was like a game for us—this copal is still used to pray, for ritual cleansing, and to cure—then my father would go to sell it [the copal] at El Porvenir, at Motozintla. Even all the way to Huehuetenango [Guatemala] did my father walk to sell his copal. Only young Francisco followed in his footsteps as a copalero. And up to his old age, before he died, he went down to Moto [Motozintla] with his copal pellets.

But I was telling you about the time when my parents came to this Sierra. Then it was only bushes. They did not know whether they were in Guatemala or in Mexico—they were Mam and were looking for a piece of land. Then they were given their documents, which stated that they would be Mexican. But Tacanecos were always looked down on. When I was a child I was told I had better not say they had come from Tacaná—there was no reason to say it.

I grew up speaking only Mam. It was not until I went to school that I learned Spanish and not very well, all mispronounced. Then there was no school here in the village. We had to walk to the municipal capital, leaving before sunrise. There were only four grades—in the fourth grade we obtained a certificate. I still chatted in Mam with my friends, and the teacher only laughed. He came from the coast land and did not understand much. But my brother Juan had to go through the prohibition [against speaking Mam]. From the government came the order that the language should be thrown away, that it was no good any more. Teachers punished whoever spoke Tokiol, Mam.[2] They hit them with a cane and sent them out to stand in the sun. That is what my brother said to me. I did not live through it. I had already left to study in Tuxtla.

I wanted to study, to know more. Then some missionaries came to the Sierra. They were from the Reformed Church of America [Iglesia Reformada de América]. They were very good people. That Don Juan Kemper [one of the missionaries] would ask lots of questions—it was around 1930. Don Juan realized that I was clever, and he told my father he could take me to Tuxtla so that I could continue studying. My father did not really want me to—he wanted me to work the land, to go down to the finca. But life at the finca was very harsh. I wanted to learn. I wanted to be a teacher and teach children. That is why I left and went to Tuxtla, where I studied at the school near the old market. About five of us went from the Sierra. We were at a public school but were still studying the Bible. No, those missionaries did not convert us. I had been born in the Presbyterian church. My parents were converted here in the Sierra. They were among the first Presbyterians here in this colony. But back then it was different. They still killed a chicken, killed a sheep in the cave just a short way from here, to make an offering to God, like in the Old Testament—so they said.

The Gospels [were] spread a lot throughout this Sierra. We stopped celebrating the saints' festivities, but we were always patriotic, always participating in patriotic matters—March 21, the birth of Benito Juárez, September 16, Independence Day. We always celebrated them.

I got to meet Lázaro Cárdenas there in Tuxtla. "Tata Lázaro,"[3] as we used to call him, was the best president of Mexico—he did care about poor people. At that time you could talk to presidents, not like nowadays when you can wait for days on end in Mexico City, and if you are not somebody important, well, you are not received. Then I was able to greet him. I shook his hand and told him about the problems in the Sierra—that Grajales, who was then governor, was with the rich. He listened to me; many people came near.

I was already keen to do something for the Sierra. I had learned. I knew that the way they lived in fincas was not fair, not fair the way we were in the mountain with no water, no electricity, like wild animals. I wanted my children to live better.

Then I looked for a wife in Tuxtla. I no longer wanted a wife from the Sierra. I wanted a town person who could read. I had already been with a woman and had had a girlfriend there at La Grandeza, but I was not happy. I wanted a town woman, so I went to find María. I brought her here to the Sierra. She was also Presbyterian. I met her at the church, there in Tuxtla. So she was able to educate my children in the Gospel. She was afraid to come to the Sierra—she thought she would not get used to it. It was difficult at first. She did not know how to grind her corn or carry water—but eventually she learned, and she has been a good wife.

I always knew I would come back. That is why I had studied, to teach Sierra people. In 1938 I obtained my appointment as a teacher. Back then you did not have to study much to become a teacher, not like today. First I was sent to Valle Obregón, then to a colony in La Grandeza. I was also in Bejucal. I got to know the whole Sierra. It was not until 1968 that I retired. I would teach in Spanish but did not scold those who spoke the language. I did not think it was good to lose it [the Mam language]—it was our root; it should not be forgotten. I taught my children Mam. It was difficult because María speaks only Spanish, but they did learn a bit. To Juan, the eldest, it has been quite useful, for that is how he got his appointment as a bilingual teacher.

At church the [Mam] language is also spoken, and from Guatemala they brought a Bible in Mam, because, over there, there are only idiomistas. The pastor would tell us we should not forget our custom, our tradition, what was our history. But you can see that the young ones gradually forget.

. . . Look, I have always been in the opposition. Since Cárdenas died we have not had a good government—all corruption, and those of the PRI [have been] just robbing the people. That is the way it has been for years—that is the way I have seen it, and I am an old man. Since I was in Tuxtla, I was eager to know other organizations. Then, I began to read *El Machete* [a journal of the Communist Party], which talked about how we the poor should get organized. Then I brought it here to the Sierra. I was the one who spread *El Machete* throughout the Sierra. Then I was told that Communists did not believe in God and did not like religions, that they would close our temples, like in Grajales's times. Then I stopped and did not distribute *El Machete* any longer.

. . . But I have always been doing my bit to make things change in the Sierra. When I was a governing elder of the Presbyterian church, I talked a lot with the people to make them understand they should no longer accept being treated like animals. And now as an old man, I have joined the PRD, and here we are trying again. Little by little we are achieving something, and now with Civil Resistance more people are understanding that things can be changed—little by little, little by little . . .

Chapter 1

THE POSTREVOLUTIONARY NATIONAL PROJECT AND THE MEXICANIZATION OF THE MAM PEOPLE

While sitting in front of a fireplace and chatting with a group of peasant colonizers of Las Margaritas rain forest, I was told for the first time by an elder Mam about the "Law of Government," which had forbidden them their language and burned their costumes. Over there, by the rivers Santo Domingo and Jataté, where the Sierra Madre seems so far away and the history of the Mexican Revolution remains only a story told by the elders, the past weighs heavily on some. Resentment colored Don Manuel's chronicle about the time when "language was kept locked and time took us to oblivion."

I found this history of violence and prohibition told all along the Sierra Madre. Whenever an elder Mam described the past, it was divided into two broad periods: before and after the Law of Government. Some, having a better memory and knowledge of dates, placed this milestone during the 1930s, and a name was sometimes remembered—Colonel Victorico Grajales. Because the Mam peasants themselves acknowledged this historical milestone, I take as the starting point of this book the year 1933.

Oral history as well as regional historiography point to the 1930s as the time when revolutionary reforms reached Chiapas. The 1910 Mexican Revolution, considered by many historians a turning point that marked the beginning of modern Mexico, did not have an impact on Chiapas's economic and social life until years later.[1] The social upheavals that shook Chiapas between 1910 and 1920 were part of a shift in the balance of forces among groups in power. After a few years of struggle, the conservative sectors, known as Mapachistas, finally allied themselves with the revolutionary president Venustiano Carranza. The historian Thomas Benjamin describes the role of indigenous and peasant groups in this struggle: "They were flung into a storm of destruction and suffering. They fought on both sides. Many abandoned their master and rejected their debts, refused to pay rent, invaded lands, and even some of them overthrew local powers. Still, this was not their struggle, they had not rebelled" (1995:165).

The saying "the Revolution did not reach Chiapas" had become a commonplace, for the conservative forces organized in the Mapachista movement bargained their loyalty with the federation in exchange for economic privileges (García de León 1985; Benjamin 1990). By the beginning of the 1930s about sixteen families still controlled the state economy, monopolizing 75 percent of all arable land (Waibel 1946). Those governors who tried to achieve some reforms, such as Carlos A. Vidal (1925–1927) and Reymundo Enríquez (1928–1932), were not able to promote comprehensive land reform, and their support for workers' organizations favored the co-optation of unions and independent organizations that were beginning to form (Spenser 1988).

The state government of Victorico Grajales (1932–1936) is remembered for its "modernizing" impulse, but this impulse did not include agrarian reform, and at the cultural level it represented the total denial of indigenous traditions, which were considered contrary to national integration and modernization. The son of finqueros from Chiapa de Corzo, Grajales had a contradictory discourse that simultaneously promoted "socialist education" and protected the interests of the large plantation owners and of the cattle breeders. During his administration, cattle breeders of the Central Depression, the lowlands of central Chiapas, became municipal presidents and deputies.

Wanting to understand and contextualize the frequently mentioned Law of Government and Grajales's contradictory policies, I rummaged through the municipal archives of Siltepec, Mazapa de Madero, and El Porvenir and traveled to the state capital in search of contemporary documents that could give an account of his integrationist zeal. Relying on bits of government reports, town hall acts, official diaries, newspaper reports, and recollections of old people, I attempted to reconstruct the encounter of Mam peasants with the postrevolutionary state and, through it, with the Mexican nation. By compiling the testimony of Mam peasants with respect to that historical period, I aimed to approach regional history from the bottom, from the everyday lives of Sierra inhabitants. I am not interested in finding through oral history a "faithful representation of reality" but the way in which contemporary Mames imagine their past.

The scarce historiography on the region tends to represent Sierra inhabitants as mere objects of economic and social forces (Medina 1973; Velasco 1979; Paniagua and Toledo 1989), as a background for political power struggles among the ruling class (Benjamin 1990, 1995), or, at best, as an amorphous mass called "the peasantry," which in certain historical moments becomes the political avant-garde of progressive movements (García de León 1985; Spenser 1988). The methodological challenge is twofold: to recognize in Mam people social subjects who have taken an active part in the construction of their own history and to recognize the existence of social processes that determine and limit their actions.

Writing a regional history from the perspective of the subordinate classes does not necessarily entail disregarding government sources, for as Indian historiography has demonstrated, counterinsurgency literature often says much about the consciousness of subordinate groups (Guha 1988). Ranajit Guha's proposal is to reread such documents searching for elements that can help us to understand the experiences of those groups. In the specific case of peasant rebellions, the consciousness of the rebel may be revealed in the counterinsurgent discourse:

> It is, of course, true that the reports, dispatches, minutes, judgments, laws, letters, etc., in which policemen, soldiers, bureaucrats, landlords, usurers and other hostiles to insurgency register their sentiments, amount to a representation of their will. But these documents do not get their content from that will alone, for the latter is predicated to another will—that of the insurgent. It should be possible therefore to read the presence of a rebel consciousness as a necessary and pervasive element within that body of evidence. (Guha 1988:13)

The specific documents analyzed here refer to a rather recent history, and I was able to compare them to the oral history that I recorded among Sierra inhabitants; the historical imagination of these Mam peasants, together with my own, wishes to account for the way in which the encounter with the Mexican nation has been lived on the southern border of Chiapas. Thus, although following the chronological order of official historiography, I integrate new voices in a broader narrative about the regional history of the Sierra Madre of Chiapas.

Forced Integration into the Nation

The Law of Government to which Mam testimonies refer was not actually one law but a series of dispositions taken by the administration of Grajales, to "civilize Chiapas Indians" and integrate them into the new postrevolutionary nation. Although this integrationist project had begun at the national level in the 1920s, in Chiapas it took on particular strength in 1933.

The ideological and political project of the federal government after the 1910 revolution had, among its priorities, the consolidation of a Mexican national identity (Gamio 1917). Cultural and economic policies enforced for that purpose had direct consequences for the lives of indigenous peoples in general and of the inhabitants of the Chiapas southern border in a very specific manner.

In 1917 Manuel Gamio, considered the father of Mexican indigenismo, called in his book, *Forjando patria*, for a cultural homogenization of the country in order to construct a modern nation. Indigenous cultures were seen by Gamio as aberrations of pre-Hispanic cultures, which, if not integrated into the national hybrid mestizo culture, were condemned to isolation and extreme poverty. This perspective guided the efforts of the Office of Anthropology and Regional Population of the Republic (Dirección de Antropología y Poblaciones Regionales de la República, a direct predecessor of the INI), created in 1917 and headed by Gamio. This institution had among its goals the "preparation for racial fusion, for cultural integration, linguistic unification, and the economic balance of indigenous populations," stating that this was "the only way in which they [the Mexican people] would form a coherent and well-defined nationality and a real fatherland" (INI [1918] 1978:26). In 1921 the Ministry of Education was established, responding to the need for a policy of integration that would promote "national values" and achieve linguistic homogenization throughout the country. The "national project" promoted by the revolution eventually reached Chiapas, almost two decades late, and was characterized by limited land distribution and by campaigns for the "Mexicanization" and "integration" of the indigenous population.

In December 1932 the governorship of Chiapas was assumed by Grajales, who had supported Carranza's forces. From that time forward, two characters are dominant in the memory of Mam peasants: Col. Victorico Grajales (1932–1936), with his unconditional support for large landowners and his campaigns of forced acculturation, and the president of Mexico, Gen. Lázaro Cárdenas (1934–1940), with his peasant populism.

In contrast to Grajales, Lázaro Cárdenas del Río was of humble origins and was elected president after a political and military career that began when he joined the revolutionary forces as a teenager. His government was characterized by the development of "mass politics" that supported the organization of popular sectors allied with the governing party.[2] Cárdenas's personality, described in several accounts by Mam peasants, helped his government to earn widespread popular support.[3] He toured the country, reaching the most isolated communities and establishing a direct relationship with the people, workers and peasants alike. Those who have analyzed the impact of Cardenism in the consolidation of the postrevolutionary state describe this "mass politics":

> Cárdenas went in search of the masses and established a strong link with them. This electoral tour as well as his later tours during his government were seen as a way to be personally acquainted with the living conditions and the needs of the people, to study the problems of each region and the way to solve them. During his tours, he patiently listened for hours to workers and peasants, to small landowners, and so on, who told him about their problems and complaints. "They have so many needs," Cárdenas used to say, "they lack so many things, that the least I can do is to listen patiently." . . . The aim of these tours was also to "educate the people in order to obtain their cooperation," . . . although some think that what Cárdenas did was to check personally that his orders were being carried out, and even to control local authorities. (Anguiano 1975:47)

Such attitudes toward the popular sectors, together with the concessions Cárdenas started to grant to indigenous peoples in the agrarian and labor areas, clashed with the vision of Chiapas's governor, Grajales, on *indios* and threatened his economic project that privileged finqueros and cattle breeders. The tension between the state and the federal government is reflected in the economic as well as the political discourse.

These simultaneous discourses challenge the idea of the state as a monolithic space and highlight the contradictions between the states and the federal government. In fact, because of the contradictory political attitudes and policies Sierra peasants had to face during that period, they commonly recall Grajales's government and Cárdenas's presidency as widely separated in time:

> During the government of Colonel Grajales, things were tough, we thought that things would change after the Carrancistas won, but not at all, it even got worse. Grajales sent us the Law of Govern-

ment, which forbade us the Mam language and defended plantation owners, finqueros. . . . [M]any peasants died at that time. As years went by, something changed a little bit; it was later, when Tata Lázaro came, when they really began to treat us as people.[4]

Although Grajales and Cárdenas disagreed in their perspectives on the so-called indigenous problem, both shared the certainty that indigenous peasants had to be integrated into Mexican national identity. For Cárdenas, indigenous people were, above all, agrarian proletarians who had to become productive citizens of the nation: "The program of Indian emancipation is in essence that of proletarian emancipation in any country, but we must not forget the special conditions of their climate, their background and their real needs" (Cárdenas 1940). As for Grajales's government program, on the one hand, it reproduced the postrevolutionary populist discourse, claiming to fight against "religious fanaticism" and for socialist education and the rights of proletarians, while, on the other, it prompted land and tax policies that favored the local oligarchy. It was the discourse and practice of a new Chiapas political class, born from a counterrevolutionary revolution.

One of Grajales's "religious defanaticization" campaigns, Decree 132, pronounced the abolition of the names of saints in the villages and municipalities of Chiapas. In the Mam area, the municipalities of San Martín Mazapa, San Isidro Siltepec, San Francisco Motozintla, and San Pedro Remate became Mazapa de Madero, Siltepec, Motozintla de Mendoza, and Bella Vista (*Periódico Oficial del Estado*, February 28, 1934:2). This campaign went to such extremes as closing churches, expelling from the state all Catholic priests, and burning religious images in several towns. In the Mam region, both Catholic and Presbyterian churches were temporarily closed, but residents decided to open them a few days later (Mazapa de Madero Town Hall Acts, October 13, 1934).

Socialist education was declared official throughout Chiapas. The state education reform policy stated, "As for the philosophy held by schools, it will be: (a) socialist, (b) against religion. As for its form, it will be: (a) of action based on work, (b) self-educational, (c) coeducational, (d) affirmative" (Grajales 1934:46). Paradoxically, these reforms were accompanied by a land policy quite contrary to the "socialist ideology" that permeated Grajales's political speeches.

In the first year of his government Grajales released landowners from paying taxes and proposed to Congress a new system of measuring land values to be used for tax purposes, as the crisis had undermined the value of land (Grajales 1933:30). At the same time, "socialist education" promoted the forced incorporation of "Indians to the national culture," establishing ten Hispanicizing centers and forbidding the use of indigenous languages in public schools. This campaign affected the indigenous population of the whole state but was particularly harsh in the border regions, where the "Mexicanization" policy fulfilled the political function of establishing the nation's limits. Indigenous languages spoken by the border inhabitants of Chiapas, such as Chuj, K'anjobal, Jacalteco, Cakchiquel, and Mam, were considered to be of Guatemalan origin, and, in contrast to Tzotzil, Tzeltal, or Tojolabal, which were spoken in the highlands and in the rain forest, to represent not only cultural backwardness but also antinationalism. In the border zone of the Sierra, Hispanicizing campaigns had strong anti-Guatemalan connotations:

> There was a government that agreed with the teachers to forbid children to speak the Mam language, Tokiol. When children were talking their language, teachers got up and punished them, and told them not to speak that language, because if they continued, they would send them to Guatemala. That was the reason for the end, and up to this day, little Tokiol is spoken.[5]

> Things started to change because of the Law of Government, even I lived through it, when it changed to Castilian [Spanish], whoever spoke the language, beware, he was thrown into jail. In that time the government officials told us, "Why are you speaking this, if you are not Guatemalan, you are Mexican."[6]

Yet in some communities integrationist policies were rejected by the people, who continued to transmit knowledge of Mam to their children at home and refused to send them to school.

> My grandparents spoke the language [Mam]; they came from Guatemala, from a place called Tacaná. In the course of time, Mam language remained in this country. People of that time did not like their children to go to school; instead of sending them, they said, let the books remain there, and sent them to shepherd or hid them. I used to run away to prevent those books entering my head. At school, they wanted us to throw the language away, but we did not go to school and kept speaking the language at home.[7]

To reinforce the integrationist policies, the Department of Social Action, Culture, and Indigenous Protection (Departamento de Acción Social, Cultura y Protección Indígena) was created in Chiapas on April 18, 1934. The decree establishing the department offers this justification:

... The largest social problem which overwhelms and arrests the economic evolution of the state of Chiapas is the existence of great masses of indigenous people, which, amounting to 38 percent of our population, are a weight for the collective progress and the greatest obstacle against the coordination of all sectors of social life, which aims at the achievement of the constructive program of the Revolution. (*Periódico Oficial del Estado*, April 18, 1934:3)

Three weeks later, a circular was sent to the Siltepec municipal president's office, announcing that the new department would start operating in the Sierra region as part of "the program of revolutionary promotion of the state's present Government and will aim its action at tackling openly the great social problems of the state, mainly those relating to the incorporation of Indians to civilization" (Municipal Archives of Siltepec, May 7, 1934).

On October 3, 1934, the Central Committee for Clothing the Indigenous Student (Comité Central pro-Vestido del Alumno Indígena) was created within the Department of Social Action, Culture, and Indigenous Protection. The committee worked intensely among the Sierra Mam, replacing the traditional costumes with "civilized clothing." Governor Grajales stated in a letter to the municipal president of Siltepec, dated January 26, 1935:

The Committee for Clothing the Indigenous Student has been constituted in order to accomplish the noble task of modifying the primitive costume worn by our indigenous races, starting this campaign with the children of our schools, who are easier to alter in their habits. . . . On November 20, the day of our Revolution, we carried out the first distribution of clothes to indigenous boys and girls with the greatest success, for, contrary to the resistance against the modification of this habit that we expected, all came willingly to change their clothes, destroying the old ones. This has encouraged us to proceed with our campaign and we are preparing another distribution of 5,000 sets of clothing for the next month of April, which can arouse greater interest among Indians and facilitate the task of civilizing them through clothing. (Municipal Archives of Siltepec, January 26, 1935)

The testimonies of the older generation of Mames, however, point out that this campaign to "civilize through clothing" was not always as peaceful as indicated in Governor Grajales's letter.

Mam men. Since 1934, when the "civilize through clothing" campaigns were carried out, Mam clothing of the colonial period has not been worn in the Sierra Madre. PHOTO BY RICHARD CISNEROS LÓPEZ.

I remember when the law came that forbade the costumes; they collected women's *cortes* [traditional skirts] and the *calzones rajados* [split breeches] of men and burned them in the center of the town square. An elder refused. He did not want to take off his costume. Then the policeman came and poured oil over him. We were all on the square. I was still a child, and he told him, "Either you take it off or I throw you into the fire, you are a hard-headed Indian." The poor old man took off his calzón rajado, crying.[8]

The peasant men and women of the Sierra did not freely choose to become part of an imagined community called "Mexico." Neither did they choose to abandon their traditional clothing and language or cease to define themselves, at least in public, as Mam indigenous peoples.[9]

Mam Women and the Myth of *Mestizaje*

The experience of Mam women during this period was marked by the profound gender and race content of the nationalistic discourse. The myth of the mestizo as the core of Mexican identity had specific consequences for the daily lives of Mam women. Indigenous women suffered in a special way the consequences of the "campaigns to civilize through clothing," for they became spaces of struggle for identity on the part of Indian and mestizo men:

> When the Law of Government came, I forbade my wife to take off her corte. I did not want her to be taken for a *ladina* [non-Indian woman], offering herself around to men. But the government men came and threatened to set fire to women if they did not throw away their cortes.[10]

Even women's clothes were taken away, or were set on fire; it was the law of government. As one informant said, "From the government came the law of taking away women's clothing, because before that it was only the corte, throw away that corte, burn it. And besides do not dare speak in that language, throw that away too, now only Castilian." [11] The way in which women's bodies became a space of expression for national or ethnic identity has been analyzed by various studies exploring the close link between nationalism and sexuality (Parker et al. 1992; Nelson 1995).

During this period, the mestizo, symbol of the cultural and biological merging of Spanish and indigenous peoples, or *mestizaje*, still colored the national discourse on "the Mexican." In this sense, indigenous women's bodies were literally conceived as the epicenter of the nation, from which would emerge the Mestizo, who would form the cosmic race described by José Vasconcelos ([1925] 1992).

Vasconcelos, who participated in the creation of the Ministry of Education and served as minister from 1921 to 1924, played an important role in the so-called mestizophilia that marked nationalist postrevolutionary ideology (Basave 1992). He institutionalized the discourse on the existence of a mestizo nationality and wrote about mestizaje as a worldwide tendency to form a new superior race:

> The different races of the world tend to mix more and more, until they form a new human type, composed by the selection of each of the existing peoples. . . . [A] fifth universal race will be formed, stemming from the preceding races and improving on all the past. (Vasconcelos [1925] 1992:103)

Although Vasconcelos's biological perspective, in which the mestizo was the result of the genetic merging of the "two races," was being replaced by a social perspective in which the mestizo was seen as a cultural merging (Gamio [1935] 1987), biology still seeped through the reproductive discourse of postrevolutionary nationalism. An article written in 1934 by

Mam woman in the municipality of El Porvenir. Indigenous women have played an important symbolic role in the reproduction of the nation through the ideology of mestizaje. PHOTO BY RICHARD CISNEROS LÓPEZ.

Angel M. Corzo, general director of public education during Grajales's administration, points out:

> In almost every indigenous race of this country and probably in the Americas, there is a custom which is like an inviolable law: that which does not allow their women to procreate with ladino or white men; any woman breaking this law will not only be expelled from the tribe, but sometimes even killed. We know this fact; we know also that the only way to achieve a slow but firm progress of our race and the construction of a nation is mestizaje; yet, we have done nothing to alter this custom which thwarts a large part of our civilizing activity. (*La Vanguardia* [Tuxtla Gutiérrez], March 4, 1934)

Taken to extremes, this perspective might be interpreted as saying that, for the construction of the new nation, indigenous women should willingly serve in procreating "the Mexican mestizo." As Andrew Parker (Parker et al. 1992:7) points out, "Where the heterosexual family played such a central role in the nation's public imaginings motherhood could be viewed as a national service." Paraphrasing him, we might say that when interethnic mixing plays such a central role in the national public imaginings, giving birth to a mestizo could be viewed as a national service.

Whereas in other contexts racism has been characterized by its segregationist impulse, in some Latin American nations where mestizo identity has been the crux of nationalist ideologies, the discourse on the need for "racial interbreeding" has deeply racist connotations. The political implications this discourse can have for indigenous women are apparent in a Guatemalan landowner's comment in an interview with Martha Casaús:

> The only solution for Guatemala is to improve the race, to bring stallions to improve it. I had in my lands for many years a German manager, and for each Indian he impregnated I gave him fifty extra dollars. (Casaús Arzú 1992:279)

In the case of indigenous women laborers in Soconusco, this "national service" was usually not voluntary. "The civilizing action through interbreeding" was assumed by many overseers and landowners on coffee plantations, where women who came to harvest coffee with their husbands were considered property. Testimonies of elder Mam women tell of the young women's fear of the landowner and his employees.

> We women also worked as hard as the men, but on top of that, we had to make tortillas; we got up at three o'clock in the morning and we sat down when the sun was set. Life in the finca was hard, but the harshest was when the owner or the overseer took a fancy to a young girl; then it had to be endured and she did what they said. In the farms many children started to be born a lot whiter. . . . [M]any of those children no longer learned Tokiol.[12]

This custom was also followed by recruiters and minor employees in the plantations. Resistance usually brought a violent response, as described by Erasto Urbina, head of the Department for Indigenous Protection, which was created in 1937, in a report on working conditions among Soconusco laborers:

> Proceeding with our task of observing all the procedures followed in the supervision of our Indians at the plantations, . . . we managed to catch up with them at a spot called San Nicolás, where they then stopped to partake their first meal of the day; and when we inquired from some of them why their clothes were stained with blood, they answered that they were beaten by their truck drivers, for having prevented these men from consummating a disgusting act with their

women after noticing that one of them had a face wound caused by a machete blow inflicted by the driver Jesús M. Cordero, who was transporting them on behalf of the *habilitador* [labor contractor] Silviano J. Ruíz to the plantation La Granja. (Urbina 1944:15; cited in Spenser 1988:268)

Still, mestizaje was not always the result of violence. Contrary to what happened on plantations in Guatemala, where the oligarchy was endogamous and intermarriage with the indigenous population almost nonexistent (Casaús Arzú 1992), among Soconusco landowners there were several mixed marriages, although always between European, American, or mestizo men and indigenous women. More research is needed on the role played by these women in the new domestic unit and the implications these marriages had for the shaping of a regional mestizo identity. There is a popular saying that "the child of Indian women with a finquero is a *tapachulteco*," referring to the inhabitants of Tapachula, the largest mestizo town near the coffee-producing region. Yet, because of the racism prevailing among much of the bourgeoisie and middle class of Tapachula, these roots are seldom acknowledged. On this point, a landowner's wife told me:

My mother-in-law was a pure Mam Indian; she used the cloth and spoke the dialect, and she married my father-in-law. He was a very simple person, had come from Corsica at the beginning of the century and bought the plantation. She came down from La Grandeza with her brothers to harvest coffee, but he met her and took her. Then they married and had four children. This happened among many landowners, but they do not tell it because they are ashamed to acknowledge their Indian blood.[13]

This common event has been little studied but constitutes an important part of the historical shaping of the southern border region. Mam women, those who stayed in the plantations as well as those who returned year after year to their communities, lived the encounter with the nation in a violent manner.

Federal and Local Indigenismos

The fissures in the power structure, resulting mostly from internal struggles between federal and state governments, allowed Mam peasants to seize new spaces to confront Grajales's antipeasant policies. As soon as Cárdenas assumed the presidency in 1934, he began to receive complaints from unions and peasant organizations in Chiapas that Governor Grajales "saw unions as a threat to the stability of his government and from the beginning set up obstacles to their development" (Liga Central de Comunidades Agrarias del Estado de Chiapas to Cárdenas, December 11, 1934, Archivo General de la Nación). In response, Cárdenas remonstrated with Grajales several times and finally sent arms to rural communities to help them form "social defense guards" for protection from the "white guards" created by landowners with the support of the state government (Benjamin 1995:214; field data).

At about the same time, with the support of the federal government, the Indigenous Workers Union (Sindicato de Trabajadores Indígenas [STI]) was formed in December 1936, with a membership of approximately twenty-five thousand. The STI was to oversee contracts, minimum wages, and transportation of workers. Although it has been described by certain researchers as a strategy to control salaried work and make sure landowners would have enough workers for the coffee harvest (see García de León 1985), this union was an important symbol for Sierra peasants, who heard for the first time about their rights as workers:

> When the Workers' Union of Soconusco was formed, we were able to claim our rights. Then the owners could not treat us in the same way and we knew we could complain. President Cárdenas himself gave the order; he ordered that all rural and town workers should be organized. Lázaro Cárdenas's government, he was really a good president, he was really the great president who fought a lot for the people, for the benefit of the Mexican nation.[14]

Yet Cárdenas's preoccupation with workers' rights came with an integrationist policy that still considered it necessary to integrate Indians into the "progressive" national culture.

At the state level, although "forced integration" measures took on a particular impetus during Grajales's administration, succeeding governors shared his point of view: the economic backwardness of the state was closely linked to the existence of indigenous cultures. Even measures that were intended to "protect" Indians were based on the concept of indigenous peoples as childlike. During Amador Coutiño's temporary government (1936), the Court Law for the Underage and the Disabled (Ley de Tribunales para Menores e Incapacitados) was published, which stated in part:

> That there are in all states of the Republic, especially in ours, a group, unfortunately rather large, which breaks the law due, not exactly to unhealthy atavisms, or degenerations of a pathological

nature, but simply driven by their absolute lack of perfect knowledge of their life situation and especially due to the conditions of mental retardation in which they develop, to such an extent that actions that would seem monstrous to a civilized man, are absolutely normal to them, and by this absolutely unimportant; that is to say, that while committing real crimes, they do not achieve, because of their coarseness, their mental feebleness and other circumstances, a whole understanding of the unlawfulness of the deed; among such groups must be considered the large conglomerates, almost the whole mass of the Indians of our state, who have ancient theogonic preoccupations, fanaticisms stemming from times prior to the conquest. . . . These individuals in certain circumstances must be protected by similar tutelary laws, for before penology, they must be considered as under age or disabled. (*Periódico Oficial del Estado,* October 24, 1936:1)

Although the main objective of these tutelary laws was to consider indigenous people's "ignorance" as an extenuating circumstance when judging an offense, they were actually never applied, and most frequently the fact of being indigenous was enough reason to be imprisoned without trial for months on end (field data). The Court Law for the Underage and the Disabled was above all a political measure to acknowledge constitutionally the "Indian's inferiority."

Under Governor Efraín Gutiérrez (1937–1940), the indigenist discourse in Chiapas underwent several significant changes, and in agrarian matters there were some responses to land demands from the incipient peasant movement. An agronomist by profession, Gutiérrez had worked for the National Agrarian Commission (Comisión Nacional Agraria) in Michoacán from 1928 to 1932, when Cárdenas was the state governor, during which time he became very close to the future president. When Cárdenas came to power, he named Gutiérrez general secretary to the Agrarian Department, which exerted a great influence on Gutiérrez's perspectives on the indigenous and peasant question.

Efraín Gutiérrez took office as Chiapas's governor in 1937 with the open support of Cárdenas, in an atmosphere of intrigue and discontent among the more conservative sectors of Chiapas's oligarchy. Grajales's allies failed in their attempts to murder his successor, and Grajales was deposed as governor before his term was over, for he had refused to turn over the government to Cárdenas's candidate.

From his first day as governor, Gutiérrez decided to make his program of government as different as possible from that which had been promoted by Victorico Grajales. Indeed, in his first public account, Gutiérrez made obvious his disagreement with Grajales in relation to the indigenous population as "a weight for collective progress":

> The government I am heading reiterates . . . that the concept that Indians are a negative factor for our country's progress is false and deceitful. On the contrary, it is a beautiful vital force that must be fostered with great care, with love and sincerity, destroying from its root the whole system that since colonial times has been depriving them for the benefit of a handful of opportunists. (Gutiérrez 1938:18)

To signal the new turn in indigenist policy, in 1937 Gutiérrez replaced the old Department for Social Action, Culture, and Indigenous Protection with the Department for Rural Education and Indigenous Incorporation (Departamento de Educación Rural e Incorporación Indígena). He replaced many of its employees and named as director of this new institution Erasto Urbina, a staunch defender of the rights of Soconusco laborers. At the same time, he created the first state-supported institution for anthropological research, the Office for Indigenous Culture (Dirección de Cultura Indígena), to carry out "studies in research on our different races, their habits, ways of life, evolutionary social state, and so on" (Gutiérrez 1937:n.p.).

Nevertheless, in the Sierra region there were no substantial changes in cultural policies during this period, and Mazapa de Madero's town hall acts contain accounts of the Hispanicizing campaigns that rural teachers still carried out among the Mam population (Mazapa de Madero Town Hall Acts, November 2, 1938).

The most significant changes during the Gutiérrez administration were in agrarian matters, achieving the largest ejido land distribution since the victory of the revolution. The ejido altered the relationship between Mam peasants and the state and gave a new structure to their community, thus marking a new stage in the region's history.

From the Finca to the Ejido: Economic Integration

It was under Governor Efraín Gutiérrez that Sierra Madre peasants came in contact with Cárdenas's populism and grew conscious of their rights as citizens. Demands for lands and improved working conditions were attended to for the first time by state representatives. To understand the importance of both demands for Sierra inhabitants, we must consider the way in which plantation work had marked their lives.

During the twentieth century, the life of Mam peasants was closely linked to the coffee-growing economy. We might say that their economic integration into the nation preceded their political integration. Mam laborers were contributing to Mexican agroexports well before being clearly conscious of their identity as Mexicans.

> My grandfather used to tell that when he came down to the finca he met many workers who spoke Mam and came from Guatemala, but at that time one could not see a difference, one did not say you are Guatemalan and you are Mexican, one only said you are Mam, that is what they said.[15]

Thus coffee plantations, more than the corporate community, were for many decades the primary space of social reproduction for the indigenous peoples of the Sierra Madre (Hernández Castillo 1994).

Although, according to historical documents, coffee was first cultivated in Chiapas in 1846 by an Italian landowner named Manchinelly (Waibel 1946:168), it was only by the end of the twentieth century that it became the main crop of the Chiapas coastal region and the backbone of the regional economy. The signing of the Boundary Treaties (Tratados de Límites) in 1882 and 1894 between Mexico and Guatemala put an end to the insecurity of property titles in the border region, thus intensifying foreign investment in the coastal zone, known as Soconusco, and the Mariscal District valleys. The historical link between the Sierra and Soconusco was thus established, which still rules the economic life of the Mam population. Subsequent coffee-growing expansion more strongly linked this region with national and international markets. Coffee produced in Chiapas was exported to Germany and the United States, and the Soconusco economy, as well as the living conditions of Sierra peasants, began to depend on the fluctuation of the international price of coffee.

The Sierra Madre and Soconusco were then sparsely populated regions, which created the need to "import" labor from Guatemala and the Chiapas highlands during harvest time. To facilitate access to this labor, Soconusco landowners requested that the government promote the colonization of the Sierra, so that laborers might have a piece of land to cultivate when the plantation did not require their services.[16]

On December 15, 1883, General Porfirio Díaz's government published the Colonization Law (Ley de Colonización), which promoted the occupation of national lands near the recently created border. At that time the

K'anjobal-, Chuj-, Jacalteco-, and Mam-speaking populations, originally Guatemalan, settled along the Chiapas border, later "naturalizing" themselves as Mexican citizens. This same law authorized the work of *compañías deslindadoras* (surveyor companies), with which the state signed contracts. The company Lands and Colonization from Chiapas, Mexico Limited (Tierras y Colonización de Chiapas, Mexico Limitada) opened the best arable lands in the state, and by the beginning of the twentieth century, haciendas and plantations owned 3,029,138 hectares, representing 87.84 percent of all arable lands in the state (Pedrero 1984:37). According to a report of the German consulate in 1927–1928, quoted by the German geographer Leo Waibel, by that time there were ninety-four coffee plantations in Soconusco producing 227,040 quintals of coffee annually. Of these, two were owned by Germans, twenty-five by Mexicans, thirteen by Spaniards, ten by Americans, eight by Frenchmen, four by Englishmen, and two by Swiss (Waibel 1946:188). Waibel also points out that at that time a hectare of coffee required one-half of a permanent laborer, and one and a half during harvest time, so that the whole Soconusco region, with about twelve thousand hectares, needed between five thousand and six thousand permanent laborers and between fifteen thousand and eighteen thousand during the harvest.

Mam peasants who had colonized national lands found in these plantations a means for subsistence. In many cases the properties of plantation owners extended all the way to the Sierra, and although such lands were useless for coffee growing, landowners rented them to their own laborers, so that they could plant corn for their own consumption while waiting for the harvest.

> The owner of all these lands here in El Porvenir was a German. He ruled here and our grandparents paid a duty for the land, to the rich man, the owner of the plantation Germania. To till the soil one had to pay a duty. One had to go all the way down to the coast to pay to the rich man; it was difficult because it was far; then the inhabitants were just a few. . . . They all put their share; it was then twenty centavos, forty centavos, fifty centavos, to have the right to sow a little piece of land.[17]

This system was maintained even after the Mexican Revolution, for the Agrarian Law instituted on January 6, 1915, did not affect the interests of Soconusco plantation owners and established that *peones acasillados* (workers living on the finca) had no right to demand land, but only peasants living in villages or settlements on national lands. Later, with the state

Agrarian Law of 1921, the *latifundio* was still protected, since "small property" was limited to eight thousand hectares, contrary to the hundred hectares stipulated for the rest of the republic (García de León 1985:2: 224). Three decades after the revolution was begun, Mam peasants continued to be tied to the plantation through a system of debts inherited from father to son; working conditions were inhumane, for "virtual slavery conditions prevailed in Chiapas," as described by a report of the Department of Indian Affairs of the Federal Government after touring the Soconusco (*Excelsior,* March 3, 1934).

In 1935 Governor Grajales modified the Agrarian Law and established that up to five thousand hectares could be owned in mountain lands. At the same time, the fertile lands of sugar, coffee, and cocoa plantations were accepted as mountain lands, which allowed a single plantation owner a property up to five thousand hectares (*Periódico Oficial del Estado,* February 12, 1936). The *enganchamiento* was conceived by Grajales as a form of agrarian credit. Through this system, which began with the first coffee plantations established in Chiapas, recruiters toured all indigenous villages, paying in advance a certain amount of money and forcing the workers to remain on the plantation until the owner considered that he had worked enough to repay his debt. Such debts were thus passed on from generation to generation and allowed the owners to have cheap, secure labor. This form of "agrarian credit" supported by Governor Grajales was declared "an illegal practice for the exploitation and control of indigenous population" by Governor Enríquez a few years later. Grajales also praised the migration to plantations as a form of "cultural integration." In the second public report on the state of his government, he said:

> Among dispositions issued concerning indigenous protection, it has been taken into account that the approximate amount of one million pesos distributed as advance payments to Indians constitutes the agrarian credit of indigenous zones, and the annual migration to Soconusco of ten thousand Indians slowly facilitates Indian incorporation into the culture. (Grajales 1934:30)

Thus tacit collaboration sprang up between the state and plantation owners to "facilitate Indian incorporation into the culture" through labor in plantations, and elders' testimonies tell us about its effect on plantation life after the alleged victory of the revolution. For example:

> After the Carrancistas won, poverty continued. I was orphaned and worked at the finca La Fortuna; we slept in the *galleras,* as they called them, mere planks; if it rained one could not sleep because

the water came in. The owner was called Guillermo; I think he was from the United States, because plantation owners were from abroad, all foreigners; they did not care about us; they gave us food like pigs, just throwing it; that is where I worked; I grew up there, in the finca La Fortuna.[18]

Life in the fincas thus makes up an important part of the oral history of Mam peoples; together with the testimonies on the "Law of Government" and "the burning of costumes," chronicles about life in plantations are the stories elder people tell constantly to explain "the suffering of the past."

In the Sierra corn did not grow; there was little land and nothing grew. To be able to live, people went a lot to the plantation, to earn and buy their corn. Life in the plantation was very difficult; one had to work from three o'clock in the morning until sunset. Those times were harsh; if one worked one ate, if not one did not.

Owners are rough; if one did not work as they wanted, at their will, they gave no food. When I grew up, we earned one peso per box. My father also worked in the plantation and in his time they paid fifty centavos a box.[19] My grandfather also went there, but I do not know how much he was paid; he said it was very little, scarcely enough to return home after the harvest. That is what my grandfather told me.[20]

When speaking about "plantation times," older people tell about overseers who raped women; about the day when a landowner, Juan Pohlenz, chose to burn his own coffee plantation rather than let the government give it to his laborers; about *enganchadores* (recruiters) who combed the villages during festivities to pick up *bolos* (drunkards) and assured them the next day that they had been paid in advance; about the owner of the Genova plantation who made a pact with the "owner of the mountain" and became rich by extracting gold from a large cave; about when eight-year-olds managed to fill half a box of coffee. These and many other stories are told on rainy nights, in front of the fireplace, when older people tell new generations about the suffering of the past.

The distribution of ejido land did not mean the end of plantation work for Mam peasants. Yet historical discourse assumes that peasant landownership significantly distinguishes "plantation times" from "ejido times," as if they were two distinct stages not overlapping in time.

The first ejidos of the Sierra region were founded at the end of the 1920s, in the municipalities of Motozintla (four), Mazapa de Madero (one), Amatenango de la Frontera (two), and Bella Vista (one), comprising 21,112 hectares of national lands (*Periódicos Oficiales del Estado*, 1925–1929). It was under Governor Efraín Gutiérrez that the first idle plots on coffee plantations were expropriated and the most significant land distribution of the postrevolutionary era was achieved. During his administration, 349,130 hectares were distributed, benefiting 29,398 peasants, as a response to 261 petitions of the 424 that had been presented (Gutiérrez 1941:34). In the Mam region during this administration, 26,899 hectares were distributed in the municipalities of Bella Vista, Frontera Comalapa, Mazapa de Madero, Motozintla, and Siltepec, benefiting thus 1,812 peasants (*Periódicos Oficiales del Estado*, 1936–1940).

The ejido established a new type of relationship between indigenous people and the state, which became, through its institutions, an interlocutor for Mam communities, which until then had been forgotten and isolated by government policies.

> Before that these lands were national, but then the government gave the law that ejidos had to be made. Then we began to fight for our lands, to travel to Tuxtla to get papers, to cooperate so that a representative could go, and so those of the Agraria gave us our ejido and each one has his plot. Those who came later were *avecindados* [peasants who live on ejido lands but without land rights], but now the land is not enough for our children, or for our children's children.[21]

Under Gutiérrez, however, land distribution was not limited to national lands. It also affected plantation owners' idle lands, for the latter evaded agrarian policies by distributing their large properties among relatives or by selling them to private small owners before they were expropriated. In some cases, they sold their worst lands to their own laborers.

> When the German owner of the Germania plantation saw that his lands would be taken away if he did not cultivate them, he decided to sell us the Sierra lands, which we were already renting from him. Then a meeting was organized. They invited young people so that they were more numerous, and first there were twenty, then even forty, and all cooperated and they named a representative who went to speak with the German owner of Germania, and that is how our fathers bought these lands of El Porvenir.[22]

The establishment of new ejidos on national lands near plantations was in the long run a benefit for Soconusco plantation owners, for they provided ready labor at harvest time.

To put an end to the enganche, which had been supported during the

Municipal head town of El Porvenir. Its lands were bought by Mam peasants from German finqueros in the 1930s. PHOTO BY RICHARD CISNEROS LÓPEZ.

preceding administration, Gutiérrez decided to create, on July 28, 1937, Free Employment Agencies (Agencias Gratuitas de Colocaciones), under the Department of Social Action, Culture, and Indigenous Protection (Alcance No. 30; *Periódico Oficial*, July 28, 1937:1–5). In his first public address, he explained the need to create this new institution for defending the rights of rural workers:

> Having realized that the system of enganchamiento to recruit workers for plantations in Soconusco and other coffee-growing areas was exploitation, . . . I decided that there should be direct supervision by the state government, in order to achieve fairer and more humane conditions for laborers. This is the aim of the creation of the Free Employment Agencies. (Gutiérrez 1937:8)

But, in spite of Gutiérrez's good intentions, the Free Employment Agencies became an instrument for plantation owners and made obtaining workers even easier. In the case of the Agencia de Colocaciones established in Motozintla, its employees were old enganchadores, who did not much alter their habits or their attitudes toward the Sierra peasants.

> Later enganchadores became government employees; there in Motozintla there was an agency, it was called of Employment; it was supposed to help workers, but nothing changed; galleras were

still the same, and nobody paid the minimum wage; on the contrary, they lowered the wages because there was a crisis in the whole country.[23]

Acknowledgment of workers' rights and the creation of new supervisory institutions that were not accompanied by the necessary mechanisms for sanctioning violation of the new regulations (contained in the Federal Workers' Law of 1931) achieved no substantial changes in the lives of Soconusco workers and became part of the new postrevolutionary populist discourse. What became very clear indeed was that, from the 1930s on, state institutions began to have a more constant presence in the Mam region, through their agrarian officials, their credit institutions, and their Hispanicizing programs.

The ejido also restructured the geographic space of Mam settlements. From the beginning of the twentieth century, Mam who colonized the Sierra lived in scattered settlements and relied on the markets of "large" villages, Motozintla (San Pla) and La Grandeza, as well as the buildings of Soconusco plantations, for social interaction (Waibel 1946; field data). With the creation of ejidos, the population tended to concentrate around ejidal agencies. Years before, in a press interview, Angel M. Corzo, general director of education in Grajales's administration, had already pointed out the need for concentrating the population in order to facilitate its control by the state:

> The office I am heading is designing a scheme to ensure the cultural raising of the numerous indigenous race . . . and, most important for Chiapas, the formation of new communities and villages, where they can gather and live in a different manner from that to which they have been accustomed until now, scattered in the mountains and perhaps in the most barren places. Chiapas urgently needs to join the activity of the indigenous race to that of the rest of its population, in such a way that it becomes an element for organized production and is controllable by the government. (*Semanario Popular* [Tuxtla Gutiérrez], May 27, 1934:1)

Along with concentrating the people on ejidal lands, the government of Lázaro Cárdenas promoted the incorporation of Chiapas peasants through the League of Rural Communities (Ligas de Comunidades Agrarias). In 1938, with the support of Cárdenas, the National Peasant Confederation (Confederación Nacional Campesina [CNC]), linked to the government party, then called the National Revolutionary Party (Partido

Ejido Malé, El Porvenir. The system of scattered settlements, questioned by Angel M. Corzo in 1934 because it did not allow population control, is still common in the Mam area. PHOTO BY RICHARD CISNEROS LÓPEZ.

Nacional Revolucionario [PNR]), was established.[24] In the new ejidos, local power elites began to take shape that favored a few peasants with credit support, facilitation in bureaucratic matters, and so on.

Referring to the new relationship between peasants and the state after the creation of the ejido, Armando Bartra points out:

> This reformed peasant is still an exploited worker, but now his relationship with capital has become more complicated; in order to subsist, he must sell, buy, fall into debt. . . . [H]is contact with capital is no longer limited to his relationship with the boss who hires him as laborer, for now his boss has multiplied, the state and its agencies are his new bosses, but also the private engineer or the multinational company who finance and buy his product. Exploitation takes on many forms. (1985:18)

This situation became more acute in the Sierra Mam ejidos, established at the higher elevations and on national lands that were not suitable for corn or agroexport crops, such as coffee and cocoa. Plots provided barely enough for subsistence, and the main crop, potatoes, had a limited market. The living conditions of the "reformed peasant" are described in testimonies collected among Chiapas Mames.

Now we have the ejido, but we also still suffer, waiting here for corn; but where is the corn? Here in the Sierra corn does not grow well. And that is why I said, thanks for the potatoes. With potatoes we manage like this; that is why we do not stop working here, all the time. Here we just have work, and on top of work, more work. . . . This morning there was a snowfall [hailstorm] but a big one, one cannot even walk. Difficult times have begun; from now until May there is a lot of it, and in May one can already see the crop, in the potatoes, in the milpa, and if it freezes in May everything is lost, and then what are we going to eat? Haaa! That is why we even cry.[25]

Corn, the Mames' staple food, had to be brought up from the lowlands of Comalapa, which were inaccessible to those who lacked transportation. Moreover, some did not have the money to buy it. Potatoes then became the main crop, but they were at risk from frost. With no food or money, the Mames had to return to the plantations, as in the past, or migrate to the towns, as a high percentage of the Sierra young people are doing now.

Thus the Mam people of the Sierra Madre were transformed into *ejidatarios* (ejido holders). The state began to refer to them as peasants, and in official documents dating from the 1940s, there are no more references to their cultural identity as Mam. In fact, by 1950 the official census in municipalities historically inhabited by the Mam reports only Spanish speakers. Possibly many of the Mam speakers did not declare themselves as such to government representatives, because of the fear provoked by "Mexicanization" campaigns. Sierra inhabitants began to identify themselves publicly as "peasants"; nonetheless, the Mam language continued from generation to generation but now clandestinely: "Then Mam began to be spoken only at home, only among the family, because in feasts or places where there were many people, sometimes one met teachers or government people and there could be a punishment."[26] The Mam language went from the public sphere to the private, and became at the same time a language for religious ritual.

Presbyterianism and a New Mam Identity

The 1930s saw the consolidation of Presbyterianism in the Sierra region. Victorico Grajales's anticlerical campaigns were directed mainly against the Catholic Church, which was seen not only as an ideological source of "fanaticization" but also as a political and economic institution whose power had to be reduced (Benjamin 1995). In this context, Protestant denominations represented a countervailing force and thus were not touched by Grajales's secularization campaigns (field data). At the national level, they were even supported by Cárdenas, who viewed the task of translating the Bible into Mexican indigenous languages as a possible contribution to the indigenist policy promoted by his administration. In 1936 President Cárdenas met the Protestant missionary William Cameron Townsend, founder of the Summer Institute of Linguistics, in the Nahuatl village of Tetelcingo, and offered him government support for the institution he planned to establish in indigenous communities. Townsend describes the encounter in his diary:

> For almost an hour we had the never dreamt of privilege to receive in our facilities the greatest ruler of this land. . . . When he looked at the garden he asked emphatically whether the young people we were trying to bring to translate the Bible would help the Indians in the same way we were doing it . . . This is precisely what Mexico needs—said the President, bring as many as you can obtain. (Rus and Wasserstrom 1979:142)

In addition, the presence of the Presbyterian Moisés Sáenz as undersecretary for public education in Cárdenas's administration eased relations between the state and Protestant missionaries.

Protestantism made its way into Chiapas through the Mam zone at the beginning of the century. During the incipient stage of this new religion, the local population did not identify it with any Protestant denomination, although it had its origins in contact with Guatemalan Presbyterian missionaries. Testimonies collected among descendants of the founders of the first congregation describe how it happened.

> In the year 1901 a gentleman called Octaviano Hernández came from Guatemala to preach the gospel. But as the people were all indigenous and only two persons could half speak Castilian, this gentleman only left the Bible. But when ashes fell from the Santa María volcano of Guatemala, there were huge earthquakes and houses collapsed; it was then that the late Pablo de la Cruz, who was municipal president and knew some Spanish, began to teach his people in the dialect. He taught the Bible because he saw that misfortune was on the village and it was perhaps the coming of our Lord Jesus Christ.[27]

Thus a popular religious movement with no international links began to emerge. It was an interpretation of the Bible based on their own con-

Presbyterian Church of Espíritu Santo. This is the first Protestant church in Chiapas, established in 1920 in Mazapa de Madero. PHOTO BY RICHARD CISNEROS LÓPEZ.

ception of the world. This movement was institutionalized when in 1920 the Presbyterian missionary José Coffin, a member of the Gulf of Mexico Presbytery, visited the Sierra. He organized the assignment of the Mazapa group to this denomination and on June 6 founded the Presbyterian Church of the Holy Spirit (Iglesia Presbiteriana del Espíritu Santo).

By the late 1920s and early 1930s the first American missionaries began to visit the region. Juan and Mabel Kempers were members of the Reformed Church of America, which worked with the Presbyterian church. At that same time, there was a large migration of mestizo Catholics from the municipality of Cuilco, in Huehuetenango, Guatemala, so that the population became divided into two large groups, Catholic mestizos and Protestant Indians.[28]

In contrast to other regions, where being Protestant implies a certain degree of acculturation, in the Mam region Presbyterianism paradoxically began to be identified as a component of ethnicity.

> All Protestants were indigenous; there was not a single Castilian, for Castilians were Catholics, but with a Catholic religion different from that which our ancestors had before the volcano erupted.
>
> The relationship between Catholics and Protestants was very ugly, because the poor indigenous people practiced their cults in a little house belonging to the municipal president and the Catholics came to throw stones on the house and they suffered. That is the way the Presbyterian Church was founded. But by then many preachers had gone out to preach the gospel; they organized the indigenous people of El Porvenir, Malé, Canadá, La Grandeza, Pacayal, and Bella Vista, and then they went over there and organized Pacayal, Frontera, and Amatenango and reached all the way to Comitán.[29]

The mestizo population identified being Protestant with being Indian: "Our brothers also had to withstand insults and derogatory words. Very often people shouted at them in the street and called them Indians" (Esponda 1986:32). This "Protestant" religion, which was not yet identified with Presbyterianism, shared much of the ritual characteristics of indigenous traditional religion: "Our parents used to tell us that the first Protestants would go to a cave on a hill nearby and sacrificed turkeys or sheep because they said it was holy command in the Old Testament."[30] Thus this new type of popular religiosity preserved many of the elements of the traditional religion known locally as "costumbre."

Presbyterian missionaries played an important role in the criticism of

"Hispanicization" campaigns. It is interesting to note that, contrary to the general censure of "Protestantism" for undermining the cultural traditions of indigenous populations (Pérez and Robinson 1983; Stoll 1990), in this area Presbyterianism promoted the preservation of the Mam language and censured the integrationist policies of the government.

> The Gospels were already here when the language was forbidden; I was aware because we used to go to school, here at the primary school, and our teacher, who was called Eulogio García Jacob, scolded us a lot and even went as far as hitting us because we spoke the language. He told us, "Do not speak the dialect to me because only 'guach guach'—one does not even understand it—and I do not want such things here; here we are going to speak Castilian so that you learn, you remember the lessons; that is why you cannot learn."
> When Pastor Coffin found out he told us: "No my children, because you are forgetting your dialect; you should speak Spanish, but you must also try not to forget your dialect, because it is an inheritance God left all of you." And thus he always taught us we must keep our dialect, not forget it, because it was an inheritance and then we should not forget it.[31]

This does not mean that Presbyterian missionaries never attacked either directly or indirectly aspects of traditional religion.

> This village [Mazapa] then lived, as all other villages in the same area, sunken in ignorance. Superstition had taken the shape of religion and thus the great number of shamans [chimanes] who fed superstition and maintained a constant fear among villagers of the region, persons who celebrated feasts and gatherings that were given a religious character, and because of that there was much alcoholism together with the tragedies that come with it. (Esponda 1986:26)

Yet, with respect to the Mam language, the Presbyterian church as an institution was much more respectful than the Chiapas government, particularly during the first decades of the twentieth century.

Mexican identity was imposed not only by means of symbolic violence through education but also by means of physical coercion. Nevertheless, Sierra inhabitants found in the new religious groups a safe space where they could speak the Mam language and reconstruct their folk religion. And Presbyterianism legitimated for the first time the use of the Mam language as a legacy of their ancestors.

This first stage of the imposition of the national project was followed by a stage of negotiation. The Mam population has not been isolated from the Imaginary Mexico described by Bonfil (1987) but has been marginally incorporated into the nation, for many have joined the official party and obtained small concessions in exchange for votes. In that sense, when speaking about the construction of the nation along the southern border, we can speak of a process of negotiation and conflict (Rosaldo 1993). In a subtler manner, Presbyterianism brought to the Sierra a nationalist discourse that did not oppose an ethnic identity but contained it together with a Presbyterian identity. For José Coffin, "being Mexican, Mam, and Presbyterian posed no problem." [32] Since the foundation in the Sierra region of the first Mam Presbyterian church, Mam converts have claimed to be nationalist and even place a Mexican flag next to the pulpit. This institutional line, born from the agreements between Presbyterian leaders and postrevolutionary governments, is present in the discourse of the oldest Mam Presbyterians.

> The Presbyterian Church is national; it is not true that we are controlled by "gringos." We celebrate March 21 for the birth of Benito Juárez, who supported the foundation of our church; we are more Mexican than Catholics who criticize the government. [33]

Ethnic resistance was achieved by maintaining and reinventing Mam identity as different, but there was at the same time a reproduction of dominant values related to the respect for the state and the reproduction of the political system.

Presbyterianism during the postrevolutionary period was widely accepted in indigenous communities, which were beset by the integrationist policies and anticlerical campaigns of the Mexican state, as well as by the rapid changes wrought by the ejidal system. Indigenous tradition in the form of interiorized culture shaped the way in which the Mam appropriated Presbyterianism, giving birth to a new kind of popular syncretic religion better adapted to the "Modern Mexico" they had to face. Presbyterianism became what Jean-Pierre Bastian (1990:20) has defined as "a more efficient space for resistance and/or adaptation to modernity than popular Catholic religions."

Nevertheless, this new form of religion was re-created mainly by those sectors of the population that both remained in their Sierra lands and managed to "adapt" to the changes through their new ejido communities. In many cases, this population appropriated the new religious ideology by incorporating it as a component of their ethnicity. Other sectors that did not benefit from ejido distribution assumed their new "peasant" identity, created to a certain degree by the same postrevolutionary discourse.

The integrationist policies of the 1930s had as their main objective the construction of a homogeneous Mexican national identity. For the inhabitants of the southern Mexican border, incorporation into postrevolutionary Mexico resulted in the imposition of the Spanish language, the prohibition of their traditional costumes, forced secularization, and, for some women, even "justified" rape. All this in the name of building a mestizo Mexico, both homogeneous and modern. To claim their agrarian rights and to benefit from the ejido land distribution, Mam peasants had to accept a Mexican identity that in turn denied them the right to cultural difference.

Chapter

2

THE MODERNIZING PROJECT

BETWEEN THE MUSEUM AND THE DIASPORA

The 1950s are remembered by Soconusco finqueros as times of plenty, when agroexport products reached their highest international price as a result of the rapid economic recovery of post–World War II Europe. For Sierra peasants, it was a time of darkness in a literal sense, for these were the years when onchocercosis, known locally as the "purple disease," reached alarming levels, causing blindness in thousands of peasants. If "the burning of costumes" marked the historical memory of old Mames during the 1930s, the trauma of the purple disease marks the testimonies of the 1950s.

Although they share the same geographic space, finqueros and Mam peasants reconstruct their pasts with very different narratives. Some finqueros refer to Miguel Alemán (1946–1952) and Adolfo Ruíz Cortínez (1952–1958) as the Mexican presidents who brought real progress to the region; their testimonies refer to the construction of the Pan-American Highway, which made it easier for them to convey their products; the electrification of the Soconusco and Mariscal regions; the so-called Green Revolution, which brought improved seeds and fertilizers; and respect for "private property," which was finally supported by the federal government. During the 1950s, Chiapas coffee growers produced a yearly average of seventeen thousand tons of coffee, with an international demand well above local production, thereby living up to the expectations of modern Mexico (Renard 1993).

But peasants talk about a different reality, and although names are absent from Mam testimonies, facts are remembered. They recall when the government announced that there were no more lands to be distributed and gave finqueros papers stating that nobody could touch their properties and when the government, through the CNC, distributed seeds and fertilizers to those who joined them; but, above all, they remember when the purple disease blinded their children, relatives, and friends and when going to plantations meant returning with a swollen face, dark skin, and lumps on the neck that little by little took away the light. It was a time of fear, which has not quite passed, for the purple disease is still there, hidden in the mosquitoes that are endemic to coffee plantations, able to manifest itself at any moment.[1]

These stories reveal two views of modern Mexico, in which the so-called stabilizing development of the 1950s and 1960s was perceived by the peasants from the Sierra and by the finqueros of the Soconusco coast in strikingly different ways.

In this chapter, I analyze how Mam peasants appear once more in the "official history" by being included in the "national heritage" displayed in the new National Museum of Anthropology. In the 1950s and 1960s anthropologists created an image of the Mam for national consumption; organized expeditions with the aim of "ethnographic and archaeological rescue"; and wrote museographic scripts. During these decades, Sierra inhabitants were confronted by a modernizing project that, while "recovering the national heritage," simultaneously promoted modernization through road construction and through the Green Revolution. Tradition and modernization were not opposed in the new political discourse that used the reconstruction of a common past for "all Mexicans" as a means to maintain its hegemony, while also promoting a development project that excluded the great majority of the Indian population.

I also analyze the exodus of the 1960s, when hundreds of Mam peasants abandoned the Sierra and settled in the southwestern region of the Lacandon rain forest, following the colonizing campaigns promoted by the government. In the context of migration, new religious identities and new forms of self-conception as a collectivity began to emerge. Ironically, while anthropologists were freezing in time the reality of Chiapas indigenous peoples with static representations in the Ethnographic Hall of the museum, the diaspora to the rain forest was beginning. The Mam have migrated, converted to new religious ideologies, and developed new contesting discourses against a nation-state that has excluded them.

The "Stabilizing Development"

The 1950s began with a new collaboration between Soconusco fin-queros and the federal government. In the preceding decades, Chiapas landowners had faced President Lázaro Cárdenas's populist measures; and finqueros of German origin, the temporary expropriation of their lands during World War II by President Manuel Avila Camacho (1940–1946). After such experiences, local finqueros viewed with pleasure the agrarian counterreform promoted by the administrations of Alemán and Ruíz Cortínez. This period has been characterized as a time of "maintenance and strengthening of the political system," as the aim was not to transform but to stabilize (Pellicer de Brody and Mancilla 1978). In that sense, the priority was investing in land production and its technological development. To achieve this, the trust of large-scale producers had to be recovered.

Protection of the improperly named "small property" to which Soconusco finqueros refer became effective with the publication of the Regulation for Agrarian and Livestock Inalienability (Reglamento de Inafectabilidad Agrícola y Ganadera) (*Diario Oficial*, September 23, 1948), as well as with the modifications of Article 27, sections X, XIV, and XV, giving the right of appeal to those who possessed certificates of inalienability and were threatened with the loss or dispossession of their lands or water. Land reform in Chiapas had been extremely limited, but with the modification of Article 27, the conditions for a neolatifundism were established. Constitutional modifications stated that improvements on property would protect it from expropriation, even when the size exceeded that authorized by law, which was 100 hectares of irrigated land and 300 hectares of commercial crops (Gutelman 1980). At the national level, 11,975 certificates of inalienability were given, protecting more than one million hectares (Gutelman 1980:11). In the state of Chiapas, Alemán's administration protected with land and livestock inalienability certificates 63,552 hectares, and later Ruíz Cortínez added 69,466 more.[2] In the Soconusco region, new coffee emporiums were created, such as that of Juan von Bernstroff, who, protected by the new law, bought the Guanajuato, San Juan Chicharras, Acapulco, El Final, and Santa Elena fincas, on which he carried out the necessary improvements to protect them from land claims. This new latifundism was characterized by discontinuous dispersed lands and by extensive family holdings, in which several members of a single family appeared to be "small-scale owners" of several properties.

Irrigation works were also a priority in the modernizing project of that decade, and technological development of land replaced land distribution.

In Chiapas, construction of the Malpaso dam began on the affluents of the Usumacinta and Grijalva Rivers.

For Soconusco coffee growers, the opening of the Pan-American Highway represented considerably lower costs for bringing their products to the marketplace. Under Governor Francisco J. Grajales (1949–1952), a pact was signed by the Ministry of Communications (Secretaría de Comunicaciones) and the Chiapas government for the construction of vicinal roads (*Periódico Oficial del Estado*, March 13, 1950). Under this agreement, the Motozintla-Huixtla road was constructed, linking the Sierra Madre to the coast, which made the transportation of seasonal laborers to Soconusco much easier. Between 1949 and 1958, the paved surface increased nationwide by 223 percent (Cline 1962:64). Branch roads became symbolic markers through which the nation-state extended its influence to the remotest regions of the country.

Under Miguel Alemán's administration, the National Coffee Commission (Comisión Nacional del Café) was formed, to help coffee growers modernize their production systems and ease agrarian credits. Fertilizers and pesticides made their appearance in Chiapas lands, substantially increasing output. Most of the Sierra highlands ejidatarios did not come in contact with the so-called Green Revolution until the mid-1970s, when governmental institutions started to provide counseling for marginalized communities. In the lowlands, near the Sierra, the CNC took on the task of predicating the distribution of agro-chemical substances on active participation in its organization.

As a result of the development of irrigation works and the use of agrochemical substances, as well as high international prices for agricultural goods, crops attained a growth index never before witnessed in Mexican agriculture: production increased by 71 percent between 1940 and 1970 (Pellicer de Brody and Reyna 1978:32). Coffee reached unheard-of prices when quotas linked to the International Coffee Agreement were relaxed, and the price continued to increase from 1950 to 1958.

Yet Mam peasants benefited very little from this "agrarian boom," for they still did not receive the minimum wage and had to compete with thousands of Guatemalan peasants who were willing to work long hours for low wages. In one of the new agreements between Chiapas finqueros and the federal government, the Ministry of the Interior (Secretaría de Gobernación) granted landowners the right to import up to twenty-thousand Guatemalan laborers at harvest time (Wasserstrom 1989). Some explain this measure as a governmental strategy to redirect the labor force from the highlands to the Grijalva Valley, a region located in the center of the state that was beginning agrarian development (Rus 1994). But Sierra inhabitants did not have the same opportunities as the Tzeltal and Tzotzil of the highlands, for the Grijalva Valley was too far for them to migrate seasonally. Mam peasants were forced to accept the low salaries offered on the coffee plantations, and in the 1960s many of them chose to migrate permanently to the rain forest region.

Ruíz Cortínez continued Alemán's policies, granting sixty thousand certificates of inalienability to alleged small-scale owners, which increased inalienable lands to 5,300,000 hectares (Gutelman 1980). His support of agroexport producers was strengthened by the publication of the Agrarian Credit Law (Ley de Crédito Agrícola), whose goal was to support those producing for "the national interest" whether for domestic consumption or for export. Few ejidatarios benefited from the new credit institutions, as their subsistence production was not considered to be in the national interest.

To implement development in indigenous regions of the country, on December 2, 1948, the National Indigenist Institute was established. The creation of the INI fulfilled the international agreements undertaken during the First Inter-American Indigenist Congress (Primer Congreso Indigenista Interamericano) held in Pátzcuaro, Michoacán, in April 1940, where Latin American governments agreed to create ad hoc institutions for addressing the needs of indigenous populations. At the same time, this new institution would serve as a mediator to "integrate" indigenous groups into national development. The INI was created at a time when the state had to reconstruct its hegemony after the popular rejection provoked by agrarian counterreform in the rural world.

The INI had as predecessors a number of governmental institutions whose main goal was "the integration of Indians" into the national project.[3] The openly integrationist perspective of Manuel Gamio was softened in the legal amendment that created the INI, which does not mention the need for cultural fusion but states that "the culture of these indigenous groups preserves characteristics that can be used in support of the national culture, for they will still provide it with the profile that sets it apart from all the other peoples of America and the world" (*Diario de Debates*, December 24, 1948; quoted in INI 1978:338). Thus the INI fulfilled the double function of conveying development to rural zones and rescuing from indigenous cultures "those characteristics" that could be integrated with the nation's cultural heritage.

By the mid-1950s, under the influence of Gonzalo Aguirre Beltrán, indigenist thought underwent an important change, incorporating an analysis of the relations of domination at the regional level. This new indigenism placed indigenous communities in a wider context, where urban centers benefited from the unequal economic exchange with rural communities. This new model, inspired by Aguirre Beltrán, centered its criticism on local power groups and did not yet question the role of the state or capitalism in structuring relations of domination. It must be acknowledged, however, that in Chiapas the INI played an important role by censuring the racism and the semifeudal relations still prevailing in the highlands and in the Soconusco region. Struggles between the federal government, represented by the INI, and local interests, often represented by state officials, have marked the history of indigenism in Chiapas and tell us about power relations in the state itself.

The limits of indigenist analysis at that time were set by the people's participation in the construction of a homogenizing and modern national project. Aguirre Beltrán's book *Regiones de refugio* (1967) set the bases for the establishment of the Indigenist Coordinator Centers, which are still the INI's main organizational structure.[4] Integrationist campaigns of the 1930s and 1940s, carried out by the Department of Social Action, Culture, and Indigenous Protection, as well as by the Central Committee of Pro-Indigenous Clothing, were so effective in the Sierra Madre that for several decades the region was not considered indigenous. It was not integrated into the CCI's model until 1978.

Anthropologists in the Sierra: The Mam People as Health Problem and as National Heritage

After the Mexicanization campaigns of the 1930s, the Mam disappeared temporarily from official documents, which began referring to them by the generic name "peasants." Neither censuses nor governmental documents refer to Mam indigenous people in the 1940s. Unlike the Tzeltal-Tzotzil region of the highlands, where the 1930s produced a large bibliography on its inhabitants, the Chiapas Sierra Madre has not been a center of interest for local anthropological research. Precisely because the region was not considered indigenous, it did not attract the attention of culture researchers. Rather, until the 1950s, it was geographers and travelers who described the Mariscal and Soconusco regions.[5]

Anthropological writings of the 1950s and 1960s drew on the fieldwork of two interdisciplinary groups: the first went over the Sierra in 1945 to sanitize the region that would be crossed by the Pan-American Highway, for onchocercosis was epidemic there; the second traveled in the region in 1967 to collect samples of local material culture for the Ethnographic Hall of the new National Museum of Anthropology. Both groups made journeys of between one and four months, which explains in part why these anthropologists are considered "Sierra travelers" rather than researchers (Fernández Galán 1995). Although not extensive, these investigations were significant, for they indirectly represented official recognition of the existence of a Mam population in Mexico. The differing objectives of these government-sponsored groups symbolized the contradictions of researchers moving between integrationist nationalism and critical Marxism.

The goals of both investigations, the construction of a road and the construction of a museum, are closely linked to the consolidation of the postrevolutionary state. Tradition and modernity are both inseparable elements of the new nation under construction. The need felt by modernizing projects to appeal to tradition is analyzed by Néstor García Canclini (1995:107), who points out that, "not only in the interest of expanding the market, but also in order to legitimize their hegemony, the modernizers need to persuade their addressees that—at the same time that they are renewing society—they are prolonging shared traditions. Given that they claim to include all sectors of society, modern projects appropriate historical goods and popular traditions." Thus the Mam were appropriated as part of the cultural heritage of a nation-state which until then had denied them the right to exist as a separate cultural entity.

Partly because of the short duration of their fieldwork, few Sierra inhabitants remember the presence of these researchers in the region. In contrast to Sylvanus Morley's and Alfonso Villa Rojas's experiences among Yucatán Mayans (see Sullivan [1989] 1991), or those of Frans and Gertrudis Blom among Chiapas Lacandones, the presence of these two teams of researchers left no trace in the historical memory of Mam indigenous people. Some old people remember when some young people went through El Porvenir and Miravalle, wanting to buy cave pots and "ancient" cloths. Many remember the doctors who came to fight the purple disease, but nobody mentioned the name Ricardo Pozas or Isabel Horcazitas. Because of this, we have but one version of this encounter, that of the anthropologists.

In Motozintla, in Don Pompilio Montecinos's old drugstore, among earthen figures he has been collecting for several years, lies a dust-covered book titled *Un reconocimiento de la Sierra Madre de Chiapas: apuntes de un diario de campo* (A Trip through the Sierra Madre: Notes of a Field Journal; 1978). To those who ask about it, Don Pompilio proudly shows the dedication signed by its author, the archaeologist Carlos Navarrete. This book is one of the very few mementos still left in the Sierra of these two research teams.

Still, pioneer writings resulting from such projects reminded the rest of Mexico that the Mam existed. In spite of the motivations of those who financed the expeditions, the writings of Ricardo Pozas (1952a, 1952b) and Andrés Medina (1973) denounced the forced acculturation campaigns against the Mam population and the inhumane work conditions on coffee plantations.

It was the purple disease that, after a decade of indifference, forced the Mexican state to remember that the Mam lived in one of the last enclaves of the Sierra Madre. Although this disease, transmitted by the so-called coffee mosquito (*Simulium* and *Simulium caidum*), was first detected in 1920 among coffee plantation laborers, by 1952 it had acquired the characteristics of an epidemic, with fifty thousand cases, mostly among the Sierra Madre and Soconusco indigenous population (de la Fuente 1952:50). Already in 1940, the First Inter-American Indigenist Congress in Pátzcuaro had sent a call to Latin American governments to support medical, parasitological, and social investigations of onchocercosis.

In 1945 Avila Camacho's administration was faced with the problem of onchocercosis when planning the construction of the Pan-American Highway in the Soconusco region. If adequate sanitation of the zone were not achieved, the new road network might spread the disease throughout the state. Thus, before construction could begin, the Pan-American Sanitation Office (Oficina Sanitaria Panamericana) undertook an interdisciplinary investigation among the onchocercosis-infected population, a high percentage of which was of Mam origin.

The interdisciplinary team was composed of a geologist, an archaeologist, a botanist, two agronomist engineers, two doctors, a physical anthropologist, and four ethnologists. The latter's main task was to find out whether there was any relation between the cultural habits of infected indigenous groups and the spread of onchocercosis.[6] The only known results of these investigations are found in an honors thesis in physical anthropology by Felipe Montemayor (1954) and two articles by Ricardo Pozas (1952a, 1952b).[7]

Montemayor's work is based on a case study from a mestizo population in Acacoyahua, a village in the coastal region of Chiapas; still, he makes several comparisons with the epidemiology among Mam peasants, the sector most severely affected by onchocercosis. In his conclusions Montemayor rules out the importance of cultural factors in the spread of the disease and points out that it is not the culture of Mam peoples but their poverty and extreme marginalization that have contributed to making this group the worst hit by the epidemic. His thesis ends with a denunciation of working conditions on plantations and the state's indifference to the situation of indigenous peoples:

> After the preceding brief considerations, it is obvious that oncho-cercosis only acquires acute manifestations in places where people stagnate under the most dramatic conditions of penury and neglect; in the very poor villages of the Soconusco Sierra and the promis-cuity of the galleys in plantations, where *peones enganchados* live in a situation akin to that of concentration camps. The proof of it is that many German and Japanese finqueros, in spite of having been infected with onchocercosis, have never shown serious eye or skin trouble. Acacoyahua peasants, having a level of existence slightly above those whose living conditions are terrible, withstand the disease. The conditions of this Mexican group living under exploitation and neglect, most of them indigenous people, make them an easy prey to all disasters and diseases, not only onchocercosis. The fact that this disease has more alarming manifestations, such as blindness and the purple disease which shock those who see it, leads one to think that this is the greatest problem in this region, while it is in fact only one of the numberless enemies harassing one of the many Mexican groups who live ignored by their own fatherland, victims of exploitation, extreme poverty, ignorance and unsanitary conditions . . . indigenous peoples, culturally and economically the most forsaken and weak of all Mexicans. (Montemayor 1954:96)

Montemayor's denunciation echoes the many testimonies of Sierra inhabitants about disabilities caused by the purple disease. For several years, working in a finca posed the risk of losing one's sight and becoming seriously ill. Don Gregorio, sixty years old, who lost his sight because of the purple disease, remembers:

> I was about thirty when I fell ill. My three elder children were already born, Gregorio, Juan, and Francisca. I went down to the fincas every year after All Saints' Day [November 1 and 2]. One year, after I came back, I began to see that my whole face was swollen and became purple, then my skin sagged, like that of an old man. Juana and I were very scared, but then nothing happened and I felt all right. Several months went by until I felt some lumps on my

head, right here, and some time later I started to see all blurred. The health center was already near here, in El Porvenir, but there was no doctor, only an aide, who did not know and gave me some drops that did not help. Little by little, light was leaving me, and one day I was not even able to see Juana's face, only shadows moving. Juana cried a lot, and I contained myself, but I knew I would be no good any more either, either to her or the children, because I could not go down to the finca. Who would buy their corn? . . . Thus started my sadness, and this sadness has slowly dried me.[8]

Although since 1935 health authorities in Chiapas had declared the old districts of Soconusco, Mariscal, and parts of Comitán and La Libertad as an onchocercosis-infected area (see Reglamento del Departamento de Salubridad Pública, Art. 4o. Gobierno del estado de Chiapas), in 1950 indigenous groups in the region still lacked any medical attention. The only health centers were in large villages, such as Motozintla and Huixtla, and in the town of Tapachula. What was a curable illness in better-served areas became a devastating epidemic for Sierra Madre peasants. The "purple disease times" are mentioned in almost all testimonies collected among Mam people between the ages of sixty and eighty.

Life at the finca was always harsh. My grandfather went down to harvest coffee and suffered very much; my father also went down, but I lived the times of the purple disease. They were the worst times. It was when my brother-in-law, María's husband, went blind, and I also caught it, but my face only was swollen like a toad. Then there was no doctor like today. One got well all by oneself, if it was God's will, or died. There was no pay to go down to the doctor at Motozintla, and the owners did not care if we got ill, although they knew it was on the coffee plantations that we caught the disease, they did not care, for them we were not people.[9]

It was the contact with this reality that marked many of the anthropological studies of the 1950s and 1960s. They could not be limited to the ethnographic description of "closed communities," when the experience at the finca inscribed every aspect of indigenous daily life. Pretending to understand Sierra reality without considering temporary migration to Soconusco was absurd, and the recognition of this fact is reflected in the studies of both Pozas and Medina.

Although Pozas's academic orientation was influenced by Sol Tax and Robert Redfield, under whose direction he worked in the highlands of

Chiapas in 1943, his first studies combine Redfieldian functionalism with a Marxist tradition born from his political activism (see Medina 1994). He took an active role in the teachers' movement and joined the Revolutionary Students Front (Frente Estudiantil Revolucionario), which was linked to the Communist Party; these experiences determined his Marxist tendency, reflected in his concern about the living conditions of Mam peasants.

Both papers published after Pozas's work in the campaign against onchocercosis touch only lightly on that health problem and instead center on a description of Mam peasant life. Pozas characterizes the Mam at the end of the 1940s as immersed in a rapid process of change produced by the mobility of the group, their relationship with the mestizos at the coffee plantations, and the influence of governmental and religious institutions on cultural life (Pozas 1952a, 1952b). Using a functionalist theoretical framework, he characterizes these cultural changes as the result of a process of cultural contact. According to a chart developed by Redfield, the Mam, together with the Chiapenecas, are at one end of the folk-urban continuum, representing the groups that are almost incorporated into urban culture, while at the other end are the Lacandones, organized in totemic clans and still using the bow and arrow. Nevertheless, Pozas goes beyond the idea of transculturation as the result of cultural contact with urban regions and emphasizes the importance of power relations.

Pozas describes how governmental policies split Mexican and Guatemalan Mam. He refers to the way in which the Mexican government forcibly imposed incorporation on indigenous groups of the border by forbidding them the use of traditional costumes and, thereby, distinguishing them from Guatemalan Indians. As for the Guatemalan government, it took measures that increased the difference between Indians and non-Indians, by excluding the former from compulsory military service. Starting from his analysis of these political differences, Pozas relativizes the importance of the traditional costume as an element necessary for identity. In his writings he describes how traditional costumes were worn by Guatemalan Indians in order to avoid military service, yet temporarily discarded when crossing the border to avoid Mexican immigration authorities. The construction of different nation-states and their relations with indigenous groups, according to Pozas, offers a new area of research.

This change occurred rapidly because of a fixing of limits between Mexico and Guatemala, which determined the separation of the Mam into two groups, one of which remained in the neighbor coun-

try. Finally, we must underline the need for comparative research
of both parts of what was until recently one single people and one
single culture, which would provide an abundance of material for
the study of transculturation I am sketching in this short paper.
(Pozas 1952a:27)

If we compare these studies with the hegemonic anthropological analyses of the 1940s and 1950s, we see that Pozas was well ahead of his time, going beyond descriptions of self-contained communities and descriptive ethnographies that misrepresent communities as static and isolated in space. His papers include a historical national context and, in some senses, even a global one, which allow us to place Mam peoples within a wider social dynamic. He points out, for example, that one of the elements that influenced the migration of Mam peasants toward Mexican territory at the beginning of the twentieth century was the Brazilian revolution, which had greatly depressed Brazilian coffee production, thus causing an increase in the international price and a greater demand for labor in the recently established coffee plantations of Soconusco (Pozas 1952a). His criticism of the devastating force of the capitalist system and the extreme marginalization of indigenous groups in this system is further developed in his paper on the Mam on coffee plantations (Pozas 1952b), which denounced the unfair working conditions that still prevailed in Soconusco.

Pozas used his knowledge of fincas in a novel that has become a classic of Mexican literature, *Juan Pérez Jolote* (1948). But, unlike his literary writing, which centered on the life history of a Tzotzil, his papers on the Mam do not refer to individuals, or even communities, for the Mam are an anonymous, homogeneous collective entity, with no internal stratification and only the beginning of a religious distinction between Protestants and traditionalists.

In 1962 Pozas would publish "Los Mames," a "museographic script," which was apparently based on his field experience during the 1940s and used as support material for the ethnographic section of the Museum of Anthropology. This essay contains a great deal of information that Pozas had left out of his 1952 paper, including discussions usually contained in traditional ethnographies: life cycle, economy, and religion in historical context and the struggle for land and political organization. We learn that by 1945 the Mam language had almost disappeared from the Sierra and was only spoken by old people. The traditional costume consisted of "a cloth skirt, which is a piece of cloth made in Guatemala, woven on a Spanish pedal loom, . . . the main colors being blue, green, and red. The cloth is held with a sash, richly woven in wool of different colors and anthropomorphic and zoomorphic designs, as well as stars and stylized flowers" (Pozas 1962:20). This costume was still worn by older women, while men had completely forsaken their traditional clothing.

If this script had actually been used in the Ethnographic Hall of the museum, museographers would have had to find a creative way to include change and mobility in their representations, instead of simply showing a dummy dressed in the Tuzanteca fashion and displaying a few isolated utensils, as they finally did in the section dedicated to "The Maya in Chiapas."

Pozas's script speaks about a Mam double economy, based on subsistence crops, mainly corn and potatoes, which they cultivated on their small plots of land, and the wage labor in Soconusco's coffee plantations. It refers also to the historic right of indigenous peoples over the land and their struggle to attain agrarian rights in the face of the limitations imposed by the state through inalienability certificates.

At the time Pozas wrote, Mexican anthropology was divided into two lines of thought: the Mesoamericanist line, combining ethnohistory with archaeology to reconstruct the history of old Mexico, closely linked to the Museum of Anthropology; and the indigenist line, led by Manuel Gamio, whose concern was solving the contemporary problems of Indian peoples, as was that of the INI. Although Pozas was much closer to the second line, in his desire to develop a critical applied anthropology, a historicist calling was always present in his writings.[10] Notwithstanding their different critical positions, both camps to an extent served the pressing needs of the Mexican state, with Mesoamericanists contributing to the construction of a glorious past for the modern nation and indigenists integrating native and peasant sectors with national development.

Mesoamericanists received special support during the administration of Adolfo López Mateos (1958–1964), who had been a member of the Vasconcelist youth movement in the 1920s. Influenced by José Vasconcelos's nationalist discourse, López Mateos conceived of creating a museum displaying the "cultural roots of Modern Mexico," those components of the cosmic race imagined by Vasconcelos.[11] This ideology explains the apparent contradiction in the fact that his administration should promote the construction of a museum acknowledging the multicultural formation of Mexico while developing an integrationist indigenism. What García Canclini calls the "dramatization of cultural heritage" consisted in displaying and cataloging the different indigenous cultures, not to acknowledge their existence as differentiated entities, but to represent them as components of "the Mexican," still conceived as a fusion of all the cultures ritualized in the museum. The building itself represents such a fusion of past and present of modern Mexico (García Canclini 1995:110). Teotihuacán, Olmec culture, Maya preclassic culture, Tzotzil Indians from the highlands, Mam from the Sierra, Pedro Ramírez Vázquez's modern architecture—all were an integral part of "the Mexican." The final goal of this "repertory" was, as specified by López Mateos himself, "that on leaving the museum, the Mexican feel proud to be Mexican" (García Canclini 1995:132).

After the new museum building was dedicated in September 1964, there were still several "field trips" designed to gather more exhibition material for the Ethnographic Hall. Thus anthropological investigation, based mainly on "field trips" rather than "long duration fieldwork" became one of the budgetary priorities in the cultural policy of López Mateos's presidential period. On this subject, Medina, one of the anthropologists who participated in such trips, remembers:

> López Mateos built the museum with a strong nationalism; it had to display our national roots, these components of the Cosmic Race. We knew that such a concept was anti-indigenist, but that is the way nationalism was at that time. Money is given, for this investigation required loads of money, a lot of money to buy objects and travel around the country.[12]

One team traveled the Mam area from September to December 1967 under the direction of the Yucatecan anthropologist Fernando Cámara Barbachano. In the groups were two linguists, Otto Schumann and Robert Bruce; four ethnologists, Jesús Muñoz, Bolivar Hernández, Juan Ramos, and Andrés Medina; and, later, two archaeologists, Carlos Navarrete and Lorenzo Ochoa. Subsequently, Medina's ethnographic notes (1973) and Navarrete's journal (1978) would be published, as well as two linguistic papers, one on Tuzanteco by Schumann (1969) and the other on Huehuetán's Nahuatl by Bruce and Carlos Robles (1969).

Linguistic investigations during these trips had a partially classificatory role in identifying indigenous languages spoken in the coastal zone and the Sierra. Schumann found three variations of the Mam language, one spoken in the Mariscal zone and part of Soconusco, another in the region called Ojo de Agua, and another in Chicomuselo, in a village called Monte Sinai. They also found Tuzanteco in the Tuzantan region, Waliwi (a variation of Nahuatl) in Huehuetán, Mochó in Motozintla, and Tectiteco in Mazapa de Madero and Amatenango de la Frontera.[13]

Graphic representation of the Mam people in the Ethnographic Hall of the National Museum of Anthropology. The Mexican nation is represented by a map with the different ethnic groups depicted in it. PHOTO BY SAMANTHA R. DE LA GALA.

None of the papers resulting from this trip considers the degree to which these classificatory terms may be self-ascriptive. Years later, in 1978, we find that the Indigenist Coordinator Center founded in Mazapa de Madero only acknowledges the existence of three ethnic groups in the Sierra region, Mam, Mochó, and Cakchiquel, with the last term referring to Tectiteco (or Teco) speakers.[14] In Chapter 5, we shall see the meaning these categories have in the daily life of the Sierra peasant.

Also, according to Schumann, these investigations had another, undisclosed goal: presenting results and "fictitious projects" to American foundations in order to obtain funds for the museum. The irresponsible nature of these "field trips" and the pragmatic point of view of museum officials are acknowledged by the participants themselves.

> Museum people thought of linguistic research in terms of collecting data for the museum and also with the aim of selling projects; one report was given to the museum and other copies were sent to the United States, as a way of saying: see, this is what we do over here. They did not think of linguistic rescue, and besides, what could we have done in such a short time? One cannot work on a language for under six months or a year and start to do a good job; frankly, no. I consider the research I have done a real wonder; who can achieve in two months research on a Mayan language? No doubt it has mistakes, being a two-month job.[15]

Yet, as in the case of the papers on the onchocercosis brigade, the final papers of the participants in this team were very far from the central goals of those who financed the trip. This is particularly true in the case of Medina's article "Ethnographic Notes on the Mam from Chiapas," which has become a fundamental work for the study of the Chiapas Sierra Madre. Like Pozas, Medina was trained in two traditions. He graduated from the National School of Anthropology and History, where he actively participated in student politics; and while an undergraduate student, he was linked to the project "Man and Nature" that the University of Chicago was developing in the Chiapas Highlands under Norman Mackown's supervision. He later did postgraduate study at Chicago.

The paper he wrote with information collected during his Chiapas field trip was published six years later (1973), and according to an interview with the author himself, during this period he was influenced by the Cuban Revolution and student militancy, which led him to analyze his data from a different perspective. With his new critical vision of indigenous reality, he contextualized the life of Mam peasants within a wider historical process. His article couples field information with a historical account that covers colonial times, the independence and revolutionary periods, and the capitalist development of his own time. This historicist perspective, which was beginning to be popular during the 1960s under the influence of "dependency theory," is more innovative than the papers of preceding decades, which were centered on community studies; nevertheless, although he gave priority to the study of historic processes, Medina leaves out much field information on everyday life, which would have been useful for understanding life in the Sierra.

Comparing information contained in his field journal (which I was allowed to read) with the essay published years later, we see that in the latter the Mam are no longer the main interest of his work but have become a pretext for approaching broader "social processes," such as "the marginalization process stressed by the establishment of a plantation economy" (Medina 1973:161).

Neither Medina's field journal nor his anthropological essay acknowledges the Mam as individuals; we may ask, where are the experiences of Don Guadalupe Torres, Profesor Solórzano, Don Francisco Ramos, Don Rutilio, and Doña Elvira to be found? In the 1973 essay, we are told about an anonymous collectivity, "the Mam," who are facing Soconusco capitalist development and the rapid marginalization processes by which they "lose" their culture. This social object, "the Mam," who in the published paper seemed to be there in Sierra communities, acculturated and marginalized, but still present, had to be looked for by anthropologists "house by house, asking people," as Schumann said. This search is mentioned throughout his field journal: "Asking for Mam-speaking places we were sent to a small hamlet called Chiquihuites, four leagues from Unión and in the highest region" (October 24, 1967); "In order to rescue traditional culture we will have to study isolated hamlets away from the municipal capital" (October 24, 1967). Later, during an interview, Medina explained this experience of "looking for the Mam":

> The Mam were small groups in the mountains. I remember I went to Siltepec, for example. I was told there are Mam here, but they are over there, in that little house you see over there, far from the village. In the case of Siltepec, that was the impression I got. They were in corners, in islands within that large sea which were the peasants who were changing.[16]

The process of change is indeed present in his essay as well as in his field journal, but we do not find a texture in his ethnographic description of this change, a concrete sense of the way Sierra inhabitants are experiencing it. If he had come nearer to this change, he would have perceived that many of the new generation were leaving the Sierra and trying to find other prospects in other regions of the state. By this time the dichotomous community-plantation was no longer the center of Mam life, and the diaspora to the rain forest was slowly beginning.

The definition of "indigenous identity" that guided the field expedition, also present in Medina's Chiapas essay, refers to a sum of certain cultural traits, such as language, traditional costume, religious ritual, and a certain political organization of colonial origin, the presence of which determines the existence or nonexistence of such an identity. In this sense, we cannot hear the voices of social actors, the way in which they imagined themselves as a community. What they were looking for were "material objects," "cultural traits," "indigenous languages." The point was to rescue for the museum a fading culture.

> The point was to recover something of what was being lost. Back then the word was that the indigenous world was disappearing, and in my paper I maintain this element. . . . [T]he indigenous culture was disappearing, and some of it had to be rescued to keep in the museum. . . . [T]he aim was to rescue indigenous culture; thus photographs had to be taken, people had to be interviewed, objects had to be bought; it was like a search for accessible elements, at our disposition to be registered.[17]

This zealous search, however, did not allow the researchers to see or hear other things. In the field journal, we find these silenced voices:

> Don Francisco wears a *paliacate* [handkerchief] tied around his head, his voice and movements were extremely calm. *I do not remember what we talked about*, I only took some photographs of him and his wife, who was wearing a piece of industrial cloth tied around her waist, which resembled at a distance one of the cloths presently used in Guatemala. (December 4, 1967; emphasis added)

This "indigenous world" in which the museum was interested was harder to find than they had thought, and the field journal records the frustration:

> We visited the village of Chahuité, the first on the Guatemalan side, wanting to buy the cloths used by indigenous groups, but all we could find was a merchant selling radios and pieces of cloth for urban suits. . . . In the village itself [referring to a later visit to Silte-

pec] I did not see anything indigenous; on Saturday when I went out there was a market in the center of the small village, in front of the town hall, but it was next to nothing. (December 4, 1967)

Although this research was not particularly fruitful for the museum's goals, for Medina it turned out particularly suggestive of what he calls "marginalization processes." His field journal shows permanently the tension between the institutional goals of the trip and the author's interests. After one of the organizing meetings at which Cámara Barbachano gave them "charts of social change," Medina pointed out, a bit disillusioned: "The cells of social and cultural change of the rescue project . . . are very general and exhaustive; they give a very general idea of the situation of a settlement, but they do not provide the necessary information to reveal something about the social structure, or any other systematic aspect of the population's life" (Field Journal, September 26, 1967). Years later, this is the way Medina would describe the differences between Cámara Barbachano's interests and his own:

Cámara was interested in our buying traditional things, collecting what was indigenous. I bought Indian textiles, sashes, pots, copal sold in Motozintla, saddles, comparing the types of copal, prices, small details like that. This information was useful for museum collection; but, of course, that was his interest, mine became having an idea of the culture of the region, how to understand what happened in the different regions, why it happened. Of course, I was interested in asking indigenous people about the culture of the region, and I discovered a very complex, very rich region, for example, Chinese migration; commerce was controlled by Chinese. When I was at La Grandeza, I lived in the house of a teacher and she belonged to one of the Chinese families; they met to play canasta as a way to maintain the links between the Chinese of the region. Even in Tuzantán, the largest store belonged to a Chinese man, who had children with several Tuzantán women. Then for me all those details were new and important.[18]

On December 4, 1967, after several days of a fruitless search for "traditional culture," Medina reflected in his field journal: "In museographic terms, results have been poor, but as for the social point of view and the process of cultural change, several very interesting problems can be perceived, and we suggest a longer and more detailed research with better-defined theoretical goals." That the project was so superficial and disorganized (a common source of frustration for the ethnologist) prompted him to follow his own theoretical preoccupations:

> The main characteristic of this collective trip has been the major absence of a fixed plan, for Cámara seemed to change his mind every day, making up a plan at a time, changing it, the next day forgetting what he said, and for this reason we had done what we chose. (Field Journal, December 4, 1967)

Guided by his own interests, the author approaches interethnic and class relations in the region, reporting the way that different ethnic groups fill different social strata and geographic spaces. The indigenous groups, living in the highlands, on the slopes, and in the narrow valleys of the highest lands, are land laborers; the poor mestizos, living almost always in municipal towns or in larger population centers, are usually intermediary merchants and fill minor political positions; the Chinese and Lebanese immigrants are also in larger settlements and control a large part of the regional commerce; the ladinos (Mexicans of Spanish origin) live at the fincas on the coast and in the lowlands and, together with German immigrants, control coffee production and export; and finally, the politicians and the capitalists from Mexico's center fill major administrative posts and control commercial activity at the national and state levels. Such rich information about social stratification does not reappear in Medina's 1973 essay, perhaps because of a political desire to underline the contradiction of laborer/finquero and the consequences of capitalist development for the most marginalized sector—indigenous peoples. Mestizos, Chinese, Lebanese, German, ladinos—all of them disappear in the description of the 1970s, replaced by "Mam laborers," who must face "the finqueros."

Notes in Navarrete's field journal (1978), although centered on the location of archaeological sites, are an important source of information for the social dynamics of the region. During the archaeological trip, which began in Tuzantán and ended in Bejucal de Ocampo,[19] the author describes the landscape, the rapid change the region was undergoing, and the dynamics of the border region, such as the continuous passing through of illegal Guatemalan laborers who entered the country to work in the fincas.

At Motozintla, Navarrete pays a visit to the office of the local Department of Indian Affairs (Departamento de Asuntos Indígenas), where he is told of the nonexistence of indigenous languages in the region (Navarrete 1978:16). This official information coincided with contemporary reports, which had declared the Sierra municipalities mestizo. Yet, during their trip, team members found speakers of at least four different Maya languages, some of them with different variations. Navarrete acknowledges that "a large part of the population is indigenous, undergoing a process of mestization or ladinization, speaking a rather rudimentary Spanish" (Navarrete 1978:35). This archaeologist also links the acculturation process to the 1934 campaigns but also points out the importance of Spanish in the local social hierarchy. Abandoning their indigenous languages gave peasants a higher status in the local hierarchy, which is why many of the indigenous people of large villages wanted to differentiate themselves from the *naturales de la colonia* (those belonging to the colony). As in Medina's writings, Navarrete concludes by calling attention to the process of social marginalization undergone by Sierra peasants, as victims of capitalist development.

After a four-month trip on the coast and the highlands of Chiapas, the ethnographic rescue team returned to Mexico City with a few archaeological objects, a linguistic typology, and some cloths, *huipiles* (handwoven blouses), earthen pots, straw mats, and small handcrafted kitchen utensils, which were "indigenous enough." After consulting the files in the Museum of Anthropology, I found that most of the collected material has been languishing in the basement for the past several decades, as being "little representative of indigenous culture." Three of the objects obtained in this trip are currently displayed in the Ethnographic Hall: a cotton and synthetic silk cloth, yellow with red stripes (Inventory no. 71081 (64) 1.36E3-42), made in San Pedro Sacatepeques, San Marcos, Guatemala, bought by Andrés Medina; a lilac-colored cotton blouse, bought in Tuzantán, Chiapas, bought by Otto Schumann (Inventory no. 71231 [69] 1.36E3-49); and a small, black cotton sash with a brightly colored pattern, made in Guatemala and bought in Cacahoatán by Otto Schumann.

One of the museum halls, titled "Los Mayas-Chiapas," displays in a single circular platform the "traditional" costumes of the Tzeltal, Tzotzil, and Tojolabal of different regions. Only one of them has no identification: it is a woman with a long black braid, bending on her knees, with a yellow cloth and a lilac-colored blouse. None of the hall attendants knew for certain where that woman was supposed to be from. I recognized the cloth as similar to those worn by older women in Tuzantán, but I had never seen such a blouse in that region. I was asked to return the following day. I did, and the anthropologist apologized for the lack of a sign; nobody knew who had taken it away, or why, but it would be replaced as soon as possible, because she had already found the inventory card: it was a Mam woman.

Figure of a Mam woman, Ethnographic Hall of the National Museum of Anthropology. The objects in this hall were collected by the anthropologists Andrés Medina and Otto Schumann when they toured the Sierra in 1967.
PHOTO BY SAMANTHA R. DE LA GALA.

In his diary, Medina describes the actual clothing worn by Sierra women at the time of his trip:

> The fashion is polyethylene shoes, which are very uncomfortable because they do not allow feet to perspire, but are convenient for their low price and durability, and possibly also for their color. Peasant people in this region are fond of bright and lively colors, turquoise or bright yellow are abundant. Ornaments are few, only colors and the gracefulness of their movements adorn them. The most sold fabrics are those of urban origin. (Field Journal, December 4, 1967)

The ahistoricity of representations in the Ethnographic Hall, however, has been noted by García Canclini:

> It [the Ethnographic Hall] describes the Indians without the features of modernity: it describes the Indians without the objects of industrial production and mass consumption we often see in their communities today. We cannot know, therefore, the hybrid forms that the traditional ethnic assumes in mixing with capitalist socioeconomic and cultural development. (1995:130)

Thus the museographic script written by Pozas, where he describes the cultural change in that region, as well as objects brought from the Sierra, gather dust in a museum archive. Paradoxically, while the state officially acknowledges the existence of Chiapas's Mam, the identification legend is lost. A nameless figure is all that is left from the field expedition of the 1960s. After I explained to the anthropologist the reasons for my interest in the object, she kindly allowed me to review the cards of the museum inventory. When I took leave, she asked me dubiously, "Do these people really exist?" Unable to hold back a smile, I answered, "I am not too sure."

Although from different perspectives, both museum officials and anthropologists of the Chiapas field trip were preoccupied with a concept of the nation. For the former, Mam indigenous people were part of a national heritage they wanted to display; for the latter, a reflection, used to analyze the construction of the nation of which they were a part. When I asked Andrés Medina for a comment on the way he valued his experience in the Mam region and what impression it made on him, he told me:

> What I perceive is the region's poverty and above all the transformation of the zone; I had been in the Highlands and knew perfectly well all the highlands. . . . [S]till Soconusco and the Sierra Madre

were something very different. They had a great social efferves-
cence, Protestantism; I remember I was impressed by Protestantism
in that region. . . . [T]raditional villages were disappearing; they
were sort of abandoned or changing. Of course, what I felt then
was that indigenous villages were disappearing and that we were
doing something important, recovering that part. But, on the other
hand, that was an expression of wider processes; which was my real
interest? What does this tell me about what Mexico is? About the
composition of this nation? What was the question with which I left
the Escuela Nacional de Antropología? What is the nation? Who
am I within this framework, in this context? [20]

Mexican nationalism as a hegemonic ideology of the postrevolutionary state has colored the political thought of the most critical sectors
of society. The way indigenous peoples have been integrated into the
nation has been questioned, but the concept of the nation is yet to be
adequately questioned. The guiding concern of most of the critical anthropological research of the 1970s and 1980s (and even today) is how to
construct a national project more just and equitable for indigenous and
mestizo people, but the need to construct "one" Mexico is not questioned.
Nevertheless, other sectors, from perhaps politically conservative positions, have refused the idea of the nation and have found in new religious
ideologies of the Protestant line a space for organization and collective
identification outside the nation. These are Mam sectors that have been
most violently affected by policies of national integration, that have not
enjoyed the benefits of land reform until recently and whose history has
been marked by the need for constant migration, first as seasonal laborers
to the fincas and later as colonizers of the plains and the rain forest. These
Mam have been forced to leave their original communities and their eco-
logic environment and try to adapt themselves first to corn plains and then
to the rain forest.

Diaspora to the Rain Forest

Anthropologists who traveled in the Sierra during the 1960s saw everyday life in the community and caught a glimpse of Indian oppression in
the fincas, but they were not aware of an important phenomenon occurring at the very time they were in the Sierra: the massive migration to
the Comalapa plains and the Las Margaritas rain forest. The sixties were
a decade of exodus, for the termination of land distribution declared by

President Ruíz Cortínez in 1958 left thousands of peasants with no possibility of acquiring a piece of land on which to live. In the Sierra, many of those *avecindados* who dwelled there since the thirties and had been trying to fulfill the bureaucratic requirements for obtaining their land rights lost all hope of becoming ejidatarios. Many of these people went down to the region of the Frontera Comalapa corn plains, where there was also a generational pressure on land.

> Before we came to the rain forest, we went down to Comalapa. First we did not want to go that far. And we stayed there, in Comalapa, living with relatives once more, with the hope of obtaining land, but no way. Those avecindados living in Comalapa's ejidos were like us, just waiting. And in the finca there was almost no pay; *chapines* came by the truck full to the harvest, and my father's land was very small, already worked by my brothers Aurelio and Juan. There was not enough for me. And this is how I left the Sierra, the family and all; almost as an orphan I came to the rain forest.[21]

It was in the Comalapa region that some heard about national lands the government was distributing in some faraway place in the rain forest. It was the colonization campaign that the INI and the Department of Agrarian Affairs and Colonization (Departamento de Asuntos Agrarios y Colonización [DAAC]) were promoting among the landless peasants of Chiapas.

President López Mateos's administration had created the DAAC, whose main goal was to extend the agricultural frontier by promoting the colonization of national lands. This allowed the government to respond to peasant demands without being forced to touch the interests of large landowners. Most of the hidden or open latifundios were in the Soconusco region. Thus the Lacandon rain forest, already unofficially being colonized since the 1950s, became a receiving region for landless peasants (Lobato 1979).

In Chiapas in 1965, the INI and the DAAC designed a colonization project aimed at populating part of the Las Margaritas border region. The document, titled "Project to Relocate Excess Population from the Chiapas Highlands in Las Margaritas" (Proyecto de Reacomodo de Excedentes de la población de los Altos de Chiapas en Las Margaritas), explains the regional land problems in demographic terms, disregarding the problems of latifundism. This project proposed the promotion of rain forest colonization by peasant groups demanding land, as well as technical counseling to face the new environment. The four priorities established by the project were (1) the construction of a road to the Las Margaritas rain forest; (2) location and demarcation of national lands under the Department of Agrarian Affairs; (3) undertaking a socioeconomic study in order to plan all aspects of relocation, particularly to program all the activities of land settlements and services; and (4) construction of the Indigenist Coordinator Center (INI 1965). This project was only carried out in part, because although government officials promoted colonization, it was the peasants who had to achieve it by machete with no technical counseling. The construction of the border road started only in 1970 and did not reach the farthest regions until the end of the 1980s.

This migration represented a new adaptation process for Mam settlers, who in many cases had already experienced dislocation to the Comalapa plains. The difficulties of rain forest colonization colored and shaped the ways in which this new reality was perceived by migrants. The testimony of one of the new ejido inhabitants tells us about this new stage of adaptation and change:

> I heard there were good places in the rain forest, but my family did not want to come. I explained to them that Bejucal was not a suitable place, because there was no land and I could only make a living in the finca; when I returned I left all my money buying corn in Comalapa.
>
> Some told I was only going to die in the jungle and to make my children die, because there was a very large river. First I went to Bella Ilusión, and on the way we found many animals: monkeys, wild boars, wild pigs. Women and children walked crying.[22]

From the beginning of the 1960s, when the landless Mam population had first migrated to the plains region, they had had contact with a Protestant dissident group, the Jehovah's Witnesses.

> I was with my family in Comalapa living at somebody else's house when some brothers came to pay us a visit; they offered us *El Atalaya* [The Watchtower], but we could not read. Then they began coming to teach us and bring us Jehovah's word.[23]

During that transition period between the migration to the plains and from the plains to the rain forest, the Jehovah's Witnesses offered an opportunity for cohesion and in some cases were the organizational axis for colonization. In the case of one ejido of Las Margaritas region, which I will call "Las Ceibas," its founder was a Jehovah's Witness and promoted colonization specifically among landless peasants who belonged to that religious group.

> Mister Urbano Ramírez invited only Witnesses to form the ejido. This gentleman's purpose was that only persons who studied the Bible should arrive, those who were Jehovah's Witnesses; because that is the community we belong to, and that is the way it was done. As you can see nowadays, almost everybody belongs to Jehovah's Witnesses; very few people do not study the Bible. Don Urbano's purposes were achieved, and that is good, because we can see there are good results. One can direct oneself better with unity. In any matter we know that everybody will answer with the truth unanimously.[24]

The way in which historic processes have touched different sectors of the Mam population has influenced their response to the conversion strategies of different religious groups. Before the violence of "integrationist campaigns," Jehovah's Witnesses represented for the dispossessed Mam a more attractive alternative to the "outside world," because they supported the endogenous community. It was no more a way to adapt to change through new forms of religiosity than was the case with Presbyterianism; instead, it was a way to withdraw from change, as a form of protection. These Mam converts, like those who became Presbyterians, responded to their changing world by adopting new forms of religious worship, a form of protective withdrawal that, nonetheless, is change itself. Transformation was inescapable for these Mam. Before marginalization and the economic and social crisis, the Jehovah's Witnesses' millenarian proposals and their refusal of the world, modernity, and the state, represented a better option for the Mam population that experienced most severely disintegration and uprooting.

In the new geographic context, the Sierra and the "ancients' traditions" became only memories, to be told on rainy evenings. The majority of Las Ceibas inhabitants do not define themselves as Mam anymore but as Jehovah's Witnesses. Daily life has been organized under new terms and the sense of community is imagined in a different manner, as we shall see in Chapter 3.

Second Border Crossing

PEDRO

SEARCHING FOR PARADISE ON EARTH

I met Pedro for the first time one morning as I was bathing with several refugee women friends in the river near Las Ceibas. I had begun to be less embarrassed by participating in the collective bath, but because of my urban modesty, I had not yet been able to take off my shorts and T-shirt, which made the daily ritual very uncomfortable. K'anjobal refugee women usually bathed in an underskirt with the upper part of the body naked. Men passing by did not seem to pay much attention to the young and old breasts so freely exposed.

Pedro arrived on his honey-colored horse, one of the few horses in the ejido, and calmly proceeded to bathe it with soap scarcely a few feet away from us. Recent rains had already made the water rather muddy, and by washing his horse so close to us, our daily bath, though refreshing, left us that much dirtier. Some women got out of the water, while the bolder ones confronted Pedro and asked him to move downriver, where, by tacit agreement, animals were to be bathed. Mumbling between his teeth, Pedro grabbed his horse's reins and left, turning around to watch us and stopping for a while near the river.

After this unpleasant company had left, some elder women approached and asked me to wear something else while bathing, because an unmarried woman should not show her legs in such a fashion. I, who modestly had covered my breasts, turned out to be the impertinent one of the group, a bad example for other unmarried girls. This first memory of Pedro, as an arrogant adolescent who had shown little respect for the rules of the ejido and who was responsible for my being publicly reprimanded by K'anjobal elder women, made me keep away from him during my first stay in Las Ceibas.

Years later I returned to the ejido and saw that Pedro still had his adolescent looks. He was now almost twenty-two and worked as a publisher[1] for the local Jehovah's Witnesses. He had remained single, which was uncommon for men of his age. Like most young men of the ejido, he had no land of his own and worked on the coffee plantation and the family milpa until three o'clock in the afternoon, at which time he devoted himself to the activities of the religious group.

When he learned of my return to the ejido, Pedro looked for me and proposed a book exchange. He would lend me *Watchtower* and *Awake!* magazines, published by the Jehovah's Witnesses, if I would help him obtain a good English-Spanish dictionary. For the last two years, Pedro had been studying English by mail. Every two months he walked three or four hours through the forest to reach the unpaved road where he would catch a bus that would take him to the municipal capital of La Trinitaria. There he had a post office box that linked him to the "outside world."

The first time I heard Pedro speak English I could not believe my ears, for his pronunciation was better than mine, and he used "shall" for the future, instead of "will" as is commonly done in American English. I thought that through the Jehovah's Witnesses he had managed to travel to the United States, but I was wrong. Pedro did not even know the state capital, and his only contact with English speakers had taken place two years before, when some tourists had passed through the ejido on their way to the Miramar lagoon.

This was the beginning of a long friendship. For several years, Pedro's letters arrived in my mailbox at Stanford University; and in one of them he told me he was learning classical Greek so that he could read the "original" version of the Bible.

Pedro's interest in languages had led him to approach some elders and ask them to teach him Mam, and his desire to know what was beyond the rain forest led him to spend hours with the eldest men of the ejido in order to speak about the times of finca work. He longed to go back to the Sierra, whence his parents had come, to know the Soconusco coastland, where his grandfather had worked, to reach Mexico City, where he knew I had studied, and, finally, to visit the United States and practice his English. As was the case for many other young people there, Las Ceibas was too small for him.

After accompanying me to record several elders relating their experiences at the fincas and the problems of colonization, Pedro offered to tell me his story. "We young people also have things to tell you," he said. In just one afternoon, half joking and half serious, he told me why he was also Mam:

Look, the fact is that I do not remember much of the Sierra. I know my roots are there—we came from there—but I remember only a few things, as dreams.

I remember, for example, the little white potato flowers. They were so pretty when they covered the mountain. I went out with my older brother to care for the sheep—we had five of them, and my mother sold their wool in Motozintla to people coming from San Cristóbal. I also remember that when we used to go down to Moto [referring to Motozintla] on Thursdays there was a market where my mother went to sell some potatoes. People came from all over the Sierra and *chapines* from Guatemala to sell remedies, clothes, and electric appliances. I enjoyed very much coming down to Motozintla. I have enjoyed learning since I was a child.

I also remember my grandfather. His name was Pedro, like mine, and he was an idiomista. He was pure Mam, a son of Mam, a grand-child of Mam—that is why I tell you that, even if guys laugh, that I am also Mam, even if I do not speak the language. Because, after all, what is language? I speak English, and I am not gringo, right?

But I was telling you about my grandfather. He had the roughest time. My father says that in my grandfather's time the "burning of the costumes" took place—what Don Ancelmo was speaking about the other day. Do you remember? Well, it happened to my grandfather. They took the split breeches from him. I remember him already in long trousers.[2]

When my father decided to come here in search of land, my grandfather would not follow us—he was already old and was afraid of dying on the way. He wanted to be buried in the Sierra, next to my grandmother's grave. So it happened. I never saw him again. Once we came, we never went back to El Pinar, until today.

From the trip forward, I do remember—could I ever forget! First we went down to Comalapa, and there we joined other families, all of them believers. It was through a publisher that we learned there were lands here. My parents were not yet Witnesses, but they had begun to study and knew a bit about the word of God. My mother only listened because she could not read. So with Don Ulfrano they organized themselves. I only remember we spent several days sleeping at somebody else's house, at some uncle's, before starting the trip here. By then the road reached only Tziscao. From there on, we had to walk. I must have been eight, but I do remember the terrible heat and the exhaustion. I remember we scarcely ate on the way. I was very scared. I thought we were going to die, that the monkeys were going to eat us. Can you believe that? The things one thinks as a child.

So, we came first to the little plain near Santo Domingo, and then we moved here. It was by machete that men had to steal a bit of land from the forest. First, we lived in a cane and mud hut, like the *chamulitas* of Santa Elena. Then, when coffee started to be produced, they carried on their backs the material for houses. Only a few mud and cane huts were left, for those who just could not build them.

At first there was no school. I learned to read with the young women who were starting to "publish" [proclaim the Word of God]— those who could read taught it [Spanish] with the "book of biblical stories." It was not until I was about eleven that the first teacher arrived. He was Chamula and did not even speak good Spanish. We would laugh at him—you know the way children are. But when I began school I could already read and write. My father said it was all a waste of time. I had better help at the coffee plantation and study the Word of God. I was only at school for two years, and then it was all work.

The truth is that the Kingdom Hall [Salón del Reino] is the only place where young people get together. We have no dances or such mundane [nonreligious] things. We come together—unmarried men and women—in the afternoon, when there is no studying, in the house of one of us, and we play biblical games. We make a circle, and we pass around an *Awake!* or a *Watchtower* magazine, while someone outside plays nonmundane [religious] music on the tape recorder for two or three minutes. When the music stops, whoever has the magazine must answer a biblical question almost always related to the week's subject of study. It is fun to get together like this, and we learn a lot.

I like publishing very much. I can take the word of God to people, and I get to know places. I already went [have gone] to all the colonies along the Santo Domingo and Jataté Rivers. People do not accept easily the Word of God, but they listen and are respectful. They learn something, and one learns too.

I do not think that everything that is worldly is evil. Many people from here think so, but if it [the world] were evil, why did God create it? Imagine, so many things just to test us. I do not think so, do you?

Look, about the things of the ancients—I do not know too well what to think of them. I know you are very interested in them. I also like listening to the stories of the ancients. It is good to remember where the seed comes from and know what they suffered so that we can now have our coffee trees and live in this colony here in the forest. But many of the unmarried people do not care anymore. You see how they laugh at me because I spend my time listening to Don Ancelmo's stories. They say that what I need is a girlfriend. But I have always liked to learn. I think there are good and bad things. As in everything, there are things that are not useful nowadays. They knew a lot about healing with plants and that is good. But there are things that are better cured with medicine, and if we have medicine, why should we not use it? Now we have to make use of what we have. In Paradise on Earth, after Armageddon, we will not need medicine or anything; there will be no illness, or sadness, or hunger. . . . But in the meantime we have to make use of what we can, we have to struggle for life.[3]

Chapter

3

MAM JEHOVAH'S WITNESSES

NEW RELIGIOUS IDENTITIES AND
REJECTION OF THE NATION

By the mid-seventies a group of Mam peasants decided to seek new paths and abandon the Mariscal region. Crossing borders of geography and identity, about sixty families migrated to the southwestern zone of the Lacandon rain forest, the so-called Cañadas de Las Margaritas. Most of these families had previously been converted to a new religious creed, the Jehovah's Witnesses. In this chapter I explore the history of the inhabitants of Las Ceibas, one of the many ejidos founded in the borderland of Las Margaritas at that time. My long stay there allowed me to learn the history and origins of the settlement, which otherwise I would not have been able to identify as Mam.[1] After several afternoons of conversation, the people began to tell me about their Mam identity. There may be other "mestizo" communities in that zone whose history is linked to the Sierra Madre and whose ancestors defined themselves in some historical moment as Mam that the official census has not recorded. Because the official record overlooks their indigenous past, their identification as Mam is difficult. It is equally difficult to define what percentage of the Mam population has been converted to the Jehovah's Witnesses, for it is a minority group and their presence in the Sierra and rain forest regions stands out more for the confrontational character of their religious and antinationalist discourse than for their numerical importance.[2]

The Jehovah's Witnesses' millenarian ideology was born in an industrial town, Pittsburgh, Pennsylvania, with a mainly English-speaking white membership, and reached Mexico's southern border almost a century after Charles Taze Russell laid the foundation of this new organization by establishing in 1879 the religious magazines *Watchtower* and *Herald of Christ's Presence*. The Association of Bible Students, called Jehovah's Witnesses since 1932, made its first incursions in Mexican territory in 1893, and their magazines have been translated into Spanish since 1931 (Watchtower Bible and Tract Society 1985:10).[3]

Because their proselytizing efforts are conducted primarily through the written word, this religious group at first focused its attention on urban and semiurban areas, which possess a higher level of literacy. After the 1950s the Jehovah's Witnesses extended their influence to the country's rural areas, mainly among Spanish speakers.

The first publisher arrived in the Mam region by the end of the 1960s, from the towns of Comitán and Tapachula. At that time the Mam population had been almost 100 percent Hispanicized and the literacy level was much higher than in other regions of the state. Comitán publishers were the first to reach the Frontera Comalapa region and offer *Watchtower* and *Awake!* to those landless peasants who in 1973 would found the Las Ceibas community in the heart of the Lacandon rain forest. The end of this world and the beginning of God's kingdom, where Jehovah's Witnesses would live happily ever after, was announced from door to door throughout the Frontera Comalapa colonies.[4]

The historical experience of the region's inhabitants with the Mexican state as well as their exclusion from the modernizing project of the 1950s and 1960s might have aided the acceptance of the ideology of the Jehovah's Witnesses among many of the dispossessed peasants. The antimodernization ideology of the Jehovah's Witnesses, a reaction against the nineteenth century's modernist philosophy and the advance of industrialization (Beckford 1975:3), was appealing to Mam peasants, who had experienced a violent encounter with the modern Mexican state.

The millenarian discourse brought to the borderland by Comitán publishers expounded the rejection of all the institutions of this world, especially nations and their rulers, who are presented as incarnations of evil forces.[5] The need to form a new nation of God governed by a theocracy headed by Jehovah himself has led the Witnesses to reject all the "governments of this world" (Stevenson 1967; Kaplan 1989).

The voices of the inhabitants of Las Ceibas are those of a religious minority within an ethnic minority and can tell us about the experience of being marginalized among the marginalized. They are the peasants "without a culture" whom indigenism has ignored. Their histories, filled with silences, willfully forgotten episodes, and contradictions, are an integral part of the history of the "other border."

In Search of Paradise

It was in summer 1973 that Ulfrano Pérez invited seventeen family heads to get together in a Frontera Comalapa settlement. The seventeen had in common their lack of land, their status as *arrimados* (people living in somebody else's house, in this case the house of a relative or a friend), being sons of idiomistas, and having links with the Jehovah's Witnesses. All those gathered had come to Comalapa from the Sierra, after exhausting all possible means of obtaining from the government a piece of land in their communities. The eroded land of the Sierra could not support their children, and Soconusco's fertile lands, in the hands of finqueros, were inalienable. There was no other way but to search for new horizons outside the Sierra.

During one of his many visits to the Comitán Ministry of Agrarian Reform (Secretaría de la Reforma Agraria), Don Ulfrano had learned that there were national lands in Las Margaritas rain forest that could be colonized. Indigenous peoples from the highlands had already begun to found colonies in the forest, and people were arriving from other parts of the state and the country.

In this first meeting, Don Ulfrano invited participants to form a colony of "believers" in the rain forest.

> When I learned there were national lands to be distributed, I invited several people I knew, all of them believers, to go and found a colony. I thought that Jehovah God had made me find out about these lands. We knew that we had to wait for Paradise on Earth, after the battle of Armageddon, and we thought that we could wait together in the forest, far from the temptations of this world. At first there were only seventeen of us, but we soon assembled the twenty able men we needed, and more joined in, all believers.[6]

The agrarian code, modified in 1962, stated in Article 58 that at least twenty applicants and a six-month residency were necessary to fulfill the requirements for the establishment of new ejidos on national lands. The modification, made under President López Mateos, opened for colonization national lands that until then had been the property of the federal government, while reiterating the defense of latifundism (Reyes Osorio et al. 1974:701).

When the founders of Las Ceibas arrived in the region in 1973, people from the highlands and Las Margaritas—Tzeltal, Tzotzil and Tojolabal—had already established at least ten settlements in the southwestern part of the rain forest (Paz Salinas 1989:84). The best and most accessible lands had already been distributed among the first colonizers. They had received an average of twenty hectares per family (Pohlenz 1985; Paz Salinas 1989; Acevedo 1992), whereas Las Ceibas settlers obtained an average of only ten hectares of arable land, which nevertheless compared favorably to the average of three hectares their parents had in the Sierra region.

The Jehovah's Witnesses established its own method of distributing land. Contrary to other ejidos, where those who promoted colonization were able to choose the best lands, in Las Ceibas such decisions were made collectively, in an effort to give each ejidatario the same amount of quality land.

> First a group of men went ahead to find our land. We had to walk a lot because everything was settled. We went through Santa Elena, through Pacayal, through Jerusalem, we reached Loma Bonita, until we found this clearing, it was near the river and there were national lands, so we decided to make our colony here. Then we brought our families, and all together we cleared the land and distributed it, fairly we gave each one his plot. Now we were not scattered like in the Sierra. Our colony would be orderly, and we decided to build a kiosk at the center, like in Comitán.[7]

Don Angel Albino Corzo's dream, expressed in 1934, of having "new communities and villages where [indigenous people] come together and live in a different fashion" and not "scattered throughout the mountains" became a reality with the founding of the rain forest colonies. Ejidal distribution at the end of the 1930s had begun to concentrate the population around municipal agencies, but in the rain forest inhabitants of the new communities not only established concentrated settlements but also made use of urban planning whereby houses were built on a rectangular grid, forming blocks. In the case of Las Ceibas, this new design has been completed with geometrically trimmed bushes around houses and the use of cement in construction.

> At first, we lived in mud and cane houses like the chamulitas around here at Santa Elena; later, when coffee began to be produced, they carried on their backs the material for their houses; only a few mud and cane houses remained, those who just did not make it.[8]

The construction of this "jungle paradise," with pastel cement houses was possible thanks to the coffee boom of the 1970s and the arrival in 1983 of Guatemalan refugees, who provided the inhabitants of Las Ceibas with a ready and cheap workforce for the coffee harvest.

Work on the coffee fincas had marked the lives of most of the inhabitants of Las Ceibas, as it had their parents' and grandparents' elsewhere. This was their first opportunity to plant and harvest their own coffee. When this group arrived in the region, most ejidos were already involved in coffee production, having failed in growing corn and breeding and selling pigs (Preciado Llamas 1978; Paz Salinas 1989).

The shift to supporting ejidal coffee growing for export was one of the new agrarian policies promoted by the administration of Luis Echeverría Alvarez (1970–1976) before the rise of the peasant movement at the national level. The agrarian crisis and peasant mobilization had led to the government's rethinking of the antiagrarian policies of preceding administrations and to the creation of new channels to support the most marginalized sectors of the peasantry. The Mexican Coffee Institute (Instituto Mexicano del Café, or INMECAFE), created in 1958, had so far limited itself to fixing prices, but by the mid-seventies it broadened its role by creating Economic Production and Commercialization Units (Unidades Económicas de Producción y Comercialización [UEPEC]), through which it organized producers and gave them the necessary training to obtain credits (Nolasco 1985). Parallel to its technical support, INMECAFE began to support ejidatarios in the marketing of their products by offering to pay for the surplus, depending on the price of coffee on the international market.

When the first inhabitants of Las Ceibas arrived in the region in 1973, they went to work as laborers with their neighbor ejidatarios who were already planting coffee. These temporary jobs helped them to obtain their own coffee plants and become familiar with the bureaucratic processes necessary to link themselves to INMECAFE.

> When we just arrived, we began to plant a bit of corn, but we were offered jobs in the coffee plantations of those who had arrived first. This is how we started to work for them in the colonies; there we learned of the existence of INMECAFE and that we could obtain credits for fertilizers and pesticides. We were soon sowing our own little plants and Jehovah God blessed us with our *cafetal* [coffee plantation].[9]

From then on, Las Ceibas's economy was centered on coffee production. Corn, the staple food for Chiapas peasants, became secondary.

Most ejidatarios still planted their small milpas, but the state-subsidized MASECA flour was making an appearance in border homes, and the money produced by selling coffee was used to complement their corn crop with this new product.

Although the state itself promoted coffee production in the region, soon peasants were no longer depending on its support because of the inefficiency of governmental offices. Excessive bureaucracy made selling their products through INMECAFE difficult, and in general the money for surpluses never reached the peasants. They frequently resorted to local intermediaries to sell their coffee.

The arrival of hundreds of Guatemalan refugees from 1982 on introduced new dynamics into the coffee-based economy and made possible the accumulation of capital on the best-connected ejidos. As a consequence of the razed-lands counterinsurgency campaigns promoted by the Guatemalan army, whole villages moved to Mexican territory in search of shelter on the ejidal lands of rain forest colonies (Hernández Castillo et al. 1992). Indigenous refugees worked for very low wages in exchange for a piece of land to build their huts and plant their milpas. This surplus workforce allowed rain forest colonizers to lower the costs of coffee crops.

Las Ceibas inhabitants received on their ejidal lands ten families of K'anjobal refugees. Although Guatemalan peasants profess a different religious belief, they were welcomed by the Jehovah's Witnesses.

> When refugees started to come we organized a meeting to see how we could help them. We understood their suffering. We had also lived at somebody else's house in Frontera Comalapa, with no land, . . . without a house. Satan's forces had led the government of Guatemala to massacre and they were escaping, so we decided to receive them and let them build their huts in the ejido. So then the families you have met came. . . . [T]hey were not believers, but they had to learn to respect our agreements.[10]

Alcohol consumption was the main source of tension between Mexicans and refugees. Many refugees ignored ejidal prohibitions and consumed alcohol in the colony, which eventually helped to cause the deterioration of relations between both groups. Yet for five years Catholic refugees and Mexican peasants lived together peacefully, until the former decided to leave the ejido. Several families were relocated in the state of Campeche, and the others joined other camps in the region.

The departure of the refugees coincided with the collapse of coffee prices, which ended dreams of bounty in the region. In 1989 Las Ceibas peasants decided not to harvest their crop because low prices made it impossible to pay for laborers. They faced this new crisis as one more sign announcing the beginning of the end.

> People were scared because coffee is no longer valuable and they have no more money to buy their MASECA. We know that the worldly governments cause these things to happen, they fight among themselves, they do not respect their agreements and lower the prices of coffee disregarding that we may starve. But we Jehovah's Witnesses are not scared. We know that soon all this will not matter because in Paradise on Earth there will be abundance and we will need no money, we know the time is near.[11]

To confront the crisis, many local coffee growers tried to find new ways to survive by contacting the agro-ecological cooperative societies that were beginning to form in the Sierra or by linking themselves to peasant organizations to negotiate new governmental support (Limón 1995; Leyva Solano and Ascencio 1996). As for the inhabitants of Las Ceibas, they used their free time to publish throughout the region.

Everyday Life at Las Ceibas

The "coffee boom" made possible the construction of a bridle path connecting Las Ceibas to the Carretera Fronteriza del Sur (South Border Road) as well as the improvement of ejido houses. The appearance of the colony—its cleanliness, the colorful houses and their geometrical distribution, the central kiosk, and the surrounding fruit trees—contrasts with the people's precarious diet, which consists of bug-laden beans bought at very low prices from Guatemalan refugees (who in turn receive it from the UNHCR), corn cultivated in family milpas, and MASECA. The granaries are empty, and many of the people suffer from malnutrition. Nevertheless, solidarity among Jehovah's Witnesses has allowed the inhabitants of Las Ceibas to weather the coffee crisis.

Las Ceibas is different from other local communities not only because of the design and distribution of its houses but also because of its internal organization. In the new community the religious group has become the organizational axis of everyday life, and the ejidal organization mechanisms established by the Mexican government have been rejected.

> Here it is different from the way they do in other ejidos, because I had heard people choose their *comisariado* [ejidal authorities] or

their whole management in one day at the end of the month when they vote; they see how many are in favor of this one or that one; they count and whoever obtains the highest number stays, and this is the way they do it with all authorities, but here it is different. Here the procedure we have is the way we study the Bible. Ministers talk with the person they think must be [the ejido authority] and tell him it is a hard job to be commissioner but explain to him he will have everybody's cooperation. Finally the person thinks it over, and when we meet they inform us, well, here is the person who will be commissioner or any other authority.

By electing our authorities this way we have no discussions or voting because there are controversies, isn't that right, sometimes to the point of coming to blows; but that is not our case. In a very favorable way our ministers make the appointments, and this is the way it has been done and there has never been any problem.[12]

Las Ceibas inhabitants have rejected conventional popular elections, instead turning the process into a community service appointed by religious authorities. Although Jehovah's Witnesses are forbidden to take public office, at Las Ceibas the position *comisariado ejidal* (ejidal authority) is not considered a public office but a community service following the rules established by the religious group.

The way the inhabitants of Las Ceibas use their free time has changed significantly. Alcohol and music have completely disappeared from community life, and now young people get together in "social gatherings" where they organize "biblical games," as described in Pedro's testimony.

Contrary to neighboring indigenous communities, at Las Ceibas the day's work does not begin at 4:00 or 5:00 A.M. but at 8:00 or 9:00. And the workday ends at 3:00 so that the rest of the afternoon can be dedicated to individual or community study, depending on the day of the week.[13]

With the disappearance of religious feasts and alcoholic beverages, consumption patterns have also changed. Satin or silkaline is very common among Las Ceibas women, as are white shirts and ties among men, giving them an urban air that is surprising in the middle of the Chiapas rain forest.

Women have acquired a new role in the community: although they still do the housework, and also care for the family orchard and domestic animals (pigs, hens, and ducks), now they have greater participation in the religious group. They can even become circuit superintendents, and their social space has widened outside the home, as they are allowed to publish in neighboring communities. The use of birth control is allowed only if the aim is to have more time for service to the congregation. Women's interest in religious activities is striking. They are usually the majority in weekly meetings and actively participate in the question-and-answer session that follows the reading of texts. In spite of the religious group's characteristic conservatism in opposing feminist movements at the international level,[14] in the context of rural Mexico, it has broadened the universe of women's participation and revalued their intellectual capacity, giving them new responsibilities in the public sphere.

Community life is ruled by an internal law established by Jehovah's Witnesses' local authority, which forbids, among other things, selling or drinking alcoholic beverages in the ejido. Underage youngsters are not allowed to meet in public places after eight o'clock in the evening. The violation of any of the Internal Law regulations entails a private sanction the first time, a public one the second, and expulsion from the ejido the third. There is no ejidal jail as in other local colonies, and major crimes, such as theft or physical assault, are punished by expulsion. People who transgress the community's laws are taken before a special commission headed by the congregations' ministers, which decides the sanction that is to be applied.

> A person who steals can actually be expelled from the ejido, but before that a different procedure has to be followed. The person is scolded and if, after committing such a grave fault, [he] does not repent, does not humiliate himself to show his subjection to the ejido, then there is nothing to do but to expel him from the colony. That is done.[15]

The jail is in effect replaced by the ideological control of the group, which attempts to direct and rule everyday life. Such control is manifested in the people in charge, who oversee the study and behavior of all converts, every Witness being responsible for someone and at the same time under someone else's responsibility. From the moment they can read, children begin to have responsibilities within their group,[16] leading the study of younger children and teaching them to read and to write from a text called "My Book of Biblical Stories."

Some scholars have pointed out that because of this authoritarian structure Jehovah's Witnesses are welcomed particularly among migrant populations, who have abandoned their original homes and thus lost their own life structure. Comparing Jehovah's Witnesses' labor in the Mexican towns of Mérida and Guadalajara, Patricia Fortuny writes:

The Organization is authoritarian and patriarchal par excellence, but these characteristics translate into positive features for all members since they find protection and certainty there, factors absent from society at large. . . . We find similar responses in many believers who refer to the rigid norms and strict behavior demanded by the group as a positive aspect. Instead of looking at these disciplinary forms of power as constraining their life and freedom, they see them as benefits for their lives. (1995:173)

These perspectives suggest the effectiveness of the group's control strategies. Interestingly, the ways in which such religious discourse is reinterpreted, spaces of dissidence negotiated, and spaces of resistance constructed are little explored by those who are preoccupied by the way societies reestablish their "inner balance." Much of the research on the Jehovah's Witnesses among migrant populations assumes the functionalist premise that all societies tend toward an inner balance and that in a new social environment migrants make use of religious institutions in order to reestablish such a balance.[17]

It is undeniable that in many cases the religious group helps to restructure community life and establish new routines. Yet group values are nonetheless complemented and modified by the historical experiences of individual converts, and religious change necessarily takes place in a context of power relations, which will affect the way religious discourses are reinterpreted.

The Strength of Utopia and Antinational Discourse

The religious utopia promised by the Jehovah's Witnesses to their converts has been reinterpreted in different ways in different historical contexts. In South Africa and central Africa, Jehovah's Witnesses' ideology was reinterpreted at the beginning of this century and upheld as part of an anticolonialist movement called Kitawala, which presented the battle of Armageddon as the end of European control over African territories (Greschat 1967; Hodges [1976] 1985; Sholto 1977). Similarly, discourse on a new utopian society has inscribed itself on the collective imaginary of Las Ceibas Jehovah's Witnesses and has influenced the way social justice is understood.

There will be no rich and no poor; there we will need no machines, or credits or fertilizers; the earth will give us everything. In Paradise on Earth we will no longer be in families, because we will all be

young; there will be no age or class differences. That is the way we
know it is going to be.[18]

Influenced by the way in which they imagine Paradise on Earth, Las
Ceibas inhabitants criticize and challenge the reality they face every day.
For adults, utopia will be attained only after Armageddon by Jehovah's
will, but some young people wonder if this Paradise can begin to be constructed right now.

It is precisely the internal contradictions of the discourse of the Jehovah's Witnesses that allow converts to make several readings at the same
time. On the one hand, it promotes political demobilization by stating
that only Armageddon will end the injustices of this world; on the other,
it speaks constantly of the illegitimacy of the power held by nation-states
and the possibility of constructing a new nation based on social justice
that extends beyond all borders.

> The Witnesses see themselves as a new nation composed of people
> from all over the earth who have given up their original nationality,
> as it were. Whilst living under different forms of worldly govern-
> ment, they are really only temporary residents, aliens, because they
> belong to this supranational new nation, subjects of God's Heav-
> enly Kingdom, whose laws contained in the Bible they must obey.
> (Stevenson 1967:160)

Because of this attitude toward worldly governments, in several coun-
tries Jehovah's Witnesses have been considered "traitors to their country."
Judge Joseph Franklin Rutherford, second president of the Watchtower
Society, was jailed during World War II for his "antipatriotic" writings.
In one such work, Franklin pointed out:

> Nowhere in the New Testament is patriotism (a narrow-minded
> hatred of other people) encouraged. . . . Everywhere and always
> murder in every form is forbidden; and yet, under the guise of
> patriotism the civil governments of earth demand of peace-loving
> men the sacrifice of themselves and their loved-ones and the
> butchery of their fellows, and hail it as a duty demanded by the laws
> of heaven.[19]

This antistate discourse has provoked the persecution and repression
of Witnesses by all types of governments. In Nazi Germany they were
considered enemies of the Reich, and six thousand of them were relocated
in concentration camps (Beckford 1975:34); paradoxically, in the United

States they were seen as a pro-Nazi movement and were subject to several discriminatory policies (Beckford 1975). In socialist countries they have been considered the ideological bastion of American imperialism, while in capitalist countries they have been ostracized for their communist ideas (Penton 1985:146, 134). The colonial administration in Africa saw them as a source of destabilization, especially since the Kitawala movement (Hodges [1976] 1985; Sholto 1977); and ironically, during the decolonization movement several nationalist movements expelled Jehovah's Witnesses from the new nations, considering them "remnants of colonial administrations" (Hodges 1985).

Because of their rejection of national symbols, such as the flag, the coat of arms, and the national anthem, together with their refusal to participate in obligatory military service and in state parties, Jehovah's Witnesses have been identified as "the national enemy," whether by socialism, capitalism, fascism, anticolonialism, or colonialism. It is interesting to note how a pacifist movement promoting political demobilization can arouse fear in so many nation-states. Rather than the doctrines themselves, perhaps the possibilities of reinterpretation arouse the political mistrust of different governments.

In the case of Mexico, the children of Jehovah's Witnesses who refuse to participate in pledging allegiance to the flag have been expelled from public schools. Religious groups have appealed to the National Commission for Human Rights (Comisión Nacional de Derechos Humanos [CNDH]), which analyzed the cases and acknowledged that such expulsions violated the right to education of Jehovah's Witnesses' children. The CNDH recommended that the Ministry of Education put an end to such expulsions, limiting the sanction to a lower grade in civic education for all those children who for ideological reasons refuse to honor the flag (Garma 1994). That Mexican Jehovah's Witnesses put their claim before the CNDH speaks to their capacity to organize and claim their rights in certain circumstances. In Canada and the United States, the Witnesses' legal fight for freedom of religion and the right to education has contributed to some scholars' view that this group is significant in the civil rights struggle (Penton 1976; Kaplan 1989).

In Las Ceibas, Tzotzil teachers, adhering to the bilingual system of the SEP, have had to adapt to community decisions. When all registered students refused to participate in "Civic Monday" ceremonies, they finally completely discarded the pledge of allegiance to the flag.[20] For many Las Ceibas inhabitants, the state is a necessary evil that is condemned to disappear. While it exists, they tolerate it and follow all the laws that do not go against their ideological principles and accept its support, as in the case of INMECAFE, but do not expect much of it.

> When we realized that INMECAFE people were stealing the money of our sales we were not surprised; we know that worldly governments are a creation of Satan and that cheating is part of their strategies.[21]

For some, the rejection of "worldly governments" is expressed in their skepticism of the electoral process. During the 1988 elections, one of them said:

> Even if the Cardenistas had won [referring to the Frente Cardenista de Reconstrucción Nacional made up of a leftist coalition] there would be no justice, because Jehovah will not allow any man to boast he has built a just society before the arrival of God's kingdom. Only in Paradise on Earth after the battle of Armageddon will there be justice in this world.[22]

Yet there are other sectors within this Witnesses community that have another reading of the antistate discourse.

> I do not think we must obey the government if we know it is a creation of Satan, if we obey it we let ourselves be cheated. We must act according to what we believe to be just as said in the Gospels. If worldly governments are unjust we have no reason to obey them, don't you think?[23]

This rejection of "unjust governments" led the Jehovah's Witnesses of the Cuauhtémoc ejido, in the neighboring municipality of La Trinitaria, to disregard the religious group's prohibitions and vote during the 1988 presidential elections for Cuauhtémoc Cárdenas (Hernández Castillo 1989).

Some scholars have held that proselytizing strategies used by Jehovah's Witnesses, based on literal memorization of religious doctrines and not their analysis or discussion, have led to homology between beliefs and doctrines (Beckford 1975:103; Bottings and Bottings 1984:142). This logic may lead us to deny any possibility of social agency by individuals, who are then represented as mere receivers of religious ideologies. Many researchers who are former Witnesses, such as Heather Bottings and Gary Bottings, James Penton, and W. C. Stevenson, represent converts as automatons controlled and homogenized by the religious group's ideological strength, a position belied by their own personal experiences. Reading over the bodies of Mam peasants experiences lived in Canada, England, and the United States would be denying the historical dimension of the process of religious conversion.

Among some Las Ceibas elders, in spite of conversion, there still persists an old religious-magic mentality that seeps through their new forms of religiosity.

> We Witnesses cannot be "witched" because Jehovah protects us. Over there at Comalapa, a woman began to study the Bible with us, but then she did not want to continue and became spiritist. She founded her own Center. One day she was talking with the spirits of evil, with the *naguales*. They told her they could not enter her house because she had Jehovah's Witnesses books in her room.[24]

This belief that Jehovah protects his followers from the negative influence of naguales is quite common among border Witnesses. An elder from Ejido Cuauhtémoc told me:

> When I was comisariado I was very strict, and many got angry at me because I made them work in community tasks. Then some sorcerers threatened me that I would suffer some harm. One night these sorcerers appeared in the shape of dogs, but they did not come in. The next day they told me some men had been guarding my hut and that is why they were not able to witch me, . . . but there was nobody. The angels looking after their people defended me.[25]

The technological world described by Jehovah's Witnesses' publications—computers, atomic bombs, microwaves, and artificial intelligence[26]—is alien to the reality of Las Ceibas inhabitants, who reinterpret this information according to their own reference points. The perception of health dangers caused by pesticides and fertilizers is linked to their rejection of "new technology" and "modernization," a position promoted by the Watchtower Society.

Las Ceibas experience confirms once more that social subjects themselves give content to doctrines. Since doctrines are neither transforming nor conservative by themselves, it is the historical and spatial conjuncture, particularly of social groups, that provide them with content in either sense. Las Ceibas Jehovah's Witnesses have broadly developed their resistance to and symbolic rejection of governmental institutions through a Messianic discourse criticizing their present conditions and through a restructuring of community life according to their own rules. This critical attitude results from both their religious beliefs and their history of marginalization and oppression. At the same time, they have rejected and challenged other forms of productive and political organization, considering them also as "worldly things."

Las Ceibas Mam have extended the feeling of belonging beyond community, regional, or even national frontiers, to consider themselves part of a new imagined community: the Jehovah's Witnesses.

Different Contexts, Different Identities

Religious identity has become the main reference point for Las Ceibas inhabitants. Above all else, they define themselves as Jehovah's Witnesses, then as peasants, and only in certain contexts as Mam indigenous people. The persistence of some religious-magic elements within the new belief system and the reinterpretation of writings reaching the ejido do not go against this religious group's effective construction of a new feeling of belonging. The new community has been constructed based on the images brought by religious texts, by contact with the head of the organization through letters, and by local networks established with other believers in the state. Their identity as Jehovah's Witnesses is claimed even over their national identity.

We Jehovah's Witnesses have no nationality; we are all children of Jehovah God. We know that borders were invented by men; in Paradise on Earth we will all be like brothers and there will be no borders.[27]

Their close link with Jehovah's Witnesses in other countries, as well as with the General Headquarters in Brooklyn, New York, has helped Las Ceibas inhabitants to construct this feeling of belonging. Contrary to what happened in Africa with the Kitawala movement (Greschat 1967; Hodges [1976] 1985; Sholto 1977) or in the French Antilles with Adventists and Jehovah's Witnesses (Masse 1978), who remained independent from the general headquarters of their movements, Jehovah's Witnesses in Las Margaritas rain forest have not acquired an institutional independence from the New York headquarters. The international organization has granted them some independence in relation to local regional powers but not in relation to General Headquarters. In spite of its physical isolation, Las Ceibas has maintained ongoing communications with the Jehovah's Witnesses' government, contrary to other communities, where, once the congregation formed, it has developed with great independence.

Las Ceibas congregations are in the Frontera Circuit, extending from

Frontera Comalapa to Laguna Miramar, including the borderland regions of the municipalities of La Independencia, La Trinitaria, and Las Margaritas. This circuit is under the responsibility of a circuit superintendent, who visits the region once a year to assess the activities carried out and the development of the congregations. The circuit itself is part of the Comitán District, which comprises Las Margaritas rain forest and the plains and is one of the three districts into which the state is divided.[28] The three Chiapas districts are among the 124 districts into which the so-called Mexican Branch is divided, headed by three members of the Branch Committee.[29]

In Las Ceibas, the first ministers were selected by the circuit superintendent from among the oldest converts in the congregation, depending on their commitment to and participation in the religious group. From then on, any position is granted by following a complex consultation system. In the same way, periodic reports are sent on the development of activities, the growth of the congregation, the sale of publications, and circuit and district meetings. All this information is processed in a computerized system in Mexico City, linked to New York. Links with the outside world are reinforced by the distribution of periodicals such as *Watchtower* and *Awake!* that are published in New York and reach the ejido after a long trip beginning in that American city.[30]

Because of technological advances—so severely criticized by Jehovah's Witnesses—they have been able to exert an important influence over their branches in the southern border region of Mexico.

> To be ministers it is no more a matter of the whole congregation, but one goes ahead and another minister is needed because the group is increasing. Then the attitude of the person is studied, his participation in all activities: such as going to preach from house to house or doing a Bible study with another person in his own house or children's instruction, together with his growth in spirituality. All this is recorded in the central offices.
>
> Then those who are already ministers see whether they qualify and if they have the necessary amount of knowledge; then they write a report that is sent to the branch in Mexico City, to be sent by them to the World Center of Jehovah's Witnesses, in Brooklyn, New York. So that over there they decide whether they are accepted or not. It is the Governing Body who makes the assessment, but above all what we have learned in the Bible is that this appointment is by God's Holy Spirit; so that is how a person becomes a minister.[31]

This new transnational community plays an important part in the collective imagination of Las Ceibas inhabitants, as the main community with which they identify has ceased to be the "Mam people" and has become instead the Jehovah's Witnesses. History is, nevertheless, still being claimed in their narrations of origin and is recovered as a form of legitimation at certain historical conjunctures. Before the new multicultural context of the rain forest, Las Ceibas inhabitants began to assume a "peasant" identity that they opposed to the "Chamula" identity, a generic term they use to refer to all indigenous peoples from the highlands. The makeup of their colony, the use of pastel colors, their urban clothes, and their fluid handling of the Spanish language have become symbolic markers to differentiate themselves from the Chamulas:

> Chamulas live in a different way. If you saw their houses, even if they have money from selling coffee, you don't even notice it, because they still live the same. Women almost do not understand Spanish. . . . They are not very civilized, this is why it is more difficult that they accept Jehovah's word.[32]

There is, up to a point, a derogatory attitude toward the Chamulas and Guatemalan indigenous people who do not know the Word of God and are not proficient in Spanish. Yet the consciousness that they share an identity as indigenous and idiomistas seeps up to the surface when the point is to legitimize a knowledge that starts to be valued by indigenist institutions working in the region. After several decades in which their indigenous identity had brought them discrimination and exclusion, the Mam of Las Ceibas confront a new governmental discourse underlining "the value of native cultures," which is analyzed in the next chapter.

From their contact with officials of the Indigenist Coordinator Center (CCI-INI) of Las Margaritas and the indigenist radio station XEVFS, "the Voice of the Southern Border" (La Voz de la Frontera Sur), Las Ceibas inhabitants began to notice the new value being placed by the state on indigenous cultures. In April 1987 La Voz de la Frontera Sur began to broadcast in Tojolabal, Tzeltal, and Tzotzil, reaching forty municipalities in the borderlands, the highlands, the rain forest, the Frailesca, the center, and the Sierra of the state of Chiapas with a four-thousand-watt signal (Gutiérrez 1996:41). In its programming XEVFS vindicates the value of traditional knowledge of resource management, herbal medicine, and agriculture in general, while recovering the oral history of local indigenous peoples. On July 23, 1988, the first program in the Mam language was broadcast, thus beginning the radio series "Mam Word and Music"

(Palabra y Música Mam), in which Sierra Madre inhabitants share their history and experiences with XEVFS listeners. As we shall see in Chapter 5, this series was the beginning of a cultural rescue movement in the Sierra, and for the rain forest inhabitants it represented the creation of a new space where Mam identity could be reclaimed.

Las Ceibas inhabitants decided to participate in these radio programs as Mam indigenous people and have broadcast several recordings in Spanish about their problems of colonization and stories told by elders on the origins of the Mam people. Participation in these radio programs was discussed at the community level, and it was decided that they did not contravene their religious precepts, as it was only a question of remembering the traditions of the "ancients" (Hernández Castillo 1991). Their position concerning this knowledge is ambivalent: on the one hand, they reject and fear popular religiosity, while they do not deny the power of witchcraft and witch medicine; on the other, they make a distinction between the "negative" and the "positive" points of this knowledge (see Second Border Crossing).

Visitors who know nothing about the history of Las Ceibas see only another mestizo community, one of the many that exist in the region. This is how it is classified by the INI. The inhabitants themselves do not speak about their Mam identity unless directly asked in certain specific contexts. For example, noticing my interest in the narrations of old K'anjobal refugees in the ejido, Pedro gave legitimacy to his own history by claiming his Mam cultural roots.

Since the creation of the Solidarity Funds for the Promotion of the Cultural Heritage of Indigenous Peoples (Fondos de Solidaridad para la Promoción del Patrimonio Cultural de los Pueblos Indígenas) as part of the social policy promoted by Carlos Salinas de Gortari's administration, Las Ceibas inhabitants officially claimed their Mam identity by proposing a project to the INI. It was an ecotourism project that included the construction of cabins near the waterfalls and an adjacent center for handicraft training where "Mam women can recover their handicraft tradition and sell their products to visitors."[33] Cabins were indeed built, but, because of lack of funds, the project was never finished.

The Las Ceibas Jehovah's Witnesses, by broadcasting their history to Sierra inhabitants through La Voz de la Frontera Sur, temporarily established a link to those listening relatives, friends, and *compadres* who had been left behind in the Sierra and from whom they had been separated for so many years. Through radio programs relaying the stories of their origin, Las Ceibas inhabitants now vindicate themselves as Mam, peasants, and Jehovah's Witnesses, reversing the order in which they usually define themselves. A linear and essentialist perspective of identity would not help us to understand or even hear these voices that try to tell their stories. They are narrations that tell us about a sense of permanence constructed day by day, with long periods of silence and denial, continuity and affirmation.

Chapter

4

FROM MESTIZO MEXICO
TO MULTICULTURAL MEXICO

INDIGENISMO IN THE SIERRA MADRE

The seventies marked a radical turn in relations between indigenous people and the state along the southern border. Integrationist policies shifted, and the nationalist discourse about a mestizo Mexico was replaced by another about a multicultural Mexico. The change in official policies resulted from the confluence of several social forces and from structural transformations in the model of the state, which were starting to be seen under the administration of Luis Echeverría Alvarez. While the inhabitants of Las Ceibas were making their way into the rain forest to found their Paradise on Earth, Mam peasants who remained in the Sierra Madre had a reencounter with the Mexican government. Indigenist officials arrived at ejidal and municipal meetings to promote the "rescue of Mam culture." This new official indigenism was greeted at first with mistrust and surprise by Sierra inhabitants, who still remembered the violence of forced Mexicanization campaigns during the preceding decades. Yet this new discourse was gradually appropriated by a sector of the local peasantry, who began to define themselves again as Mam.

With this new definition, the heterogeneous and changing space we call "the state" became an arena for confrontations between different conceptions of the future of the nation. Following those who have challenged the unitary and monolithic character of the state, and considering it "a series of decentralized sites of struggle through which hegemony is both contested and reproduced [and] locations where conflict over power are constantly being resolved and hierarchically reordered" (Mallon 1995:10), I explore here the contradictions between integrationist and critical indigenists, as well as the way in which such opposed definitions of Mexico have influenced the local projects of the Indigenist Coordinator Center Mam-Mochó-Cakchiquel and the actions of minor officials who were appointed to promote them. Those who have pointed out the need to conceive of state institutions as ethnographic spaces point out that through the action of minor officials "the state" is represented and challenged by its citizens (Gupta 1993). Anthropologists, agronomists, veterinarians, economists, and many other indigenist officials became the incarnation of the populist state for Sierra inhabitants.

This study has proceeded on the premise that indigenist policies and actions have influenced the way in which cultural identities are constructed. It is important to acknowledge as well that the state is also formed by everyday actions through which popular movements concomitantly influence the formulation and reformulation of hegemonic projects. The "everyday forms of state formation" include speeches, actions, and rituals through which popular cultures and the state mutually constitute each other (Joseph and Nugent 1994). By means of its indigenist policies, the state established the terms by which the indigenous population would be included in the national project, but at the same time, indigenous and peasant movements took over the indigenist discourse and assigned new meaning to it. Throughout history the Mexican state and popular movements have influenced each other through "a dialectic of cultural struggle that takes place in a context of unequal power and entails reciprocal appropriations, expropriations, and transformations" (Hall 1981:233).

Characterizing the Mexican state as corporative has tended to oversimplify the analysis by underlining the state's capacity to group and control popular sectors. Conventional definitions of Mexican corporatism refer to a set of institutional agreements through which group interests are structured. On these perspectives, corporative structures represent state control mechanisms over groups and subordinate classes (Hamilton 1982; Middlebrook 1995; Garrido [1982] 1991). Although corporative policy rests on the principle that the state decides who are the legitimate representatives of a class or sector of society, its mechanisms of control are not always effective. The very same mechanisms developed by the state to incorporate popular sectors into the hegemonic project can be used by those sectors to develop counterhegemonic practices and discourses (Berzley, English, and French 1994; Mallon 1995; Rubin 1997). A clear example of these reciprocal appropriations, expropriations, and transformations between the state and indigenous peoples is the new indigenism born at the end of the 1970s. With the development of a new multicultural discourse, the state began to consider Sierra inhabitants not as peasants but as Mam indigenous peoples, creating through its institutions new spaces of confrontation. The terms of this new "conversation" were established by the state, but a "language of contention" was developed by the Mam population. On this matter, it is useful to consider William Roseberry's assertions that hegemony takes its shape through struggle, not consent:

> The ways in which words, images, symbols, forms, organizations, institutions, and movements used by subordinate populations to talk about, understand, confront, accommodate themselves to, or resist their domination are shaped by the process of domination itself. What hegemony constructs, then, is not a shared ideology but a common material and meaningful framework for living through, talking about, and acting upon social orders characterized by domination. The state claims the power to name; to create and print maps with state-sanctioned labels. Community residents can recognize the right but refuse the name, among themselves. (1994:360–361)

The way in which the conditions for this new conversation were established was also the result of a political struggle within the state between two hegemonic projects, using different paths to pursue the same goal: the integration and modernization of the nation.

Two Struggling Perspectives

After its repressive campaigns against popular, urban, and peasant movements, which peaked with the Tlatelolco massacre on October 2, 1968, the Mexican state faced a crisis of legitimacy (Poniatowska 1971; Alvarez Garín 1998). On assuming the presidency, Echeverría began reconstructing the credibility of state institutions by means of a populist nationalism that gave agrarian credits for agro-export crops, subsidized basic products, and created jobs through public investment. For Chiapas, this nationalist populism represented the defense of a hidden latifundism by giving priority to technification of land use over land distribution. President Echeverría's populist measure granting 614,321 hectares of the central rain forest to sixty-six Lacandon heads of family, instead of solving the local land problem, created new conflicts between Tzeltal and Chol people who shared the territory with Lacandon natives and were expelled after the presidential decree (Arizpe, Paz, and Velázquez 1993).

As a result of this limited land policy, the official CNC lost its ability to mediate for the peasantry, a large sector of which was seeking, through independent peasant organizations, to establish a forum for their land demands (Harvey 1989). It is in this context that we see the emergence of governmental initiatives to recognize "ethnic groups" as state interlocutors and to create institutional spaces for their representation. Within the Mexican state several sectors struggled to establish the terms in which governmental power would be consolidated and regional development promoted. Political groups linked to the previous president, Gustavo Díaz Ordaz, supported a hard line giving priority to control and repression over negotiation, while a reformist sector promoted negotiation and indicated the need to end regional *cacicazgos* (chiefdoms) in order to attain true modernization of the Mexican rural system (Harvey 1989; Fox 1993).

This reformist line underlined the need to promote the organization of ejidatarios as the next step after land distribution. In 1975 the Agricultural Credit Law (Ley de Crédito Agrario) was modified to promote the formation of regional associations of small-scale producers. Credits were granted on the condition of collective organization, which helped to create new networks of control over the peasantry after the downfall of the official peasant organization.

As for cultural policies, Gonzalo Aguirre Beltrán was still the INI's national director and promoted acculturation. Yet this point of view was being challenged by a group of young anthropologists, who denounced official indigenism as ethnocidal. It was a generation of anthropologists trained in Latin American Marxism and "dependency theory" whose points of view were beginning to gain strength at the end of Echeverría's presidency.[1] This new perspective placed indigenous peoples not only within the regional realm but also within national and international political and economic structures. Departing from a traditional Marxist perspective that saw indigenous peoples as "potential proletariats," these critical anthropologists emphasized the need to respect cultural differences.

Aguirre Beltrán still defended the position that the priority of indigenism should not be indigenous peoples but the nation and argued that the recognition of cultural differences might lead to the creation of "fictitious nationalities." African American and Chicano movements in the United States aroused fear in the INI's director, who stated in an interview with a large national newspaper:

This policy acts in favor of indigenous development not for the group itself, but rather because it is a part of the national population and the nationality. . . . The supposition that we must form an Indian power on the lines of Black, Chicano, or Red power in the United States is out of touch with reality, because the situation in other countries is very different from our reality. We are against the creation of Indian nationalities that do not exist, because indigenous people have, by and large, a communal situation or organization, and a clear national consciousness is still being formed. (*El Día*, December 8, 1972:23)

Between 1970 and 1976 Echeverría's administration created fifty-eight Indigenist Coordinator Centers, in addition to the twelve that had been founded in preceding decades, while INI's budget was increased fivefold. Such measures constituted the largest support given to this institution since its creation in 1948 (*Acción Indigenista*, no. 281, November 1976).

In view of the immoderate growth of the indigenist apparatus, President Echeverría invited several of Aguirre Beltrán's opponents to participate in the INI, and these new points of view challenged the integrationist model from inside. Critical anthropologists such as Salomón Nahmad and Mercedes Olivera began to participate in the INI and to speak of the need for a participative indigenism. This struggle between the two positions is expressed in the INI's official magazine, which supported the director's position and, in 1973, warned about the "ideological" dangers represented by the proposals of

a group of politicians, anthropologists, and sociologists with anarchic tendencies, which struggle to turn Mexico into a multiethnic and multicultural nation; to do that they propose a full respect for native cultures and the creation of an ethnic consciousness among the groups who practice it in order to transform them into small nations. (*Acción Indigenista*, no. 235, January 1973:1)

At the same time, a minority group of indigenous intellectuals educated in the indigenous institutions themselves also began to challenge the assimilationist model and to advocate respect for cultural differences (de la Peña 1997). With no wish to diminish the importance of the indigenous peoples' struggles to resist the integrationist model, we would have to explore the historical and social conditions that allowed this challenging discourse to have even the slightest influence over governmental policies toward Indian peoples. We must acknowledge too that these new spaces are opened in part because of the political need to revise the "model of the nation" after the failures of the integrationist model. For although its acculturation strategies had managed to wipe out the use of indigenous languages in entire regions, such as the Guatemalan border, most Mexican indigenous peoples, including Mam peasants, still rejected the state's "modernizing" policies and ignored many of its educational, medical, judicial, electoral, and developmental agencies, among others.

Changes in the official discourse from a mestizo to a multicultural Mexico were the result of many struggles over power and meaning. This new discourse on the nation stemmed in part from the struggles of an emerging indigenous movement and the influence of a critical academic sector over indigenist agencies, but it also represented an updating of control mechanisms by the state. Imposition did not prove to be the most effective tool for the integration of wide sectors of the indigenous population into the "national project," so it was necessary to revise the characteristics of the imagined community so that a larger number of individuals might identify with it. The new state discourse about the nation enlarged the meaning of "being Mexican" to achieve a better "citizenization" of the indigenous population that had been left on the sidelines of the postrevolutionary project.

This newly born indigenism was behind the organization of the Pátzcuaro congress in 1975, where the National Council of Indigenous Peoples (Consejo Nacional de Pueblos Indígenas [CNPI]) was formed as a new agency to mediate between indigenous communities and the state.

From San Cristóbal to Pátzcuaro

The 1974 Indigenous Congress in San Cristóbal and the 1975 Indigenous Congress in Pátzcuaro are two important events in the contemporary history of Indian movements in Mexico. The first, jointly organized by the Chiapas state government and the San Cristóbal Diocese, is considered a key historical moment for the birth of an independent indigenous movement; the second, promoted by the CNC, the INI, and the Ministry of Agrarian Reform, is seen as a mechanism of co-optation by the state after the success of the 1974 congress. An examination of the documents issued by the two congresses, as well as the testimonies of participants in both, reveals that San Cristóbal's was not that independent and that Pátzcuaro's was not that official. Both congresses were characterized by conflict and negotiation between the state and indigenous peoples.

In accordance with President Echeverría's populist policies, Chiapas governor Dr. Manuel Velasco Suárez suggested to the bishop of the San Cristóbal Diocese, Samuel Ruíz García, the joint organization of an indigenous congress to commemorate the five hundredth birthday of Fray Bartolomé de Las Casas, a Dominican bishop known as "the Defender of Indians." At that time, the social ministry of the San Cristóbal Diocese was already beginning to be characterized by the "preferential option for the poor" promoted by the theology of liberation. Bishop Ruíz approved of participation in the organization of the congress, provided it did not become a folkloric congress but a true space organized by and for indigenous peoples. Through his catechists and Diocesan workers, Bishop Ruíz summoned Tzotzil, Tzeltal, Chol, and Tojolabal indigenous peoples to participate in the congress and promoted the organization of local congresses that would discuss regional problems and prepare documents to be taken to the San Cristóbal congress (Morales Bermúdez 1992).

Perhaps because Sierra Madre communities were under the jurisdiction of the Tapachula Diocese, or because at that time they were not considered indigenous communities, Mam peasants were not invited to the 1974 Indigenous Congress. Yet the political impact of this event influenced later occurrences that did have a direct effect on Mam peasants, such as the creation of Indigenous Supreme Councils (see Chapter 5).

According to the testimony of one of its organizers, the planning committee was made up of three young university faculty members (a sociologist, a specialist in pedagogy, and a philosopher) and three priests, who, aided by a linguist, trained the indigenous translators who would help during the reflection meetings held prior to the congress, as well as during the congress itself (Morales Bermúdez 1992). The "community" reflection had two somewhat contradictory premises, partly influenced by educational methods that were in fashion in Latin America during the 1970s, the aim being to "raise the consciousness" of the indigenous population while starting from a defense of "cultural respect." Finally, the "consciousness raising" concept emerged as linked to that of "false consciousness": just as official indigenism wanted to "recover those elements of indigenous culture which proved positive," the promoters of the Indigenous Congress emphasized the need to "respect culture," providing it did not hinder the birth of a new consciousness. Those with a Marxist point of view became explicit when they tried to turn this space into a political organization, stating as long-term goals the following:

> The Indigenous Congress aims to change the present socioeconomic system into a society where there would be no private property or means of production and in the short term . . . [a]waken

the *proletarian consciousness* within us and our communities [and] [c]onstitute ourselves as a true independent organization. (Morales Bermúdez 1992:261; emphasis added)

Yet the documents prepared by the peasants themselves and presented during the congress do not evidence any political claims, and the phrases "proletarian consciousness" and "end of private property" are not taken up by indigenous representatives. Papers submitted focused on four basic claims: land, trade, education, and health. As for land, they demanded that the government restore communal lands; that the Agrarian Department solve pending business; that an underdelegation be created in San Cristóbal with indigenous employees; that there should be fair wages and taxes; and that the army not be called out during land conflicts. With regard to trade, they demanded support of indigenous markets; that CONA-SUPO provide essential products to communities and buy crops at guaranteed prices; that the creation of cooperative societies be supported; and that INMECAFE buy at guaranteed prices directly from producers, avoiding negotiations with monopolies. With regard to education, they spoke about the need to have indigenous teachers who knew their languages and habits, who taught communities about their rights as citizens, and who provided an education that responded to practical needs; they also called for a newspaper in the languages of the four participating indigenous groups. In addition, they demanded better health care services and respect for traditional medicine, as well as an efficient campaign against tuberculosis (Documento Diocesano 1979; Santiago 1980; Morales Bermúdez 1992; DESMI Archive).

Thus, except for the restitution of communal lands, none of the congress's demands were radical. Demands for cultural rights were limited to bilingual and bicultural education and the recognition of traditional medicine. Rather than an expression of the radicalizing of the indigenous movement, the San Cristóbal congress represented a rapprochement between Chiapas indigenous peoples and Governor Velasco Suárez's populism. The governor himself inaugurated the congress with a speech criticizing integrationist indigenism, which was still hegemonic in the INI:

If your wish is to join the country's economic development, such incorporation must take place in the way you want it, not as an imposition, not under circumstances that might superficially attract you through appearances. Because this culture we now call Western Culture is not the best. We must acknowledge that in your habits and customs much is respectable and positive. (Velasco Suárez 1974)

In their final agreements, congress participants acknowledged the efforts of Velasco Suárez's government:

> We see that your government is being good to us, because now we have more freedom to discuss our problems and because we see you are more interested than preceding governments in cooperating with our material needs. (Morales Bermúdez 1992:349)

Rather than the demands that were presented at the 1974 Indigenous Congress, what may have attracted the state's attention was the appeal that a discourse focused on "indigenous rights" could have and the potential danger that such demands could be radicalized. The CNC, supported by other governmental institutions, decided to organize another indigenous congress in the town of Pátzcuaro, Michoacán, exactly one year after the San Cristóbal congress. Using the same organizing mechanisms of the 1974 Indigenous Congress, the INI and the CNC organized sixty regional congresses previous to Pátzcuaro's congress, where they suggested the creation of Indigenous Supreme Councils (Consejos Supremos Indígenas) in order to form the National Council of Indigenous Peoples (*Acción Indigenista*, no. 267, September 1975). This new political body was established using the organizational model of the Rarámuris (Tarahumaras) from Chihuahua, which was quite alien to the local organizational principles of most other indigenous communities.[2]

Through the CNPI, "ethnic groups" were imposed as the organizing and identity spaces of indigenous peoples; thus Zinacantecos and Chamulas, historical rivals, were represented by a single Tzotzil supreme councillor. Linguistic classifications were taken by the state institutions as identity classifications and began to function as such, thus exerting their influence on the organizing spaces of indigenous peoples. The creation of the Supreme Councils is reminiscent of the tribal classifications imposed on African peoples during European colonization. On this point, John Iliffe states, "The British wrongly believed that the Tanganykans belonged to tribes; Tanganykans created tribes to function within the colonial framework" (quoted in Hobsbawm and Ranger 1983:252). Paraphrasing him, we could say that indigenists wrongly believed that indigenous peoples belonged to ethnic groups, and indigenous peoples decided to create ethnic groups to function in multicultural Mexico.

In a meeting prior to the Pátzcuaro Indigenous Congress, the Mam Supreme Council (Consejo Supremo Mam) was established, headed by Don Gregorio Constantino Morales, a Mam speaker native to the Horizontes community but living at the municipal capital of Mazapa de Madero. The surprise elicited by the creation of this new office, after several years of integrationist policies, is expressed by the testimony of the first Mam supreme councillor:

> I remember they called a meeting at the Motozintla auditorium. Since I had held several offices in the municipality, I was appointed to go. There were representatives from many Sierra communities, there was the representative from the government; it was under Echeverría. Then the government man asked who speaks Mam language; all were silent; nobody answered; they were afraid, or ashamed, who knows. . . . But I thought if this is my own race, if I am idiomista, why should I deny it and raised my hand. I am pure Mam blood, I told him, and right there they appointed me Mam supreme councillor. . . . We did not understand because the government first forbade the language and then wanted us to recover it.[3]

Don Gregorio attended the First National Congress of Indigenous Peoples, held October 7–10, 1975, in Pátzcuaro, as the representative of the "Mam ethnic group." The meeting was attended by some twenty-five hundred indigenous persons who allegedly represented sixty-four linguistic groups existing in national territory (*Acción Indigenista*, no. 268, October 1975). Demands emerging from this congress were very similar to those of the 1974 Indigenous Congress, although they were more specific. For example, in the demand for bilingual and bicultural education, they also suggested the creation of the Mexican Linguistic Institute, supporting a systematic study of indigenous languages; in relation to agrarian demands, they asked for a revision of the Agrarian Law to reconsider the limits of private property and to prevent the protection of latifundism; in relation to the support for commercialization, they suggested the creation of the National Bank for Indigenous Social Security and Development (*Acción Indigenista*, no. 268, October 1975:3). But the most radical demand, albeit still in very ambiguous terms, is that of self-determination, a direct predecessor of the demand for autonomy that came almost twenty years later: "This new organism [CNPI] will have as its main goals to increase and maintain the unity of indigenous peoples in order to satisfy their demands, . . . which will allow the self-determination of our communities" (INI 1978:363). Among the political demands of the document, known as Acta de Pátzcuaro, was a proposal to amend Article 54 of the political constitution to create an indigenous seat at the congress.

During its first years, the CNPI functioned as the "indigenous arm" of the official peasant organization, CNC. By 1977 one of its members was head of the Office for Indigenist Action within the CNC. Links between the CNPI and the CNC were described in 1978 by Oscar Ramírez Mijares, general secretary of the CNC National Executive Committee:

> The different institutions forming the CNC have always worked very near our indigenous comrades, following closely the different negotiations directly promoted by the Supreme Councils united in the National Council of Indigenous Peoples. The building at Calle López No. 23, which was for several decades the official seat of our Confederation, is now at the exclusive service of our indigenous comrades. With no impairment to the autonomy of the CNPI, the Confederation participates in all organizing, study, or analysis, and backs the resolution and determination of the said Council through its periodic and extraordinary meetings. (INI 1978:163)

Yet by 1979, during the Third Congress, the CNPI was openly criticizing José López Portillo's government for its refusal to redistribute land, and it made explicit its quarrel with the officialist CNC (*Uno Más Uno*, July 27, 1979:21–25).

In the Mam region, the Mam supreme councillor became a "culture missionary" expected to travel through the most distant Sierra communities to promote "cultural rescue" and implicitly to promote the new discourse on multicultural Mexico. Many of the peasants who for at least three decades had ceased defining themselves as Mam began to realize that defining themselves as Mam could offer such opportunities as scholarships, posts as bilingual teachers, funds for cultural projects, and attaining the office of supreme councillor. This does not mean there was no sense of shared common origin, everyday practices, and ways to relate to the earth that made them feel ethnically as a collectivity, but such elements were assumed as part of the life of "Sierra peasants." Identity spaces created by the Supreme Councils came to reinforce the establishment of the CCI Mam-Mochó-Cakchiquel.

Participative Indigenismo

When the central government changed, Aguirre Beltrán was replaced by Ignacio Ovalle as the head of the INI, and "critical anthropologists" became indigenist officials, transforming the integrationist model into what they called participative indigenism. Since his presidential campaign, López Portillo had adopted the proposals of "critical anthropologists" and pointed out that national unity should imply respect for cultural pluralism and announced his project to coordinate state actions vis-à-vis ethnic groups through a plan of programmed investments. A few days after he became president, López Portillo created the National Plan for Depressed Zones and Marginal Groups (Coordinación General del Plan Nacional de Zonas Deprimidas y Marginadas [COPLAMAR]), which became the axis of his social policy. The new INI director, Ignacio Ovalle, was also the head of the new governmental institution that took over the coordination of several preexisting welfare programs.

Through the CONASUPO-COPLAMAR program, thousands of community stores were opened and provided the rural areas with subsidized products. Through IMSS-COPLAMAR, rural clinics were built in the most isolated communities throughout the country. Such social policies have been seen as progress by reformist sectors within the state, whose perspectives can be summarized in the words of a high-level COPLAMAR official: "My ideological battle was to show that it is cheaper to take up the flag of popular struggle than to confront head-on. In other words, it is cheaper than buying arms" (quoted in Fox 1993:201).

The initials INI-COPLAMAR began to appear in conjunction with many infrastructure projects promoted in indigenous areas, and the INI became in a way the subsidiary of a wider program called COPLAMAR. At the same time, the INI-COPLAMAR director attained political power within the state that none of his predecessors had achieved. The COPLAMAR program cut funds from other government ministries and established new agreements with state governments, which in the preceding decades had lost control over their budgets and political decisions to federal institutions. This new political pact between INI-COPLAMAR and state governments was described by a former indigenist official:

> The creation of COPLAMAR undercuts all ministries to apply [resources] to programs defined by COPLAMAR; that is, not only the funds of other ministries are diverted, but the political struggle goes even further. I was a personal witness in San Luis Potosí. There was a meeting with the governor and the federation representatives, who as it is commonly said had always been "viceroys," since in general the governor has neither influence nor power over them. Licenciado Ovalle began to explain to the governor what COPLAMAR was, and said in a few words: "It is a bunch of money, Governor, money you will handle; that is, in the past investment was not possible if no money came from the ministries, but now their budget will be cut and it will be granted to the COPLAMAR specific regions;

you authorize it and INI invests it." This program gave such power to governors over federal representatives that the San Luis Potosí governor all but carried Ovalle in triumph all the way to his plane. That explains the INI's growth during those years, when they hired a whole generation from the National School of Anthropology.[4]

The historical link between anthropologists and the state, which had characterized the development of Mexican anthropology, became even stronger at that time: anthropologists not only took the lead in cultural policies, but also in the whole social project of López Portillo's adminis-tration. Such an alliance persisted under the next presidents, as we shall see in the analysis of PRONASOL, a direct offspring of COPLAMAR under Salinas de Gortari's administration.

Within the INI itself, the new director decided to change the long-term goals of official indigenism, as well as its methods. The basic idea that gave birth to the INI in 1948, which considered cultural homogeni-zation essential for achieving national integration, was openly criticized by the new directors, who stated in their Work Program:

> The indigenist policy of the present government has stated explic-itly the right of ethnic groups to preserve, transform, and develop their cultures, this not being a drawback for their economic and so-cial claims within the class structure of society. They complement each other. In this sense, we intend to put an end to the compul-sory measures aiming at homogenization, as well as to paternalistic measures which might displace the communities' own initiative or prevent the development of creative potential in these groups. (Ovalle 1978:21)

On this new perspective, an internal restructuring was carried out in the INI, creating new departments to promote and support indigenous cultures. Parallel to this, they created Community Committees (Comi-tés Comunitarios) that would function as consulting institutions for the INI, and through which the indigenous population could have a "larger" participation and influence in the creation and application of indigenist policies.

New departments were established in Mexico City's headquarters, and at the level of the local CCIs, new offices were created that were in contact with national departments. They founded, thus, the External Contact and Publishing Department (Departamento de Difusión y Publicaciones) and the Audiovisual Archive (Archivo Audiovisual), whose goal was to "aid the national society to recognize itself in cultural diversity and that this diversity define the Mexican people in the world" (INI 1982b:41); the Anthropological and Social Organization Research Department (Departamento de Investigación Antropológica y Organización Social), whose aim was to "suggest ethno-development strategies fitting the particular characteristics of each ethnic group" (INI 1982b:88); the Broadcasting Action Department (Departamento de Acción Radiofónica), which established a national network of indigenous radio stations broadcasting in local languages. They also created the Program for the Training of Bilingual Technicians in Indigenous Culture (Programa de Formación de Técnicos Bilingües en Cultura Indígena), whose aim was to train officially recognized "culture specialists"; the Program for the Defense and Development of Native Cultures (Programa para la Defensa y Desarrollo de las Culturas Autóctonas), promoting the support of traditional techniques, community social organization, and the recovery of historical memory.

One of the main weaknesses of this "participative" model was that policies were still being created in the country's capital by urban intellectuals and civil servants with little knowledge of indigenous reality. Out of the sixty-six Centros Coordinadores Indigenistas, not one was under indigenous management. The few indigenous personnel in the CCI were at best hired as "research assistants," which meant basically being translators for the local anthropologist. Most INI indigenous employees were in fact drivers or janitors. In spite of the official discourse on "participation spaces," the INI is still in the hands of a mestizo minority (Vargas 1994). These personnel policies, which in any other context would be called racist, have not been challenged, not even by the most critical sectors of Mexican society. Only since 1994, after the Zapatista uprising, has institutional racism been discussed in the political debate of the Mexican left. The Community Committees, which should have functioned as advisers for indigenist civil servants, were rather an administrative space in which local INI officials met "community representatives" monthly to inform them of the projects that were already being developed or decisions that had usually already been taken. As for the programs "to support and promote indigenous cultures," they have turned into an effort to institutionalize cultural practices according to the judgment and perspectives of local officials on "culture," as we shall see in the specific case of the CCI Mam-Mochó-Cakchiquel.

Participative indigenism, in spite of its good intentions, finally reproduced many of the paternalistic practices of old indigenism. When I questioned some critical anthropologists working for INI on the absence of indigenous personnel in managerial posts, they argued that indigenous people's lack of academic training prevented them from taking the reins of the new indigenism.[5] If this were true, we should question the fact that almost fifty years after its foundation, the INI has not been able to train indigenous managers able to participate in indigenous policy.

The CCI Mam-Mochó-Cakchiquel

After the creation of the Mam, Mochó, and Cakchiquel Supreme Councils, the new indigenous representatives began to apply for financing and technical counseling for their communities. The closest CCI was in the Tojolabal region, at the municipal capital of Las Margaritas, which forced councillors to make trips as long as eight hours from their communities to the indigenist offices. This logistical problem prompted Don Ismael Mateo, Mochó supreme councillor, to meet his Mam counterpart, Gregorio Morales, and suggest that they should ask together for the creation of an Indigenist Coordinator Center for the Sierra region. Later, they were joined in their petition by Cirilo Ramos Jacob, Cakchiquel supreme councillor from Mazapa de Madero.

After receiving this petition, the INI's national director sent the anthropologist Mauricio Rosas Kifuri to carry out diagnostic research prior to the establishment of the CCI. Between October 4 and 31, 1977, Rosas Kifuri traveled through the municipalities of Motozintla, El Porvenir, Siltepec, La Grandeza, Bejucal de Ocampo, Mazapa de Madero, and Amatenango de la Frontera. The aims of his research were to determine the best place to establish the CCI, to analyze the socioeconomic integration of the region, and to suggest development programs for the region (Rosas Kifuri 1978).

Previously, Governor Manuel Velasco Suárez's son had studied the region for the honors thesis required to receive his bachelor's degree in economics at the National Autonomous University of Mexico (UNAM). As acknowledged by Rosas Kifuri himself, José Agustín Velasco's honors thesis was the basic document from which he wrote his proposal for the foundation of the CCI Mam-Mochó-Cakchiquel. Velasco's thesis is an uneven document, full of official data. The developmentalist views of economists who talk about the "backwardness" of Sierra peoples mingle with culturalist views that represent Mam culture as isolated from the "cultural traits of modernity." In 1975 Velasco described Mam communities in the following terms:

Far from European settlements and Mexican government offices, the Mam (and Quiché) have retained in the treeless high regions of the Sierra their old way of life in all its purity. . . . Planting, with the coa, is here the dominant form of economy and corn is the staple crop. Also, the ways they build houses and villages are distinctly indigenous, and only their native language is spoken. (Velasco 1976:30)

When Velasco wrote this description, the Mam language was spoken only by elders, the traditional costume was no longer worn, and coffee growing was beginning to spread among local ejidatarios. When Rosas Kifuri arrived in the region after consulting Velasco's book, he found a completely different world. Like the anthropologists who came to the region in the 1960s, the indigenist official had to search for the scattered settlements of Mam peasants.

My experience with the indigenous population was with a visu- ally very clearly identified population, evidently self-manifested, as the Nahuatl, Otomí, or Tarasco peoples. In the places where I had been in the Sierra de Puebla, what I had lived as familiar history was characterized by such cultural manifestations. A bit jokingly, what I said upon arriving to the Sierra Madre was: But where are the Indians with feathers? I could not find them anywhere, since the population spoke almost no Mam and the costume had disappeared almost everywhere.[6]

The document written by Rosas Kifuri challenges many of Velasco's proposals. After a Marxist analysis of the unequal exchange in the region and the class oppression that was behind the "indigenous problem," he suggests a number of programs to be developed by the INI: a sheep pro- gram to genetically improve local livestock and support the formation of cooperative societies to make wool clothing; a forest program promoting wood industries, one of them in direct production (tree felling) and the other in wood processing, including the possibility of making handicraft furniture; a coffee-processing program so that small producers do not have to sell to monopolies; a chalk factory through school cooperative societies; support for the construction of roads and irrigated areas; a tech- nical training program; an ethnicity program based on support for bilin- gual education and a radio station broadcasting in indigenous languages (Rosas Kifuri 1978:93–107).

Sheep breeding, Ejido Malé, El Porvenir. Sheep breeding has been essential to the Mam family economy. PHOTO BY RICHARD CISNEROS LÓPEZ.

Agreements for carrying out such proposals by the Sierra inhabitants or their representatives were never sought, although these proposals became the main programs developed by the CCI Mam-Mochó-Cakchiquel after its creation on March 15, 1978. Perhaps if there had been consultation with Mam elders, they would not have imported sheep that were ill adapted to Sierra weather conditions and, instead of representing a "genetic" improvement, have caused new problems for local peasants; they might have been conscious of the serious problem that deforestation represented for this region, where it became more and more difficult to gather firewood; perhaps they would have realized how difficult it would be to promote a bilingual program in a region where children no longer spoke the indigenous language, which was still being stigmatized by the actions of immigration officials who would stop and beat Guatemalan Mam on that account.

This "participative" indigenism discussed with the supreme councillors only the place where the new CCI should be located. INI's proposal, emerging from Rosas Kifuri's document, was the village of La Grandeza, which was the largest subsidiary marketplace in the region. According to Aguirre Beltrán's analysis of refugee regions, the proposal was that "the new CCIs should be in subsidiary and not central markets, the goal being to break the line of value transfer created in indigenous population regions" (Rosas Kifuri 1978:31). This proposal was rejected by the supreme councillors, because La Grandeza was difficult to reach and far from many communities inhabited by Mochó and Cakchiquel people. The Supreme Council proposed Mazapa de Madero, a settlement by the border road, inhabited by many Cakchiquel and Mam people, only fifteen minutes away from Motozintla de Mendoza, the main local economic and political center, where many Mochó live. Don Gregorio, the Mam supreme councillor, was then municipal president of Mazapa de Madero. He convinced the ejidatarios to donate part of their ejidal lands for the construction of the CCI, on the condition that they be given preference in technical counseling and support for administrative negotiations, stipulating that the land and the building would be given to the ejido in the event the CCI was closed (Acta Ejidal, April 6, 1979, Mazapa de Madero Municipal Archive).

The professional personnel for this new CCI came mainly from Mexico City, the technical staff was hired from among the mestizo population of Motozintla, and only two indigenous persons joined the new CCI, one as a watchman and the other as a driver. According to the testimony of the first CCI director, this driver also served as translator and "certifier" of the Mam identity of peasants coming to the center.

> Look, practically the first person I hired was a local recruit. I was advised to hire a Mam-speaking driver who could become my translator and help recognize whether people were really Mam or not. Since he had worked for many years in the Sierra, this gentleman spoke Mochó, Mam, and Cakchiquel.[7]

Policies for supporting indigenous culture, created in Mexico City by the Program for the Defense and Development of Native Cultures, were difficult to apply in this region. Because of its specific history, it had cultural characteristics that did not fit the parameters of Mexico City anthropologists. This new indigenist institution arrogated to itself the right to define who was Mam and who was not.

> With the creation of the CCI I was very strict, for if they said they were indigenous population, they had to prove to me they were speakers and had to speak to me in Mam. . . . That was fun, because we applied entrance examinations in Mam, Mochó, and Cakchiquel, and they began to teach the children.[8]

This new indigenism notwithstanding, its "critical" discourse immediately established links with local mestizo power groups. Don Jorge Montesinos, then director of the regional office of Rural Development Investment Projects (Proyectos de Inversión para el Desarrollo Rural [PIDER]), member of the official party and a merchant family with great financial and political power in the region, introduced the new INI director to Sierra communities. It was Don Coqui, as he is commonly known locally, who helped the INI anthropologist to identify Mam communities.

The limitations of using indigenous language as a parameter for Indian identity became evident when they tried to give life to the School Shelters Project (Proyecto de Albergues Escolares). The aim was to create boarding school–type shelters where children of school age could live from Monday to Friday and receive room and board while being "encouraged to learn [their] own culture so that it does not die off."⁹ Such shelters would provide low-income children with easier access to primary education. This was the goal of the eleven shelters built under the auspices of the INI in the settlements of El Porvenir, Malé, Chimalapa, Carrizal, Niquivil, Francisco I. Madero, La Grandeza, Bella Vista, Nuevo Amatenango, Tolimán, and Benito Juárez. Those selected to participate in the program had to prove that they were indigenous children from low-income families. The second criterion was easily fulfilled in the most marginal region in the state; the first one, however, was quite a problem if indigenous language was to be taken as a basic standard for Indian identity.

After several vain attempts to find "indigenous children" who could participate in this program, the anthropologist Humberto Zappi Molina, head of the CCI Mazapa de Madero Anthropological Research Area, sent a written communication to the CCI manager:

> After a reconnaissance of the area under this Center's auspices and confirming that one of its characteristics is that the indigenous language tends to disappear and that it is most difficult to find bilingual indigenous young people applying for scholarships, and that there are monolingual young people (who speak only Spanish), I deem it relevant to inform you of the following: That there is a need by young indigenous people to have scholarships. That the fact of not being bilingual does not mean they are not indigenous because an ethnic group is not exclusively cataloged by its language. It is an important characteristic, but there are others which will define its being indigenous, so I make this suggestion for you to take the necessary measures and give grants to young people applying after a study of their economic situation and following the new criteria.¹⁰

The way in which children in these shelters are being encouraged to learn "their own culture" is a subject beyond the scope of this book. A future analysis of the experience of these "school shelters" is important, as hundreds of indigenous children are under the responsibility of indigenist technical personnel for most of the year.

It was this shelter program that forced the CCI Mazapa de Madero to widen its definition of Mam identity and begin to support Sierra peasants who organized themselves and applied for technical or credit counseling, whether they spoke Mam or not. The CCI Mazapa de Madero began to grant agricultural counseling, medical attention, scholarships, shelter, and support for economic and cultural projects to all peasants defining themselves as Mam, Mochó, or Cakchiquel. In theory, the CCI should have a structure for attending to four areas: promotion of production (agricultural aid, commercialization, and reforestation); social welfare (preventive medical and dental care); training and counseling (legal counseling, shelter system, scholarships); and promotion of their cultural heritage (development and promotion of native cultures). In fact, CCIs are finally organized according to available resources and generally have at least one doctor, one veterinarian, one lawyer, and a sociologist or anthropologist.

In its first years of operation, the CCI Mazapa de Madero centered its promotion of production on the sheep program and the distribution of fertilizers and pesticides, while supporting at the same time the creation of twenty-eight CONASUPO-COPLAMAR peasant stores. Its social welfare efforts were devoted to the creation of twenty-seven Rural Medical Units through the IMSS-COPLAMAR program and immunization campaigns. In terms of training and counseling, it established twelve school shelters. And the promotion of cultural heritage consisted simply in providing support for administrative tasks and following the progress of infrastructure projects. In 1980 the sociologist Rosalía López Paniagua, then head of this area, carried out a reconnaissance tour of the region in which she did case studies in twelve communities.[11]

In general, the personnel in charge of the various programs share the same view of "indigenous culture" as the rest of local mestizo society. Being "indigenous" equals economic and cultural backwardness. Only anthropologists and sociologists in charge of promoting cultural heritage usually have a more respectful attitude toward local cultures. The discourse on the necessary economic development through technical development of land use is still present in social scientists' opinions and articles, yet the discourse on "cultural respect" of the new indigenism pervades most of these officials' testimonies. The report presented by López Paniagua (1980) is a good example of this hybrid discourse on "modernization and culture." Most of her advice has to do with the need to increase the distribution of insecticides, fertilizers, and improved seeds. Although in her analysis of the twelve sample communities she mentions the land problem and Mam peasant exploitation in the Soconusco coffee plantations, the paragraphs under the heading "Possible Solutions" do not take up these problems. She criticizes integrationist indigenism and speaks of the importance of cultural respect. Under the influence of the critical Marxism of that time, this indigenist official concludes her report by pointing out: "Limitations are numerous, yet the best element for change would be the consciousness of the indigenous population" (López Paniagua 1980). To attain this consciousness, this sociologist suggests using the teachings of the Brazilian pedagogue Paulo Freire and adds as an appendix an essay titled "Concientización en el Medio Rural" (Consciousness Raising in Rural Areas) by Freire. This contradictory discourse by indigenist officials has caused very different attitudes toward the CCI among local peasants. For many, it is just one more among other governmental offices in the region that promise much but do little. Others see the CCI as "more in favor of the poor" than other governmental offices. Some young anthropologists who passed through the CCI Mazapa de Madero are remembered for their support of peasant organizations and their "consciousness raising" work on the issue of peasant cultural and economic rights.

It was one of these young anthropologists, Carlos Gutiérrez Alfonzo, who in 1988 suggested to the community committee of the CCI Mazapa de Madero the creation of a radio program called "Mam Word and Music" (Palabra y Música Mam). The new program was broadcast through the Las Margaritas indigenist radio station XEVFS, reestablishing communication between the Mam colonizing the rain forest and those living in the Sierra. Such governmental initiatives for the promotion of "native cultures" have had important consequences for the reinvention of Mam traditions.

Although "participative indigenism" and multicultural discourse have not altered the verticality of relations between governmental institutions and indigenous peoples, the new indigenist project has constructed a new image of the "state" for Sierra Madre peasants. The presence of young anthropologists and sociologists trained in the new theoretical paradigm of critical anthropology has exerted its influence on the legitimation of the image of the state as "benefactor."

In these ways the hegemonic process of the Mexican state was temporarily strengthened through the creation of new discourses on nation and citizenship. Although many Mam peasants acknowledged the inefficiency of most indigenist programs, state officials had contributed to a new image of the state, which replaced that of a "repressive machine" of the 1930s or that of an "excluding machine" of the 1950s or 1960s.

By this, I do not mean that the discourse on a multicultural Mexico is only a state strategy for its own legitimation, for these new discourses on the nation are the expression of a hegemonic process and thus necessarily include part of the discourses of subordinate sectors. Rather than the "expression of a domination strategy," the transition from a mestizo to a multicultural Mexico expresses the struggle for meanings in a force field in which both the state, through its public institutions, discourses, and policies, and its subordinate sectors, with their resistance and negation practices and discourses, have contributed to the formation of a new national imaginary.

It is not the state but rather the hegemonic process itself that has shaped these changes in the discourse on the nation; as Roseberry (1994:362) points out, "The points of contention, the 'words'—and the whole material history of power, forces and contradictions that the words inadequately express—over which centralizing state and local village might struggle are determined by the hegemonic process itself."

This complex hegemonic process has given way to the emergence of a new conception of nation and aided the production of new identities. These new identities at the same time reproduce part of the indigenist discourse on "Mam culture" and respond to and reject official definitions through new languages, rites, and cultural practices, which I analyze in the next chapter.

Third Border Crossing

DON EUGENIO

"RESCUING" MAM CULTURE

The concrete building of the Indigenist Coordinator Center, an example of the austere architecture that characterized public building in the 1970s, represented for several years the symbol of modernity reaching the Sierra. Established in 1978 by the INI to support the development of Mam, Mochó, and Cakchiquel indigenous peoples, the CCI has become, over the years, an intermediary between peasants and governmental institutions working in the region. Located on Mazapa de Madero ejidal lands, but far from the settlement, the CCI rises in the heart of the Sierra like a white elephant in the middle of a deserted plain between Motozintla and Mazapa. The "Indigenista," as it is locally known, has become a gathering center for peasants throughout the Sierra, who come down periodically to apply for credits, ask for support in commercializing their agricultural products, find technical counseling for a new crop, or simply pay a visit and say hello to friends in the waiting room.

Looking for "the roots" of rain forest colonizers, I arrived in the Mariscal region in mid-1993. My first move was to introduce myself to the regional CCI and find out whether I could have access to its records. It was a rainy morning, so common in the Sierra for at least half the year. I was waiting for the CCI director when a man of about sixty arrived for a chat. This man stood out among all the other peasants waiting in the corridors in the way he walked and looked one straight in the eyes. He was Don Eugenio Roblero. "He is a bit stuck up," those who knew him used to say. Some were disturbed by the poise with which he addressed any person, whether a peasant, a public official, or the state governor.

In my encounter with Don Eugenio, he subjected me to an in-depth interview, wanting to know who I was, what I was doing there, what was my connection to the CCI, and so on. It was one of the very few times that I did not have to explain what an anthropologist does. Don Eugenio felt he knew better than I the anthropologist's task. He had several anthropologist friends interested in "the culture." He had known the first CCI anthropologist, Mauricio Rosas Kifuri. He knew Andrés Fábregas, an old teacher of mine and by then head of the Institute of Chiapanec Culture (Instituto Chiapaneco de Cultura [ICHC]), and had had a friendly relationship with Dr. Jacinto Arias, a Tzotzil anthropologist and an official in the state government. If I was interested in "Mam culture," he was the person I was looking for. I had no reason to wait for the CCI director, who, on the other hand, was a veterinarian—"And as you know, veterinarians do not know much about culture," Don Eugenio told me.

We had a long conversation, and after I told him a little about my interest in writing a history of the Mam from the Sierra Madre, he told me he had been the first supreme indigenous councillor of the highlands (Primer Consejo Supremo Indigena de la Zona Alta).[1] He told me that his appointment came directly from the president of the republic. He was now coordinating the Mam dance groups in twenty-two communities, which were "rescuing" the culture of the ancients. We made an appointment to meet the following Friday at El Porvenir.

In spite of Don Eugenio's openness and his interest in "the culture," at first I was not keen on the idea of having strong ties to him. He was some kind of an "official informer," too close to governmental institutions to tell me what had "really happened" in the Sierra. However, I decided to pay him a visit. He was easy to find, for he rented one of his rooms to the National Peasant Confederation, the peasant branch of the PRI, and his house, bearing a large sign with the letters CNC, stood out from the others in the community. Don Eugenio, together with his wife, Doña Pina, and their children, was expecting me. We had breakfast in a small kitchen, not so different from other kitchens in the Sierra: a small traditional woodstove in a corner, a hand mill, a few low chairs, which scarcely raised us above the ground, and several dried ears of corn hanging from the ceiling. I would spend many hours in this kitchen, speaking with Don Eugenio and with his daughters, particularly the two who were critical of their father's PRIismo.

Don Eugenio had everything planned for my stay in the Sierra. He had seen me tape some political demonstrations at Motozintla and was familiar with video cameras. His plan was that I should make a film on the twenty-two dance groups and his work in "cultural rescue." It would be a difficult task, for I would have to travel all over the Sierra and reach communities inaccessible by car; yet I thought it an excellent way to get to know the region and this cultural movement linked to official indigenism. The passion with which Don Eugenio talked about "his" dance groups and the support and kindness he offered me from the first day we met made me reconsider my rejection of the "official informant" and learn about his version of the history of the Mam.

It was almost a year before I openly questioned Don Eugenio about his political ideas. My fear of jeopardizing our relationship prevented me from remarking as he praised the PRI's work, especially the qualities of the candidate for the governorship at the time, Lic. Eduardo Robledo Rincón. In his kitchen, through a secondhand television set, a gift from one of his children, we heard together of the murder of the general secretary of the PRI, Mario Ruiz Massieu, in September 1994, and we discussed the party's internal problems. With time, we learned to accept and respect our political differences.

On the afternoon when Don Eugenio told "his story," he insisted on being filmed next to the Mexican flag he kept in the CNC office. He wanted the film to demonstrate that the Mam were Mexican.

> . . . I was born in the Malé colony. My parents were born here, but my parents' parents came from Guatemala. When El Porvenir was formed, many people came from Guatemala, but at that time it was in a way global. It was not clear where Mexico would begin and where Guatemala would end. It was not known where the division was. It was sort of mixed up. My grandparents spoke only Mam, and my parents then learned Spanish. In my house both were spoken. That is why I learned a bit of Mam; when I grew up I improved it. But the language was being lost, the Mam was being forgotten. Elders say it was lost when teachers came. People were Hispanicized. Teachers no longer allowed children to speak their languages—they wanted only Spanish spoken. In that way in the mountain the Indianidad [Indian identity] was lost. But the first inhabitants who came from the Tacaná region spoke only Mam.
>
> My grandfather used to say that when a man was about to be sixteen he was picked up and sent to service in Guatemala—[so] then

they ran to the mountain; they came over here, but they did not
know if it was Mexico. When the first settlers came here they built
a little house, here, another there. The distance between two houses
being up to two leagues. Then the first settlers found out that the
owner of this mountain was a gringo.[2] The owner of all these lands of
El Porvenir was a German. He ruled here, and our grandparents paid
a tax for the land to the rich man, the owner of the Germania finca—
since at that time to work the land one had to pay a tax. People had
to go down to the coastland to pay the rich man. It was difficult
because it was far.

Then, the inhabitants were very few. They all cooperated. It was
then a matter of twenty centavos, forty centavos, fifty centavos—to
have the right to plow a small plot. Later, during Tata Lázaro's government, some lands were distributed. They did what they call a Land
Reform (Reforma Agraria). When the German owner of the land saw
they would take away his lands if he did not plow them, he decided
to sell his Sierra lands, which he was already renting. Then there was a
meeting. Young people were invited to go in larger numbers. And at
first twenty came, then up to forty, and each of them gave his share,
and they appointed a delegate to go talk to the German owner of
Germania. And this is the way our parents bought these lands here
at El Porvenir.

Then they gave us our documents as ejidatarios. But the young
people, the ejidatarios' children, are no longer getting any. They
have to organize an expansion of the ejido, but there is no point in
fighting anymore—there are no more lands, even if the comisariado
wanted to fight. Well, it is no longer possible—there is no more land
to be distributed. That is why our children are living in our shadow.
Like mine, two of them work my land—the others had to leave. Two
live in Tuxtla. They work just on business—they no longer think of
cultivating the land. I have also two others in the teaching profession,
a boy and a girl. Many of the young men and women have to go to
Mexico City, to Tecate, to the United States. But they go and come
back. They never settle.

Young people nowadays no longer know about suffering at the
fincas, like we do. I had to go to the finca with my father, and I
suffered quite a bit. I started to go to the fincas very young, at
fourteen. From the age of fourteen until I was forty-five I worked on
coffee plantations. First I worked at the finca Germania, belonging to
the German, then I enrolled in the finca La Fortuna and in a finca

called Juárez. It was very hard to be at the fincas. We were subject to the orders of the *mayordomo* [resident administrator] and *caporal* [foreman]. It was hard work, and for food we could only afford beans. We ate nothing but stale beans. Yes, we suffered a lot then. In large fincas there were *galleras* [workers' living quarters], like warehouses, where we all slept on a wooden platform, all together. There was no latrine, like nowadays—we relieved ourselves right in the bushes.

Some owners treated people well, but others cursed. Some owners were very difficult. By then, people did not last long, that is, people moved from finca to finca very often. Germans were very strict. By three o'clock in the morning we were having our breakfast—very strict. Yes, I suffered, I really suffered.

My family remained here, in the Sierra. Here we had my little plot of corn, but it did not yield. The corn did not grow, because it was not fertilized. That is why everybody went to the fincas to be able to buy corn, because corn did not grow.

One day I decided I did not want to go down [to the finca] anymore. There was a swell German who chatted with me at the finca Juárez. He said, "Your lands are rich. Because you do not know how to work, you are stupid. You do not know how to work. You have to turn over the soil, fertilize it, so it won't be exhausted, and then plant potatoes in large amounts, not half a *cuerda*.[3] You must plant from 30 to 40 cuerdas." I drew my experience from it [the German's advice], and I began to work. I had to earn my seeds and everything. I started planting my two cuerdas of potatoes.

Then came the CNC people and invited me to join the party. I did not know very well what it was all about, but they offered to help me to obtain more cuerdas of land. So I started to work in the party and gained a few more cuerdas. Then they gave me fertilizers, and I was able to harvest more. In that way I gradually increased until I was able to plant forty cuerdas of potatoes. Now with a quiet life, I did not go away anymore—with that I stopped work at the finca. The times of suffering are over for me.

Nowadays, the rich are suffering more than we. Now we are at the same level. Now the rich man has no more money, because coffee is no longer valuable. It is no longer valuable. Here we have potatoes. We have cabbage. We have sheep, and we make things go. Now it is steady, because things have changed. Now we receive support from the government. We receive fertilizer. We receive pesticide. Now corn grows better. Then everything is modernized.

It was after I joined the CNC that I was appointed Mam supreme councillor (Consejo Supremo Mam). I had always been interested in traditions, and I did not like to see that they were disappearing. From the government came the order to form councils. Under the coordination of the INI, a councillor was appointed here in the Sierra, because there was only that of the lowlands. That is how I started this work of energizing the indigenous vein. I started to go to indigenous communities, to see what they needed—scholarships to study, land property problems, also education. This way I worked for four years as supreme councillor.

On several occasions I had to go to Mexico City, [where] there was the Indigenous Parliament (Parlamento Indígena), [in which] all fifty-six Mexican indigenous languages [were spoken]. Together with other supreme councillors, I saw it was no shame to be indigenous, that it was our roots and we should not deny it. It had to be explained to my people. Then the Mam supreme councillor had to do with everything about our indigenous speech, about our language, [so] that not only Spanish is spoken. The supreme councillor has to analyze the problems of the community—see what was the strong feeling we indigenous people must have, a strong feeling toward all our indigenous brothers. The supreme councillor had to see why our language had been lost—why we had lost our habits, our parents', our grandparents' traditions. Then, at that time, I began to have a strong feeling for my indigenous language. I felt sad our habits and costumes had disappeared. Then I thought of rescuing them through dance. I began to form my own dance group here in 1981, only here in the municipal capital of El Porvenir.

I felt that a feeling came to me from Heaven that the heritage our fathers had left us did not exist anymore, [so] then, for that reason, I had to take care of them. Then I thought I want their thoughts, because traditions had been lost and they had to be rescued. So we made an analysis, and we had to see how to raise our culture, and how to rescue our language. Thus we organized the dances. At first we were only a group of fourteen, all Mam speakers, but then it spread to other municipalities, until reaching the twenty-two groups we are now. We represented life as it used to be—how people sang, how they danced, the way traditions were, so that children learn, know their roots.

We also showed the way our customs [once] were at the Festival Mayas Zoque organized by the ICHC every year. We showed it [lost customs] to the Tojolabal, to the Tzotzil, to the Tzeltal, to the Zoque—we showed them all our traditions. Then I went to other countries to tell them that the Mam still exist, still live in the Chiapas mountains. Being the dance coordinator, the Chiapanec Institute took me seriously, so that I went to represent the Mam group, and for this reason we went to Europalia 93.[4] We went all the way to Europe. We went to leave our signatures at the museums, to show how the traditions were, the labor of our grandparents—of the ancients, of our parents. There we went to show everybody. We all went— Tzotzil, Tzeltal, Tojolabal—with Dr. Jacinto Arias and his aides from the Chiapanec Institute.

Now I know my culture will not disappear. Right now I am not doing this by myself. We are doing it with the support of the INI, of the Chiapanec Institute. We know that the government does not want our customs, our traditions, to disappear. I am sure they don't, because right now it is not only we who speak Mam. I gave my advice to the municipal authorities, and in some communities now the Mam language is spoken at 80 percent [by 80% of the people in the community]. Now young people are also studying. There are bilingual teachers who can speak Mam. Then we are not going to allow our traditions to disappear. As long as I live, I am going to plant the seed. When I disappear from this life perhaps, perhaps.

Chapter

5

MAM DANCE GROUPS

NEW CULTURAL IDENTITIES AND
THE PERFORMANCE OF THE PAST

The changes in the official discourse from a mestizo Mexico to a multi-cultural Mexico created new institutional spaces wherein Sierra peasants could identify themselves as Mam indigenous people. On searching for a place in this new Multicultural Mexico, Mam peasants drew on their elders' memories and took on the task of reinventing their traditions by means of "cultural rescue" groups. In their dialogue with official indigenism, several initiatives emerged to promote the use of the Mam language and the knowledge and rescue of the traditions of the ancients. Ultimately, Mam peasants appropriated these institutional spaces for cultural rescue created by the INI and by the Indigenous Supreme Council, negotiating, accepting, or rejecting several official definitions of indigenous culture.

Those who have dedicated themselves to the task of analyzing how traditions are invented have stressed their colonial origins, linking them to strategies of control that were adopted by European administrations (Hobsbawm and Ranger 1983). Such points of view, which have played an important role in pointing out the social construction of traditions in postcolonial societies, still make a distinction between "authentic" and "invented" traditions, the first being conceived as a result of the cultural identity of peoples and the second as constructions for colonial domination.

Other perspectives have challenged this dichotomy between "authentic" and "invented," or "genuine" and "spurious" (Handler and Linnekin 1984), pointing out that all traditions are social constructions, interpretations of certain practices, and in this sense all are invented. Such perspectives note that tradition, rather than a descriptive term for an "essence," is an interpretive term referring to a process. Considering that cultures are constantly changing, conceptualizing something as traditional means giving it a specific symbolic value rather than temporality. At the moment a certain practice is conceived as "tradition" its content is altered: "Cultural categories such as traditions have reflexive character; they are invented as they are lived and thought about, people's consciousness of them, as categories, affects their content" (Linnekin 1983:250). Once the social construction of traditions is acknowledged, the challenge is to place their construction within the framework of power relations, which will help us to understand why certain inventions are legitimated while others are not (Ulin 1995).

In their preoccupation with creating a space to listen to the voices of subordinate groups, some authors have analyzed the way the past is reinvented in the historical memory of the people as a strategy to legitimate their present struggles and counter the homogenizing power of colonial and postcolonial governments (Price 1983, 1990; Rappaport 1990; Berzley, English, and French 1994). We would thus have a new dichotomy: traditions invented by "rulers" to maintain their hegemony and those invented by the "dominated" to resist. In this chapter I challenge this dichotomy by analyzing the invention of traditions as a dialectic process of resistance and reproduction in which state definitions have a productive capacity that allows the construction of certain identities, which eventually confront the same definitions that created them.

The construction of hegemony is an ongoing problematical political process of domination and struggle, which confronts the perspectives of state hegemony as a finished monolithic ideological formation.[1] Through its new indigenist policy, the Mexican state brought new words, images, symbols, and institutions to Mam lives. Within this new framework of Multicultural Mexico, Mam peasants have developed new discourses that may reproduce or reject the terms of the "dialogue" set by state policies.

The Mam Supreme Council

The creation of the National Council of Indigenous Peoples (CNPI) has been described by some analysts as a corporate measure of the Mexican state that failed to influence the political organization of indigenous peoples (Pozas 1976; Harvey 1989). Although this may be the case at the national level, in the Sierra Madre of Chiapas the creation of the Mam Supreme Council influenced the emergence of new discourses about "culture" and "tradition" that had a direct impact on the daily lives of Mam peasants. For example, after being appointed Mam supreme councillor in 1976, Don Gregorio Constantino Morales traveled to Mam communities throughout the Sierra to learn their needs and took steps to obtain scholarships for indigenous children from indigenist authorities. After finding out the communities' needs, he wrote petitions that he took periodically to the national CNPI meetings, usually held in Mexico's capital.

Although the CNPI may have become more of an administrative instrument of negotiation than a true political organization, its existence allowed indigenous people throughout the country to meet for the first time and learn about the problems they shared with other Mexicans. What emerged as a strategy of control for the Mexican state became a space of encounter for indigenous people from different regions, who expanded their perspectives beyond their community and began to place their local problems within the wider perspective of the nation. For some, like Don Gregorio, learning of the existence of more than fifty-four indigenous languages in Mexico was a revelation that made him reflect on their different experiences before forced Hispanicization.

> There in the capital I met other supreme councillors. They told us there were about fifty-four different idiomistas assembled there; imagine, some of them did not understand Spanish too well. I had heard Chamulas speak their own language, and also the Mochó very near here at Motozintla, but I had no idea there were so many idiomistas in this country. I used to think that it was good that my children spoke only Spanish, but there I saw that in other places they had not lost their language, even children spoke it, so I thought it was not good to lose our roots.[2]

Once more language was becoming the focus of state cultural policies. While during the 1930s government policy had threatened the survival of all indigenous languages, during the 1970s the official priority, at least in the indigenist discourse, was the rescue and preservation of native languages. These new indigenist policies focused on the "rescue" of Mam in their efforts to undo the damage of previously forced integration. Thus, as a result of the size of the territory inhabited by Mam speakers, another Mam supreme councillor was elected for the highlands, with its seat at the municipal capital of El Porvenir, and at its head was Don Eugenio Robledo, an old militant of the PRI and the CNC.

Don Eugenio points out that one of the supreme councillor's main tasks was to recover indigenous languages.

The Mam supreme councillor had to see everything, but especially
to see about our speaker, about our language, that not only Spanish
is spoken. . . . The supreme councillor must analyze the problems
of his community, see which is the strong feeling we indigenous
people must have, a strong feeling together with all our indigenous brothers. The supreme councillor had to see why our language
had been lost, why our customs, the traditions of our parents and
grandparents had been lost.[3]

The Mam Presbyterian population has played an active role in the cultural rescue programs promoted by governmental institutions. Because
Mam became a "cult language" during the 1930s, for a time it ceased to
be spoken publicly in most Sierra communities. Among idiomistas there
are at present several Presbyterians. In fact, at the time my fieldwork was
conducted, the Mam supreme councillor was an important Presbyterian
elder. The words of José Coffin, the missionary who in the 1930s openly rejected forced acculturation campaigns with the argument that the indigenous language was a heritage of God that must be preserved, are echoed
in the testimony of Don Nicolás Paez:

I am elder governor of the Presbyterian church here in Canadá and
I belong to the Supreme Council, which struggles for the rescue of
old-time culture, that it is not forgotten, it does not end. We are
appointed by those who speak Mam; it is our father and mother
tongue, we must not forget it; we must talk it over with our children and grandchildren, so that they know we depend on this race.
My office in the Supreme Council does not affect my religion. On
the contrary, we can give good ideas for treating indigenous people
fairly.[4]

Although the National Presbyterian church does not have a clear cultural
policy defending indigenous cultures, as does the Catholic church, several
converts have been allowed into "cultural rescue" projects, provided they
do not participate in festivities for the patron saint or consume alcoholic
beverages.

Identity spaces created by Supreme Councils were reinforced by the
CCI Mam-Mochó-Cakchiquel. As we have seen, the CCI combined
support for community development projects with "cultural rescue." Its
Promotion of Cultural Heritage program marks the difference with the
preceding indigenist model, as its primary function is to support the "cultural traditions" of indigenous peoples. Although this "new indigenism"
emerged with a more critical view of the structures of domination that

mark the everyday life of people, its vision of "indigenous traditions" is still culturalist. It looks for the "cultural specificity" in "ancient traditions," which in the case of the Sierra disappeared several decades ago. The language used in one of the projects presented to the Solidarity Fund for the Promotion of the Cultural Heritage of Indigenous Peoples (Fondo de Solidaridad para la Promoción del Patrimonio Cultural de los Pueblos Indígenas) by the CCI anthropologist of Mazapa de Madero in 1994 tells us much about a perspective on "traditions" and "indigenous identity" that still exists in indigenism today:

> Within the Mochó tribe [sic] we see that natives feel a deep reverence for ancient traditions and customs as well as the automatic respect for their advice and orders, which they must obey spontaneously, as faithful serfs and loyal "children of God," because of their mental inertia [sic] transmitted through the community parliament; integrated by the "white heads," prestigious elders who inherited their wisdom from their ancestors.[5]

In communities where traditions and old customs had disappeared, anthropologists actively supported their reinvention. Indigenist discourse and policies filled the same role given by Michel Foucault (1979) to legal discourse; it creates the same social subjects it says it represents. Yet, when acknowledging that the indigenist discourse is capable of producing new subjectivities, we are not denying that this discourse is complemented, challenged, or rejected by other discourses having the same productive capability.

Mam Dances

After the Mam Supreme Council of the highlands was formed in 1981, a "cultural rescue movement," called Mam Dances (Danzas Mames), began to emerge. Its main goal has been to represent Mam traditions and customs no longer practiced in everyday life to introduce them to new generations and perform them at cultural programs organized by the state. The Danzas Mames are peasant theater groups that, apart from dancing to marimba music, represent everyday scenes of ancient Mam life and reproduce important religious celebrations, which in most cases are no longer practiced. This movement was initially centered in the municipalities of El Porvenir and La Grandeza, and its participants were men and women between forty and seventy years of age who still spoke Mam.

This new sphere for identity formation and organization emerged under the influence of Mam supreme councillors and with the institutional support of new indigenism. Don Eugenio Robledo, the promoter of Danzas Mames, told how this project was born.

> I felt that from Heaven came to me a feeling, that the heritage left by our parents no longer existed, then for that reason I had to worry about them; I want their thought, because traditions had been lost and could not be rescued, and we made an analysis and had to see how to raise our culture, and how to rescue our language; thus we organized the dances.[6]

This testimony reminds us of *iloles*, or traditional doctors,[7] who attribute to divine revelation their decision to dedicate themselves to healing (Freyermuth 1993). Like the iloles, Don Eugenio cannot rebel against his destiny.

Having received this feeling from Heaven, Don Eugenio talked with the elders in order to recall religious festivals and harvest rituals that were celebrated in the past. Thus they managed to reconstruct "The Three Falls," which refers to the three falls of Jesus Christ in the Catholic Via Crucis; "The Saint Anthony Image" and "San Juan de Dios," in celebration of both saints; "The Day of the Corn Ear" and "The Sheep Marking," in which they represent harvest and shepherd rituals; and All Saints Day, a religious festival of the dead. They also organized performances of familiar rituals, such as "The Child's Baptism," "The Planting of the Child," "The Washing of the Head," "The Asking for the Hand," and "The Choice of a Godfather."[8]

The first problem they encountered in representing the past was that essential elements—such as traditional costumes and the marimba—were lacking. Contrary to their ancestors, however, Danzas Mames participants were able to choose their costumes: the split woolen breeches, worn by the old Mam, were replaced by a natural color cotton costume, to which were added a red handkerchief around the neck and a straw hat, attire similar to the costume worn in some Veracruz folk dances. As for the women, they added new colors to those used in the past in their cloths and brought them from Guatemala; they also exchanged the simple cotton huipiles for colorful embroidered blouses. Anthropologists also played an important role in the reinvention of the traditional Mam costume.

> At the beginning all by ourselves we did the dance, but we had no support from any institution; then once an anthropologist, who came from Mexico City, Licenciado Arturo Lomelí, he came for

a few chats, to ask whether Mam was still spoken, and he asked us if we could form some dance groups, to see how the speaker could have more support. I told him that since 1981 I have been working with the dance groups, and he liked the project. Then I asked him for help with costumes, and he got me cotton cloth. So we made men's costumes. Then about six months later we got three hundred thousand pesos to buy clothes for women in Huehuetenango, Guatemala.[9]

Gradually this movement grew, embracing the municipalities of El Porvenir, La Grandeza, Bejucal de Ocampo, and Siltepec. At present there are twenty groups, with between ten and fifteen persons each, distributed among the four municipalities: in El Porvenir, two in the municipal capital, one in Ejido Canbil, one in Ejido El Roble and two in Ejido Canadá; in La Grandeza, one in Barrio Banderas, one in Maíz Blanco, one in Las Tablas, and one in Libertad Ventanas; in Siltepec, two in El Rodeo, four in El Palmar, and one in Palmarcito; and in Bejucal de Ocampo, one in the Reforma Casbil colony (see Map 3).

In recent years some groups have been temporarily organized in the coastland because the state government, through the Chiapanec Cultural Institute, has invited them to participate in the Mayas and Zoques Dance Festival (Festival de Danzas Mayas y Zoques). Other institutions, such as the INI radio station XEVFS, the ICHC Department of Ethnic Cultures, and the PRONASOL Solidarity Fund for the Promotion of the Cultural Heritage of Indigenous Peoples, have supported and encouraged in various ways the work of Danzas Mames.[10]

The Department of Ethnic Cultures supported workshops in which the Mam language could be taught to young people and children. It also promoted the creation of new groups.

The first time I learned about the existence of Danzas Mames was when I met Licenciado Becerril here at El Porvenir. Then I asked him what his goal was, what his career was, and he explained he came for the matter of rescuing the culture and he encouraged us to participate.[11]

Since Danzas Mames received institutional support, young people and children of Mam-speaking parents who had no longer used this language have shown an interest. There are even cases of mestizo women who have decided to "convert" to Mam in order to attend the performances with their husbands.

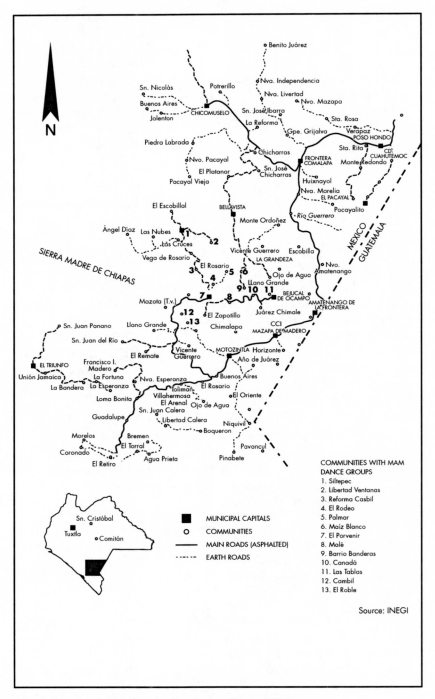

COMMUNITIES WITH MAM DANCE GROUPS

1. Siltepec
2. Libertad Ventanas
3. Reforma Casbil
4. El Rodeo
5. Palmar
6. Maíz Blanco
7. El Porvenir
8. Malé
9. Barrio Banderas
10. Canadá
11. Las Tablas
12. Cambil
13. El Roble

Source: INEGI

■ MUNICIPAL CAPITALS
○ COMMUNITIES
── MAIN ROADS (ASPHALTED)
----- EARTH ROADS

Map 3. District of the Indigenist Coordinator Center (CCI)
Mam-Mochó-Cakchiquel

My parents speak only Spanish, but my husband demanded that I speak Mam. "I am going to teach you" he said. "Little by little you are going to learn it." At the beginning I did not want to, I could not speak Mam. "You will also participate in the dance group," he told me. "That is what the coordinator is for, to teach you, but if he does not teach you, I will." Then I could not pronounce the language, now I know the names of the household animals, sheep, chicken, pigs, now I can pronounce it a bit.[12]

This testimony suggests the temporary, dynamic, and changing character of Mam identity and supports the criticism of Indianists' naturalization of cultural identities.

Danzas Mames has served as a collective reconstruction of a prohibited past that now includes memories of the "Law of Government," the "burning of the costumes," the suffering of the finca, and the years of the purple disease. All of these historical discourses have been combined into a myth of origin with which the Mam, from the Las Margaritas rain forest to the Malé mountains in the Sierra Madre, can identify. Danzas Mames performances have become spaces for representing and legitimizing a collective memory reconstructed regularly before large audiences.

Memory and Performance of Everyday Life

Dramatizations by Mam dance groups, rather than faithful reproductions of their traditions, are a way in which contemporary Mam imagine their past. It is a new ritual space in which ethnic identity literally becomes a performance, in which past and present mingle to tell us about the way contemporary Mam see their history.

The dance becomes a selective performance of the past that recovers only those practices that are considered the most significant in the "lives of the ancients." As Catherine Héau de Giménez (1994:107) writes, "Only what can be explained, justified or related to the present is remembered. Our past is articulated in the memory according to the present interests of our community, our family or our own." Given that it is the expression of a "collective memory," the struggle of interests within communities is evident in the way content is selected: for one group, religious rituals and family festivities are the most important; for others, remembering past suffering validates and leads to understanding of present struggles. The tension between these two representations of the past is always latent in Danzas Mames performances.

Gender roles and age hierarchies are also enforced in dance performances. Several performances, particularly those relating to rites before marriage, such as "Asking for the Bride's Hand," or those relating to everyday life, stress the importance of discipline and of children's obedience to their parents and women's obedience to their husbands.

Although Mam women participate importantly in the dances, none of the twenty existing groups is directed or coordinated by a woman and few women attend planning meetings, where the content of performances is discussed. As in ejidal assemblies or other meetings where community problems are discussed, a woman attends as her husband's companion and does not have the right to an opinion or a vote. This "community democracy," which has been praised by an important segment of the indigenous movement, constructs its consensus on the basis of the exclusion of women, which is why decisions, whether on agrarian problems or cultural performances, do not express the feelings of an important sector of the community.

Some women writers, such as Judith Stacey and Florencia E. Mallon, use the term "democratic patriarchy" to refer to the form in which the community consensus has been historically constructed in some indigenous regions where men, particularly older men, "were the custodians of 'legitimate' communalism, the very embodiment of communal notions of justice, of the concept of reciprocity and responsibility contained in the idea of a good patriarch. This mutual recognition of power and influence, then underlies the construction of 'democratic patriarchy' " (Mallon 1995:76). Although Mallon acknowledges that there is an oxymoronic tension between democracy and patriarchy, she states that elder men have finally managed to construct a community hegemony, which allows them to reach consensus on their decisions. A new generation of indigenous women has begun to question the democratic character of this patriarchy and to demand a larger space for participation, and so older Mam men use the dances to legitimate men's authority in the name of tradition.[13]

Many of the "uses and customs" that have been questioned by other organized Mam women are legitimated by dance performances, such as marriages arranged by parents. This practice, which has been denounced by many indigenous women as "forced marriage," together with domestic violence, justified in the name of discipline, is performed by dance groups as part of Mam "customs," and participating women neither question nor reject it.

Discourses constructed in dance groups express, then, the complexity of the struggles to define the meaning of "Mam culture and tradition." Whereas some contexts question the structures of economic domination represented by the fincas and the spiritual racism of mestizo society, thus playing a counterhegemonic role, others reproduce and reinforce women's subordination, thus echoing hegemonic discourses on gender roles.

The content of histories told by Danzas Mames depends much on the public for which they are intended. There are usually three kinds of audiences. There are performances for the community itself, generally on special occasions, such as the end of the academic year at the primary school, Mother's Day, or the celebration of a patron saint. Then there are performances at regional festivals that are directed to a wider audience, normally composed of indigenous people from other parts of the state. Finally, there are performances taped for the INI radio station that have wider coverage and give priority to elders' narrations. Although the content of performances changes, depending largely on the audience, improvisation and renewal are constant features of the art form and new memories are added day by day to stories told and performed by Danzas Mames.

XEVFS, the "Voice of the Southern Border"

A little more than a year after XEVFS, La Voz de la Frontera del Sur, went on the air in Las Margaritas, Carlos Gutiérrez Alfonzo, the anthropologist from the CCI Mam-Mochó-Cakchiquel of Mazapa de Madero, suggested adding the voice of the Sierra Mam peasants to those of the Tzeltal, Tzotzil and Tojolabal.[14] Gutiérrez Alfonzo described the origins of this new program for "cultural rescue."

> In July 1988 I placed before the presidents of the community planning committees of Mazapa de Madero an outline of the project. Contents: history and organization of the community, oral tradition, music. Participating voices and listeners: the Mam. The committees would make a list of all possible participants, would name the communities and assess the work; they suggested as broadcast time Fridays at four o'clock in the afternoon. (Gutiérrez Alfonzo 1996:70)

Gutiérrez's suggestion found a positive response in the dance groups, which Eugenio Robledo had begun to organize. Although there had been some performances, the "Mam Word and Music" program was the catalyst that consolidated the organization of Danzas Mames and contributed to the formation of new groups in the municipalities of La Grandeza and Siltepec.

The stories broadcast on radio tended to be longer than those performed in communities or during the Mayas and Zoques Dance Festival. With the usual interruptions, such as lunch and dinner, recording a program would take a whole day. Soon Comitán merchants who passed through the Sierra ejidos began to tell others that they had heard the story of "The Little Ear of Corn" in Don Luciano's voice, or a relative visiting the coast would joke about his surprise on hearing his own grandfather when he turned on the radio in Tapachula. After the first programs were broadcast, the Mam became aware that what was being spoken into the microphone might reach thousands of people—relatives who had migrated long ago to the rain forest, friends working at the fincas, or a husband selling his vegetables at Frontera Comalapa. XEVFS technicians became guests of honor in Mam communities. I was invited to one of these recording sessions when I went to the Sierra for the first time. At the request of the inhabitants of Las Ceibas, I tape recorded their stories for XEVFS in October 1989. This was the beginning of a long friendship with the station's technicians and made possible my access to the Mariscal region.

One morning in June 1990 I climbed to the top of the Malé mountain with Carlos. From its height I saw Motozintla small and frozen in time, and at that moment I decided I would live in the Sierra and write this story.

I was able to join the technical team on one of their trips through the region. By then, Noe Morales, a young Mam from the Miravalle community, had already joined the team and would later be in charge of "Mam Word and Music." It was the rainy season, which in the Sierra lasts for almost six months of the year, and it had been confirmed through the radio that we would go that day to work in Ejido El Rodeo in the municipality of Siltepec. Through some of Noe's relatives, El Rodeo people had invited the radio station to record a program on the ejido. The aim was to tape several hours, which would be broadcast later in several parts during the Friday programs.

Covered with rubber cloaks and carefully protecting the radio equipment, we walked through mud and rain to the house of the group representative, who lived far from the ejidal office on the slope of one of the adjoining hills. In the house we were greeted with hot coffee and corn and black bean tamales that the dance group women had prepared for us. After having our lunch and drying a bit by the stove, recording began. All dance group members sat in a semicircle by a table holding a bottle of Tatish, a popular cane liquor in that region made in Yucatán. After Noe introduced the dance group to the XEVFS audience, the performance began. The aim was to represent a group of friends meeting to remember how the ejido was founded and the way things were in the past. This group of friends who made up the El Rodeo dance group were in a way representing themselves.

The recording session began with people speaking the Mam language. Then someone outside the group would summarize in Spanish what had been said, without making it sound like a translation. They spoke about when their grandparents had arrived and the land had been nothing but wilderness, about the "Law of Government" that had forbidden the language and burned the costumes, about what the ancients had planted and what they had eaten, and how documents had been obtained to form the ejido. As the recording went on, the Tatish was passed around and stories became more painful, emphasizing more than before the suffering of the Sierra Mam. As Don Gumercindo told us how difficult it had been to plant in the frost-hardened land, about life at the finca, and so on, Doña Luz would repeat among murmurs and almost sobbing, "It is his truth, it is his truth, it is not only a story for the radio . . ."

More than fifty hours of tapes, which have been broadcast by "Mam Word and Music" and are kept in the station's library, represent the most complete record of Sierra peoples' oral history. This material deserves more careful analysis than I can provide here. Gutiérrez Alfonzo (1996) provides an excellent selection of the recordings, along with a discussion of his experience at XEVFS, in his thesis.

Contrary to what I would later see in performances for the community itself, the radio recordings often underscore how difficult life in the Sierra is and refer to specific problems that the "ancients" faced and that contemporaries still face today. The following excerpt from the recording I witnessed is an example.

This is a marginalized place. . . . During the rainy season, well, we cannot travel. And then during the rainy season we become sad; the corn scarcely comes in the COPLAMAR, and here we are feeling miserable. I do not know which will be the system of the governor who has taken his place right now, whether he will keep helping us peasants. I hope so. That is why we signed [voted] for him; thanks to us that man is there. And if we had not, if the peasant had said no, well, what if we change our minds. Because the majority is the basis, the main basis.

In other places, down there, it is good; buses go by any moment, by night. But here, well, in the Sierra, . . . when you get to Motozintla, it is a pity to look up. Before coming here you think twice.

Look how many remained there that time when there was a bad spell. And we are here, suffering, waiting for corn. But where is the corn? There is no corn. Fortunately, there were potatoes; with potatoes we survive. That is why we never stop working here all the time, work and overwork, more work.[15]

The radio is a good opportunity to send messages, not only to relatives in other parts of the state, but also directly or indirectly to the governor himself, to remind him of unfulfilled promises made during his election campaign. In an opinion poll conducted by the radio station to find out about the regional impact and the opinions of listeners, a woman commented:

I like to be told by the radio that the people are being cheated by the governor. These programs have helped us *to wake up*, to understand better. I would like to be taught how to work better, how others have improved, how they are organized. (Gutiérrez Alfonzo 1996:74; original emphasis)

Although XEVFS is sponsored by the INI and therefore does not air viewpoints that are critical of government policies (Vargas 1994), it does allow the voices of the Sierra and the rain forest to tell their stories and to express their opinions, and thus it has indirectly helped some listeners to "wake up." This unintended consequence created tension between the state government and the XEVFS directors under Governor Patrocinio González Garrido, and there was even an attempt to buy the station and make it part of the state government broadcasting network. To ensure that the station would remain in the hands of the INI, its directors had to watch their programs more carefully and restrict broadcasting opportunities to many independent peasant organizations who had used the medium (Vargas 1994).

Nevertheless, the recordings and broadcasts by XEVFS of many of the performances of Danzas Mames have furthered the legitimation of these groups among the population as a whole. Because of the prestige of radio among the peasant population, many young people, who thought of Danzas Mames as entertainment for old people, began to take this new organizational space seriously.

The Mayas and Zoques Dance Festivals

After 1982, when the Tzotzil anthropologist Jacinto Arias became head of the Department for the Strengthening of Ethnic Cultures of the Chiapas government, interethnic cultural festivals were organized at the state level. An old PRIist militant and a political conservative, Arias moved away from the independent positions of the state indigenous and peasant movement, especially since he was the PRIist municipal president of San Pedro Chenalhó. Yet as a public servant he did not allow his cultural policies to be influenced negatively by official indigenism. The main difference between Arias's indigenism and that of INI lies in his conviction that indigenous people should be responsible for administering cultural and development policies that affect their own people. When he was head of the Department for the Strengthening of Ethnic Cultures, his team was made up of twenty indigenous and three mestizo promoters.

It was this interest in the creation of spaces for indigenous people which they themselves controlled that led him to promote the organization of the Mayas and Zoques Dance Festivals, whose primary goal was to support the cultural expression of Chiapas indigenous peoples and to aid the cultural interethnic exchange between Mayan and Zoque groups. Contrary to other festivals organized by the state government, which openly maintain a folk character to promote tourism, the festivals are closed to the public and are political in nature. The festivals, and in general the initiatives of the department, have fostered the development of an indigenous elite within the official party, which at several points has confronted indigenous intellectuals of the independence movement.

In spite of the partisan position of the committee organizing the festivals, they are attended by indigenous people from all over the state, whether or not they are linked to the official party. Like the creation of the CNPI, the Mayas and Zoques Dance Festivals made it possible for indigenous peoples to learn about the problems of other regions while exchanging information on their cultural traditions and reinventing new ones.

In September 1994 representatives of Danzas Mames invited me to the Zoque village of Tapilula to videotape their performances at the Mayas and Zoques Dance Festival. Only those invited by the different organizations or participating communities were allowed to take photographs or videos, and they had to obtain special permits from the event's Security Committee. Carrying all of my video equipment, after driving for several hours, I arrived at Tapilula on a Thursday at midday, in the extreme heat of northern Chiapas. It took me some time to find the Sierra people among the more than six hundred participants assembled in the park. The embroidered red huipiles of the highland Tzotzil, the elegant white blouses with bare shoulders of the Tzeltal women, the colorful Tojolabal skirts, the monkey costumes of the people from Chamula—all these colors gave this Zoque village of colonial origin a seldom seen splendor.

On a wooden platform at the center of the park performances were taking place: music, dance, and theater by Tojolabal, Tzeltal, Tzotzil, Chol, Jacalteco, Chuj, Zoque, and Mam peoples. Apart from the main event in the park, some groups from San Juan Chamula were performing their religious ceremonies in front of the village church. Unfortunately, a Sierra dance group was one of the first to perform. I had not yet applied for my permit and a Security Committee member forbade me, and a Tzotzil friend from the independent theatrical troupe Sna Jtz'ibajom (the Writer's House), to videotape the performance. We both had to turn our cameras off and approach the Chol official granting the permits. The leader of the group that had invited us had to verify that we had indeed been invited, and we were allowed to videotape only the group from which we had received an invitation. In my case, each of the leaders of the ten Sierra dance groups had to come forward. Among the six hundred attendees, this was like finding needles in a haystack.

My friend went to look for Dr. Arias, and I tried to find Don Eugenio. After a laborious search, we found out that the Organizing Committee was at a special meeting that would not adjourn until the afternoon. The heat, the exhaustion of carrying the camera, tripod, and microphones all over the village, plus the frustration of not being able to videotape the festival, led me to take a seat on a bench so that I could at least watch one of the performances. To my surprise, a Sierra dance group was presenting its premiere performance of a story about labor on a coffee finca that ended with peasants organizing themselves to take over the finca. It was one of the best-received performances of the festival.

The Organizing Committee, all of them PRI people, discussed the replacement of zone coordinators locked in some warehouse, and in the meantime participants were able to give their performances contents better suited to the reality lived after the Zapatista uprising.

I managed to videotape two performances by the groups whose leaders I was able to find in time to apply for my permit. My Tzotzil friend had given up and returned to San Cristóbal on the first day of the festival. The next day, I met Dr. Arias and explained that I had come to the festival at the behest of the Sierra dance groups and, because of bureaucratic red tape, had not been able to keep my word to them. With an ironic smile, he answered, "Here we make the laws, you can use this setting to analyze the new indigenous cacicazgo in Chiapas." Arias's cynicism or honesty left me speechless.

I had promised to give each group a videocassette of its performance, and days later in the Sierra I had to explain to them that the new indigenous bureaucracy did not allow me to film. Because of my experience, several Danzas Mames coordinators decided to make their own film, for which they borrowed my video camera for a few weeks. Later I helped them to write a proposal to INI in which they requested video equipment. The relationship of Danzas Mames to the world of image is part of the ongoing contemporary history of Sierra peasants.

The Community

Danzas Mames has become an integral part of most community events, from religious festivals to inaugurations of public works. For their participation in such events, members receive no financial remuneration and only in cases when a marimba group from another community is invited will people contribute to the cost of transportation. The description of one of these performances before their own community allows us to compare the kind of stories they tell in familiar spaces with those told before wider audiences.

It was the end of the school year in the primary school of Barrio Banderas, in the municipality of La Grandeza. The Danzas coordinator, a young man who understands Mam but cannot speak it, agreed with the teachers that the community dance group would perform to support the school festival. Through relatives, an invitation was sent to the groups Maíz Blanco (White Corn), in the municipality of La Grandeza, and Laguna Canadá, in the municipality of El Porvenir. Friendly ties to the members of both groups influenced the decision to invite them. Both groups accepted and left their communities very early in the morning to attend the festival. Those from Maíz Blanco had to walk for four hours, carrying their marimba, and those from Canadá for an hour downhill on muddy and difficult paths. Their pleasure in attending the festival and showing their dances and the promise of a hearty sheep stew were the only incentives that both groups had for undertaking this journey in the middle of the May rains.

The school, situated on a flat plot and surrounded by hills, seemed to be the only building on the mountain. But if one looked carefully, one could make out houses scattered between the hills. People came down early from their houses to arrive at the school before the rain began, but they had to wait until the rain subsided to begin the festival. Performances would be on a basketball court, with marimbas placed in a corner and several large plastic sheets to protect them should it rain. Children took their places

The marimba, an essential instrument in the Mam musical tradition.
PHOTO BY RICHARD CISNEROS LÓPEZ.

around the court, organized by grade. This festival was for them, especially the performances.

Unlike other performances, those for the community were usually preceded by a short speech explaining the importance of culture and the goal of the dances. This speech was delivered in Mam by one of the oldest members of the group and translated by him or a younger bilingual member so that children could understand it. Before other audiences, it was usually not necessary to justify the importance of recovering the past, as participants in the Mayas y Zoques Dance Festival and the technical staff of the indigenist radio station share their interest in "cultural rescue." Many community people, however, particularly children and young persons, do not see why they should want to return to the times of the ancients.

Don Feliciano was asked to introduce the Barrio Banderas Danza. Using the school's old sound equipment, Don Feliciano spoke in Mam for more than ten minutes, his voice interrupted by static. After completing his speech in Mam, he translated it himself:

> We thank the teachers for inviting us here, and also our brothers from Maíz Blanco and Canadá for accepting to come in spite of the rain. We are here to remind the children where our roots come from; it is a remembering of the way our grandparents lived, so that they know we are Mam, that it is no shame, but quite the opposite. ... [W]e must always remember and never deny who we are. We are going to show you first the way the ancients used to shop. At that time it was not like nowadays; soap did not come in little bags, but was pig soap;[16] there was no sugar but *panela* [a loaf of brown sugar], money was not organized like nowadays, but was one *real*, two *reales*, one *tostón*. One sold in the market what one sowed or made with one's hands; the pot, the blanket, the copal, all was done by the ancients with their own hands, unlike today when everything is brought from outside. That you will see children in this performance, in this remembering, so that you know, so that you do not forget. . . .[17]

After this brief introduction, the Barrio Banderas group, composed of seven men and seven women, appeared. The men wore trousers and white shirts with red sashes and palm hats. Don Julián's suit was not ready, so he decided to wear a karate shirt one of his children had brought from town many years before. All the women wore green clothes they had bought in Huehuetenango with the money given them by INI; their shawls and their plastic shoes were multicolored. The group divided into two, sellers and buyers. They placed on the ground several handmade earthen pots lent by some old women of the community, copal pellets, a woolen blanket—one of those Don Cayito still makes at El Porvenir—several kinds of vegetables, and the ever popular Tatish. The performance was in Mam and dramatized bargaining between buyers and sellers. The children paid attention and laughed, and some left their places to see what was sold and bought; the teachers scolded them and made them sit again. The "market" was taken away, and the dancing began.

I recognized the song "Ferrocarril de los Altos" (The Highlands Train), one of the marimba airs most popular among Guatemalans. Then they played "El Cafetal" (The Coffee Plantation), a Colombian melody considered "the" regional song of the Sierra. It was a simple dance, men with their hands behind their backs and women holding their cloths, with the rhythm soft and movements slow. After they had danced three or four airs, the children became bored and left their seats. It was time for the next performance.

The Maíz Blanco group had decided to honor their name and perform the End of Harvest Feast. Once more, this play was in Mam, followed by a translation. This time it told the story of a little ear of corn that had appeared a few days before in the Barrio El Letrero and spoken to a little girl, giving her a message to take to all the ejidos:

> Those who know tell that this little ear of corn was angry because it was being replaced by coffee; nobody respected it any longer; nobody burned copal for it; nobody organized its feast to give thanks for the harvest. "Can coffee be eaten," it told them. "Do not be thankless because hunger might be upon you; I give you your tortilla, your *pozol*, your *tamal*; you must not forget me," so they say the little ear of corn told. Then many people began to go to El Letrero to take copal and fire to the little ear of corn, and many organized a feast that year to give thanks for the harvest. That is what we are going to see just now, how we used to organize the feast of harvest.[18]

This time the set was a bit more complicated: there was a flower arch that was prepared beforehand (and probably carried on the four-hour walk) and under it a small shrine with several ears of corn in a basket, flowers, *ocote*, and an old coffee pot where copal was burned. Men and women sat on both sides of the arch on two small benches; the men were dressed like those of Barrio Banderas, while the women had clothes of different colors, all brought from Guatemala. The performance began. A couple came to the house with several presents for the ear of corn—fruit, copal, candles. They greeted and called each other *compalé* and *comalé* (the standard Spanish is *compadre* and *comadre*), godparents, in this case godparents of the feast. It was explained to me later that *compadrazgo*, the special relationship between the parents and godparents of a child, was established not only when baptizing a child or sponsoring a wedding but also when sponsoring a feast. Those who helped to organize a religious festivity become compadres to the owners of the house. Presbyterians, of course, did not participate in these kind of performances. Guests sat down and those representing the owners of the house took out a bottle of Tatish and started serving all the guests in the same glass, one by one, and each one gave thanks with a prayer; then the Tatish was offered to Mother Earth by spilling some of it on the ground (unfortunately, on this occasion it was a cement floor, and thus Mother Earth could not receive her homage). The dialogue continued for more than twenty minutes, and the young Barrio Banderas coordinator became impatient because there was no translation. Children followed attentively everything that was going on and did not seem fretful during long dialogues that most of them did not understand. Finally the coordinator interrupted and demanded a translation. Again, the translation consisted of only one or two sentences: "They are talking about the harvest, how good the rainy season was this year and all the blessings Mother Earth has given us." Dialogues in Mam continued until the marimba broke in and dancing began. This time they danced with an ear of corn that was passed from hand to hand among all participants. Some rocked it to sleep like a baby, and some women sang to it. The children laughed, and some decided to join the dance. This time their teachers could not control them. Elders stopped the teachers from interfering so that the children could dance freely, for it was their feast after all. Some of the children asked to have the ear of corn and danced with it, while dance members smiled happily at the children's enthusiasm.

The last performance was by Laguna Canadá. Only five of its members were able to come because of the rain and because several of them had been hired as laborers on a road that would link El Porvenir with La Grandeza. An old couple and three old men made up the cast. Their costumes were also made of cotton but with different styles, some of them quite old. They wore neither a sash nor a hat. As they still had received no support from the INI, they were unable to buy their costumes and had no marimba. The Barrio Banderas marimba served as the accompaniment for their dance. Doña Natalia wore her own old cloth. She had worn it before she was married and had kept it for several decades for special occasions, its color now grayish but still bearing traces of the green it once was. The introduction was in Mam and shorter than the others. The translator related:

We are going to present the custom of June 24 that our grandparents performed to have an abundance of sheep. You children must take good care of sheep because they give us their wool to make our blankets, to sell and have a bit of money. We must take care of sheep because they give us their meat, like the one we are going to eat today. . . . [T]hey give us their manure for the milpa. When you go as shepherds, do not begin to play because the sheep get lost; we must take care of it, and thank God for our sheep.[19]

The performance began by tying a live sheep by its four legs. It was a medium-sized sheep that someone in Barrio Banderas had lent for the festival. All members of the dance group burned a little copal and lit candles around it. In low voices, as though they were praying, they spoke some words in Mam. They poured some Tatish, and the glass was passed on to each participant. Then the sheep's ears were cleaned with the liquor. One of the men took out a pair of large metal scissors and cleaned them with Tatish. Children could no longer hold back their curiosity and left their places to form a circle around the group, their teachers powerless to stop them. The tips of the sheep's ears were cut with the scissors. The animal moved and cried in pain. Blood spilled on the cement, and then two of the men in the group lit several firecrackers, which marked the beginning of the music. Once more there was dancing and the music of the marimba, but this time the Laguna Canadá troupe invited the members of the other two groups to join in the dancing. The festival ended with a dance in which all in attendance participated. The Maíz Blanco and Barrio Banderas marimbas took turns to enliven the dancing. Softer rhythms such as "La Chiapaneca" and "Ferrocarril de los Altos" were followed by tropical rhythms played on the marimba, which someone had learned on his travels to the coast and then taught to other *marimbistas*. To the same low rhythm we danced "Juana la Cubana" and other coastland airs I could not recognize.

The stories told and performed that day were all centered around the importance of self-subsistence. Nostalgia for the times when "things from outside" were not needed to live permeated the three performances. Coffee had replaced corn as the main crop in several regions, and when the price collapsed there was no more money to buy corn. The little ear of corn's threats were thus becoming real. This new crop had made them increasingly dependent on credits for fertilizers and pesticides or support for commercialization and technical counseling against the *broca* (plague of coffee). The stories told through the dances spoke of a mythical past in which a milpa economy allowed them to subsist with no need of "external" support. Soap, clothes, and blankets were made with their own hands, and sheep provided manure, wool, and food.

Cane producers at Mazapa de Madero. Productive subsistence activities, such as making sugar at home, are claimed as part of tradition by Danzas Mames. PHOTO BY RICHARD CISNEROS LÓPEZ.

Yet this vision of the past is challenged by other performances organized by younger members of dance groups. These remind the audience that when "nothing was needed from outside" people periodically had to go down to the Soconusco fincas, where they suffered ill treatment from overseers and enganchadores (recruiters).

Dispute in the Construction of Mam Traditions

The dynamic process of inventing traditions reflects other social processes in Sierra communities. Official indigenism's emphasis on cultural rescue is centered on music, handicrafts, and ritual festivities, leaving aside the historical claim for land by indigenous peoples. Some of the elders who participate in Danzas share with indigenists the idea that "traditions" refer to these specific practices of the ancients. For young people, however, "tradition" is closely linked to land rights, and this is expressed in stories told in their performances. Old men and young men agree that "tradition" also means that women should obey "their" men, stay at home, and take care of the children, animals, and family orchard.

As more young people join the Danzas, performances include new elements that tell us of different aspects of contemporary Mam life. Thus we find Sobrerón, a magical character in regional popular traditions, facing Spiderman in one of the performances.

Many of the young people who have joined the Danzas have participated in peasant mobilizations in recent years, as land distributed during the 1930s has proved insufficient for younger generations. The justification for the present struggle is partly found in past suffering, and although many young people no longer go down to work at the fincas, their grandparents' stories support their accusations of neolatifundism. Their performances at religious and family festivals focus on aspects of daily life that they see as an integral part of being "Mam" and that culturalist perspectives often disregard. "The Finca Cafetalera" (The Coffee Plantation), for example, tells about how Mam are treated by finca owners and their overseers and about living conditions in the galleras and the low wages they are paid.

This performance was presented at a school festival in a community of El Porvenir. It began with the Día de los Muertos (Day of the Dead, or All Saints' Day) festival, which marks the time when Mam go down to the finca to harvest coffee. The first part of this Danza is centered around the visit to the graveyard and food, flowers, and Tatish for the dead, following a structure similar to other religious festival performances. Yet in the space representing the graveyard men come together and begin to chat in Spanish: it is time to go to the finca, to sleep in the horrible galleras and eat bug-ridden beans. They talk about how low salaries are because of the low price of coffee. They comment on the ill treatment they receive at the hands of the overseers and on how they are making the "finquero gringo" rich while they themselves are starving. After this dialogue, which the children and the rest of the audience follow attentively—no translation is required since it is in Spanish—the trip to the finca begins. The men carry machetes at their waists and the women carry the children in shawls on their backs. Coffee plants on sticks represent the plantation; men and women begin to harvest the coffee, which they put into baskets hanging from their waists; and they wipe the sweat off their faces, representing hard work. At the center of the court they place a table with a boy and a girl of about thirteen years old, representing the owner and the overseer. Workers return with their loads, and the owners inform them that because the price of coffee has fallen even farther, they will be paid half the wages they had been promised. The men protest, and an argument breaks out. They do not accept the money. The group of workers (all men) come together and converse in Mam. The owners seem surprised that they do not accept their offer. After talking for a while in Mam, with

Mam woman washing, municipality of El Porvenir. Gender roles are reinforced by Danzas Mames performances. PHOTO BY RICHARD CISNEROS LÓPEZ.

no translation, they go to the coffee plantation and destroy it with their machetes. The performance ends when the owners run away in fear and the workers sit down at the table for conversation. The occupation of the finca is never mentioned, but the implication is clear when the workers sit at the owners' table.

Although young women participate in such performances, and in the case of the "Coffee Plantation," one of them plays the role of the owner, none of these plays questions the exclusion of women in organizational spaces. Only the mestizo woman, the owner of the finca, is represented with some kind of power, albeit to oppress her workers. Questioning class oppression and racism does not imply criticizing gender subordination, even in dance groups some of whose members are young people with secondary school education who in some cases have temporarily migrated to urban areas to study.

"Espera en la Reforma Agraria" (Waiting in the Land Reform Office) tells of the Mames' struggle for land and with the Mexican bureaucracy. Some Danza participants who belong to agro-ecological cooperative societies have also organized performances about the ill effects of pesticides on their health and on Mother Earth's.

What emerged as a space closely linked to the official culturalist perspective has acquired a dynamic of its own and has become in many cases a space for criticism and questioning of the state and the system in general.

> But Mam life is not only tradition. We are also peasants who do not have enough land; but who has it? Well, landowners do; they have the best lands. I understand about eight people have Mexicans under their domination; they do what they want; I understand the rich get richer every day and the poor become poorer.[20]

Testimonies such as the one above tell us that being Mam means not only speaking the language and celebrating the festivity of the little ear of corn but also working at the fincas and fighting for land.

In the new political context that developed after January 1, 1994, a large number of Danzas Mames members began to participate in peasant mobilizations within the framework called "peaceful civil resistance." Civil resistance, which is discussed more fully in Chapter 7, has included closing of roads, occupation of fincas, and assuming municipal presidencies, in support of Zapatista demands and in rejection of an election process considered fraudulent. Within this context, cultural identity has become for some a key element for political organization. An example is the kidnapping by the Mam Supreme Council of government officials at the finca El Edén, in the municipality of Tapachula, as a way to press for the distribution of this finca, owned by an American, John Heidegeith Smith. The Mam supreme councillor of the Soconusco region, Ancelmo Pérez, states that this extreme measure was taken after their land demands had been ignored for several years (*El Observador*, January 22, 1995:1). Generally, this type of action has been claimed by peasant organizations, even when having indigenous language speakers among their militant members. Now this right to the land is claimed not only as peasants but also as Mam. One ICHC official who has worked in the Sierra for several years, describes this transformation in self-identity:

> When they become conscious that they are Indians and that if they ceased being it, they would only be forced to be in the middle, then they accept their Indian identity; and when they tell them, you are an Indian, well yes, I am an Indian, they answer, and they begin thinking as Indians and claiming more respect as Indians. . . . [A]nd now Indians are rebelling; they are Indians who, when not fighting for their land, are fighting for respect for their culture; they fight in many ways, but they are now conscious of their Indian identity.[21]

I do not mean by this that Mam dance groups are a consciousness-raising strategy promoting political mobilization. Reality is much more complex than that. After all, the Danzas can be analyzed as one part of the hegemonic process of new indigenism trying to modify its discourse; yet they are at the same time spaces for identity construction that can be used by sectors of the Mam population that are beginning to question the state. The marginal participation of women in this movement and the reinforcement of gender inequality also point out the limits of resistance in these new cultural discourses.

In the last chapter we shall see how different sectors in Danzas Mames have taken different positions toward the state since the Zapatista uprising. The different ways to construct the past and conceive of oneself as Mam have marked the different political options of Sierra inhabitants and, to a certain extent, the way they imagine their future.

DOÑA LUZ

ORGANIZING FOR WOMEN'S RIGHTS

After living for almost a year in the Sierra, I heard about a "cultural rescue" movement that was not linked to official indigenism. It was composed of agro-ecological cooperative societies that, in tandem with their work, promoted the recovery of cultural traditions. Up to that point, my research had focused on what I called two circuits of social relations, the twenty-two communities participating in the Danzas Mames and the Presbyterian communities made up primarily of Mam peasants. These two "circuits," together with the archival research that I was pursuing in Mazapa de Madero, Siltepec, Tuxtla Gutiérrez, and Mexico City, left me little time to concern myself with the "nonofficial cultural rescue" movement.

The participants of the Mam dance groups organized by Don Eugenio Roblero told me about the existence of Motozintla Sierra Madre Indigenous People (Indígenas de la Sierra Madre de Motozintla [ISMAM]) and Nan Choch (Our Mother Earth), two organic cooperative societies founded with the support of the Catholic church, whose aim was also to recover the traditions of the ancients, but particularly from the standpoint of respect for Mother Earth.

Don Eugenio's close links with PRI had aroused some uneasiness among those Danzas Mames participants who were not PRIistas and were afraid that their performances would turn into folk shows for official ceremonies. Some of these peasants mentioned other efforts in the region to recover the "ancients' knowledge." Some of them had thought about the possibility of approaching the cooperative societies, but so far contacts had been limited to technical counseling on the growth of organic vegetables and compost making.

The influence of the agro-ecological movement began to be seen in the performances of Danzas Mames. Some performances included criticism of the use of pesticides and fertilizers, explaining the problems that agrochemical products caused for the land and the health of peasants. When I asked about the new content of their performances, they explained that they had "taken" them from an ISMAM festival, which one of them had attended at the invitation of a cousin. My interest in complementary and sometimes contradictory discourses about the "Mam tradition" led me finally to approach these agro-ecological cooperative societies.

After introducing myself to Father Jorge Aguilar Reyna, adviser to IS-MAM and Nan Choch, and after explaining the broad outlines of my research, I managed to obtain an invitation to the ISMAM Anniversary Festival, which would be held in the newly bought coffee processing factory in the town of Tapachula. The festival was attended by some five thousand peasants from all over the Sierra, counting members, relatives, and friends, as well as foreign buyers, agronomists on the technical staff, special guests from other organic cooperative societies from throughout Mexico, priests linked to the social programs of the Catholic church, and the odd, out-of-place researcher like myself. It was an event that included sporting competitions, talks by the oldest members about the benefits of organic agriculture, theatrical performances on the ancients' respect for Mother Earth, songs in Mam and in Spanish, and the annual reports of the cooperatives.

I felt lost among these people. Father Jorge introduced me to some of the cooperative society leaders—"This is an anthropologist called, What did you say your name was? Who is researching on, What did you tell me you were doing?"—an introduction that opened few doors for me. After I had wandered through the coffee warehouse and had sat for a while indifferently watching a basketball game between ISMAM and Nan Choch members, a woman with a child of about two years old sat down by me. It was difficult to guess her age—was it twenty or maybe even thirty? Her sun-withered skin betrayed the youth of her movements and the spark in her eyes. Her name was Luz, and her husband was a Nan Choch member whom she had not seen since that morning. Her child was uncomfortable in the heat of Tapachula, for they came from the Sierra and were not used to hotter coastland temperatures. Tired of looking for her husband in the warehouse and the courtyard, Luz decided to sit down and spend some time with me. She knew that Joel, her husband, would show up as soon as the arts festival began, for they had planned to join in.

The festival lasted two days, and during that time, Luz and I talked about Nan Choch, her life, my life, her problems with her husband, who drank too much, my recent divorce, and so on. We had a common interest: our concern about women's rights and our wish to support organizations fighting for them. Luz participated in the Women's Pastoral of the Catholic church and, with other Nan Choch women, was trying to promote greater participation of women in the cooperative. I told her about the Women's Group of San Cristóbal de Las Casas, a nongovernmental organization devoted to preventing sexual and domestic violence against women, in which I had been a volunteer since 1989. She was enthusiastic about learning of our efforts and invited me to participate in some of the meetings of their newly formed organization.

Through Luz, I became acquainted with the accomplishments of the Women's Pastoral and the way in which peasant women, Mam and mestizo, have succeeded in including in the platform of organic cooperative societies the importance of giving new value to women's work. Her testimony, reconstructed from a brief interview and several informal conversations in different contexts, tells about how some Mam peasant women have organized and successfully reshaped their identities as indigenous people and as women.

Look, the truth is I do not know the exact date of my birth. My mother could not read and did not register me. This has caused me trouble, because I do not have a birth certificate, and living at the border, at times immigration officers stop us and want to send us to Guatemala. This is why now I have obtained my voter credential. In case I get stopped, I can show something. They wrote in it that I am thirty. I must be about that [age].

My parents were also born here. We were born right on the border. My grandparents came from the other side, but at that time it was all the same thing. Today one can hardly see in the mountains where Guatemala begins and where Mexico ends. At that time you can imagine, there were not even migration posts.

My grandparents spoke Mam, but my mother did not learn it. She lived through the times of prohibition and spoke only Castilla [Spanish], so I did not learn it either. I can understand a little bit. My grandmother who lives over there at Niquivil—I understand her a little bit—she speaks all mixed up, a bit of Spanish and a bit of Mam. For the festival performances, I had to learn my words in Tokiol. I knew some of them [in Tokiol], but others I did not.

When I went to school all my schoolmates spoke only Spanish—only some of their parents or grandparents were idiomistas. I only studied for three years. I scarcely learned how to read a bit. They took me out because I had to help my mother at home. I have seven brothers and had to make tortillas and take care of the sheep.

I also had to go down to the fincas some three years in a row. I would help my parents. I was only nine when I went down the first time. I did not like it—life was hard at the galleras, and food was bad. When I turned thirteen, I did not want to go down anymore. My parents wanted to force me to go, but I would not let them. My brothers could go down if they wanted to. I would stay to keep the sheep. That time they beat me hard, for being saucy. From then on, I got only blows. I learned how to say no and stand the blows.

Then they tried to marry me by force, like they did with my mother, but I would not let them. The parents of some boy who lived in the colony went to ask my hand. They came with their rum, their bread, their crackers—and along came a godfather who spoke well to ask my hand. I told my mother, "Do not bother to receive them because I am not marrying." But they did receive them and accepted the gift. And I made them ashamed, because in front of everyone I said I would not marry, because I did not love the boy and they would have to tie me to take me. That night they hit me with a rope. My father hit me hard, and my mother [watched] just silent in a corner. She understood me because she had been married by force. That was the custom then.

I found my husband myself. He was a catechist and so was I. We were both studying the word of God and analyzing our situation. There was not yet a TCO,[1] but we already had [developed political] consciousness and discussed poverty in the Sierra and rich people's injustice. When we were engaged, he was very happy that I participated, and he helped me understand things. So I married happily, thinking I had really found my partner. Things changed [however]. He does not like me to travel. I go to Motozintla to workshops, and now with the conflict [the Zapatista Uprising], I have been going to the Women's State Convention [Convención Estatal de Mujeres]. [But] now he does not like me to participate.

This is the problem we have in cooperative societies. We have learned much—to cultivate while respecting Mother Earth, without harmful chemical products, to find a way out of poverty in collective work, to be proud of our culture, not to be ashamed to say we are

Mam, that we are indigenous from this Sierra. And much is talked about [concerning] woman's dignity. But for our partners, it is still difficult for them to support their wives' participation. We have to make them conscious—talk more with them, organize workshops— so they understand we are persons too, so that we can progress more together. But you have seen that woman here at Tonicaque, [how] her husband beat her because she absolutely wanted to go to a workshop at Motozintla. That is why we want to organize in Nan Choch workshops, so that we can think together how to do it, how to change. That is why I have my children help me from an early age. I will never say this task is not for them because they are males. They are all the same.

Many of the ancients' things are worth rescuing, but bad habits must also be changed. [The] women's situation was very hard—they were married by force. It was customary that in the ceremony, when they [suitors] asked for the bride's hand, the father would beat his wife in front of the guests for not having taken proper care of the girl, for if the young man had been able to court her, it was because the mother had not taken care of her. It was only a custom, even if the father agreed to his daughter's marriage. [And] the mother had to be beaten for people to see that the man made himself respected— just imagine.

Life is very difficult there in the Sierra, especially in colonies where coffee does not grow. The few vegetables we grow do not last long, so we cannot do like ISMAM members who sell their coffee abroad. We can only take them down here to Motozintla. We have opened a stand in the market, on Thursdays, but people do not very well understand about organic crops. If they see a larger vegetable somewhere else, well they go and buy it, even if it has pesticides. That is why I believe that if we women also get organized and start to work on wool it might help. Nowadays we do not know very well how to card and weave it—that knowledge has been lost, but we can learn from our Tzotzil sisters from the Highlands. We can help each other. We taught them how to grow healthier sheep and to make compost, and they [can] teach us how to weave. It looks difficult, but I think it can be done. Don't you think so?

Chapter

6

ORGANIC GROWERS

AGRO-ECOLOGICAL CATHOLICISM AND THE INVENTION OF TRADITIONS

We are the guardians of the earth, and not poor little bastards used by rulers to justify their budgets and their speeches.
EDUARDO MORALES, MAM MEMBER OF NAN CHOCH

In the last two decades we have witnessed the emergence of a number of social spaces in the Sierra, some complementary and others contradictory, within which there have been efforts to recover, re-create, and thereby reinvent Mam cultural traditions. Several organic growers' cooperative societies,[1] like the Mam dance groups, have been formed whose organizing principle is the "rescuing" of their cultural roots. They constitute a minority of the Mam population that to a certain extent has fared a little better in the economic crisis caused by the neoliberal policies of recent administrations. Of course, the activities of these cooperative societies—such as ISMAM, with 1,878 members, and Nan Choch, with 266 members—cannot be thoroughly representative of the Sierra Madre population; yet their various strategies for economic and cultural survival have had an important impact on the way other sectors of the Mam population are imagining their identity. In this chapter I explore the way in which a particular sector of the Mam population has appropriated agro-ecological ideology in the reconstruction of ethnic identity. With the support of Catholic priests and nuns, these peasants have found in agro-ecological cooperative societies, not only an economic option, but also a space for organization and political learning, from which they have started to reconstruct their collective identities. This new organic growers' movement, which has also taken place in other regions of Mexico, has expanded its struggle beyond land demands, pointing out the need to appropriate the production process as well as commercialization. The formation of these organizations has been interpreted by several researchers as the emergence of "a new peasant movement." Many of these researchers, however, in an attempt to underline the importance of community values of reciprocity recovered by peasant agro-ecology, have concluded that this "strategy of resistance" is based on an indigenous worldview, without sufficiently analyzing the diverse social forces that have converged to make it possible (Hernández Navarro 1991; Toledo 1994). The specific case of the organic growers' movement in the Chiapas Sierra Madre, for one, cannot be understood without taking into account the encounter of Mam peasants with a socially committed Catholic church.

The history of Mam agro-ecological cooperative societies begins with an encounter between poor peasants in search of options and a group of priests and nuns influenced by the teachings of liberation theology. These Mam peasants, accustomed to working from dawn to dusk on coffee plantations in the coastal region of Chiapas, have had long experience in struggling for a better life; the nuns and priests, who wanted to go beyond grand theories of macroeconomic problems, were seeking possible solutions to local problems. Hence in this encounter we find that influence has been reciprocal. Mam peasants have taken the methodology of popular education promoted by liberation theology and applied to it their own meaning. They have reinvented a "Mam utopia" by taking elements from agro-ecological ideology, thus recovering a past that had been denied to them; and, at the same time, they have found economic options that are less predatory and that have allowed them greater political independence. The clergy, starting from their analysis of the problems of Sierra indigenous peoples, have widened their views from the critique of the state to a critical examination of a whole pattern of development; they have learned from elder Mam a sense of *communality*[2] that goes well beyond cooperative systems and have called into question the role of a committed church facing new processes of economic globalization.

Yet it has been an unequal encounter, colored by power relations. Marginalized peasants have had to negotiate with a clergy that, although critical and committed, is backed by an institution with political and economic power. Being part of a hierarchical and authoritarian institution, the clergy's zeal has been tempered, even restrained, by relations between the Catholic church and the state. Indeed, when analyzing the endeavors of the Foranía de la Sierra,[3] we should keep in mind the words of Daniel Levine:

> Although analysis must go beyond the formal limits of institutions, the continued impact of institutions cannot be ignored. Institutions are more than just machines for grinding out documents or allocating roles and statuses in a formalized way. They are vital, changing structures that help form the contexts in which experience is lived and judged. They provide identity, continuity, and nets of solidarity that are much valued by members, despite possible rejection by group members of specific institutional leaders or positions. (1992:15)

My analysis here takes into account this tension between institutions, as producers of meaning, constructors of spaces, and possessors of forms of control, and Mam peasants, as social subjects who retake, bargain, or reject meanings and practices promoted by institutions.

The Foranía de la Sierra: The New Social Ministry

The state's acceptance of the right to cultural difference coincided with Chiapas Catholic church's calling into question of evangelical methods used among the indigenous population. Starting from a process of self-critique, the need arose to develop social pastoral work that would take into consideration the cultural traditions of Chiapas peasants. The influence of the Second Vatican Council in 1962–1965 and of the Medellín Episcopal Conference in 1968 was felt throughout Mexico, but it had a special impact on the southern Pacific region, formed by the dioceses of Oaxaca, Tehuantepec, Tuxtla Gutiérrez, Tapachula, Tuxtepec, San Cristóbal de las Casas, and in the Mixe and Huautla de Jiménez prelacies, which have a high concentration of indigenous people.[4] The so-called preferential option for the poor, promoted by the liberation theologians, had particular influence on the work of the Diocese of San Cristóbal, headed by Msgr. Samuel Ruiz; that of Oaxaca, under Msgr. Bartolomé Carrasco; and that of Tehuantepec, under Msgr. Arturo Lona. The so-called Indigenous Congress of 1974, held in San Cristóbal de las Casas (see Chapter 4), marked the beginning of a new pastoral ministry serving indigenous peoples, which promoted a new reading of the Bible in the light of everyday experience but at the same time rejected acculturation strategies of the state and of the traditional church, while suggesting the use of indigenous languages in evangelization. Bibles that had been translated into local indigenous languages by linguists from the Summer Linguistic Institute in the 1940s began to be used by Catholic priests, who also produced new translations to use in their work among indigenous peoples.

The Mam region is under the jurisdiction of the Foranía de la Sierra, which is directly dependent on the Diocese of Tapachula. Although in this diocese, Catholic hierarchs used to view (and still do) the new pastoral line with indifference, and sometimes even rejected it outright, many of the priests and nuns were influenced by the new Latin American theological debate. The direct influence of liberation theology came via the Diocese of Huehuetenango, Guatemala, geographically closer than that of San Cristóbal, in which Maryknoll church members had begun promoting a holistic program encompassing the social, spiritual, and economic spheres among Mam, K'anjobal, Chuj, and Jacalteco peasants, which included concern for their social situation and a search for options.

From 1950 until 1970 the Sierra region had been the responsibility of three itinerant priests, who were barely able to minister to the more than three hundred communities scattered throughout an area of 2,200 square kilometers. These priests offered the sacraments to the peasants but paid no heed to the conditions in which they lived. Indeed, at the time, because of the government's acculturation campaigns, the local people were not even recognized as Mam.

The arrival of Father Antonio Stefan at the parish of Motozintla, center of the Foranía de la Sierra in the early 1970s, marked a shift in the church's mission in the region. With the support of Franciscan missionaries, he prompted the construction of a catechist school to create secular agents of the church, natural leaders who might return to their communities to encourage biblical and social reflection.

> At that stage came a priest to the Foranía who had been educated with the spirit of a new religious consciousness; he was a biblicist who was in charge of training courses, Father Antonio Stefan. Such training courses started to change things, not only to satisfy the intellectual need for knowledge, but also one of the criteria for Bible studies stressing the search for justice; then comes all about the Exodus, the New Testament, in accord with liberation movements in Latin America.[5]

During this time more than forty cooperative societies were established, which failed in the long run because of a lack of organization, but also because they were not able to compete with CONASUPO, state-subsidized stores.

Many of the secular agents trained in the Foranía became members of independent peasant organizations, such as the Organización Campesina Emiliano Zapata (OCEZ) and the Organización Proletaria Emiliano Zapata (OPEZ), which employed land invasions, seizures of municipal presidencies, and closing of roads to demand fairer land distribution and the democratization of municipal power structures. The state government responded by repressing their demonstrations, and under Gov. Absalón Castellanos Domínguez (1982–1988), several local peasants were murdered by government forces. In 1985, in Amatenango de la Frontera, three secular agents who were involved in the peasant movement were murdered by the police after they tried to seize the municipal presidency. Such experiences led Foranía's clergy to rethink their promotion of social awareness; although it had succeeded in creating a new consciousness, it had not been accompanied by a comprehensive search for solutions to local problems.

The clergy decided to form working commissions that could address specific problems. Thus were established the Evangelization Commission (Comisión de Evangelización), in charge of promoting biblical study; the Health Commission (Comisión de Salud), whose aim was to place illness in its social context; the Human Rights Commission (Comisión de Derechos Humanos), to denounce human rights abuses and to educate peasants about defending their rights; the Women's Support Commission (Comisión de Promoción de la Mujer), whose aim was to reappraise women's role in the family and the community and to promote greater social participation; and, finally, the Cooperative Societies Commission (Comisión de Cooperativas). The Cooperative Societies Commission was supported by the Center for Community Promotion of the Tehuantepec Diocese, whose goal was to find new economic options in the face of the coffee-growing crisis and the failure of the government's development policies.

This new structuring of the Foranía's work coincided with the development among followers of liberation theology of a critical stance toward the Marxist perspective, which centered its analyses on the capitalist state and on its overthrow as the strategy for social change.

Socialism and capitalism share the same modernizing perspective, which sees technological development as an option. Within liberation theology, critical thinking had been limited to the social structure, the analysis of the state, its repressive policies and its impoverishment policies, but the new agro-ecological Catholic thinking goes well beyond these; it is the same critical point of view, but not only with respect to the state, but also to modes of production. ... It is said that the eighties were the decade of great reflections on macroeconomic problems: economic blocs, the United States, the Soviet Union, capitalism, colonialism, transnational corporations, market economies, and so on. The decade of the nineties is marked by attempts to solve local problems without losing the global perspective. Then agroecology emerges as a response which tries to provide options for local problems; agroecology is a criticism of the technological path, of modernization understood as all those technological programs which come, are imposed and produce poverty, indigence, indebtedness, and destruction of the land.[6]

This testimony is a reflection of the new religious ideology in the Foranía; it reformulates a philosophy promoted by liberation theology between the 1960s and the 1980s, critiques a development pattern based on predatory technology, and brings its analysis up-to-date by including the local impact of transnational capitalism.

In 1985 the Cooperative Societies Commission held a meeting to discuss the problems of the region's small producers. It evaluated the failure of the forty consumption cooperative societies (community organizations that collectively buy basic products) and proposed the creation of new cooperative societies for production that would not depend on government credit or subsidies. The first local problem to be faced was the decline in the price of coffee on the international market and the future of the region's small-scale producers.[7] It was estimated that coffee production by hectare using agrochemical products took more than 50 percent of the growers' total income and that, in spite of fertilizers and pesticides, average production by hectare was thirteen sixty-kilogram bags of parchment coffee, whose value was well below production costs (Sánchez 1990). Furthermore, it was determined that agrochemical products had caused a series of skin and lung ailments, which had already led some small producers to stop using them.

In an effort to promote the rescue of traditional agricultural practices among younger Mames, Foranía's priests sought the wisdom of elder Mames. For Mam peasants, who for decades had been denied a voice, this new strategy indicated a reappraisal of traditional knowledge and the creation of spaces in which their opinion took on legitimacy.

All workshops turned often to the testimony of elders, to see how it was done before. In fact, many of the written notes always contain old people's testimony; how crops were produced in old times, why this method of production was abandoned, the impact of fertilizers, how it changed many habits in communities. For example, the question of sheep, because sheep provided fertilizers, manure, they were placed in pens, and by rotating them it was a self-sustaining system. For a time a pen was in a certain place, it fertilized the land, you only had to water it. Let us say that they were put together little by little and small experiments were explored which would later provide a guideline to be followed.[8]

Through these workshops the clergy became aware of the historical plundering of the Mam population and of their incorporation into the Mexican nation by violent means. Cultural rescue became an integral part of the planning process, not only from the culturalist point of view of indigenism, but also as a way to relate to nature and to recover a collective history so as to strengthen group identity. The participants agreed to complement coffee crops with corn and beans, so as to avoid the negative consequences of monoculture. They also agreed to halt the use of all agrochemical products and to study techniques of organic agriculture, including how to protect the land, compost, and build terraces and nurseries. This event coincided with the fortunate arrival of several agricultural technicians from Chimaltenango, Guatemala, who had fled their country to escape the violence. These men had experience in the management of organic agriculture and joined the team advising the Cooperative Societies Commission.

Thus several experiences converged in the creation of organic growers' cooperative societies. Advice was sought from the Union of Indigenous Communities of the Istmo Region (Unión de Comunidades Indígenas de la Región del Istmo [UCIRI]), formed by Oaxacan Zapotec peasants who had been involved in the organic culture of coffee since 1981; and a visit was made to the Irlanda plantation, Chiapas's pioneer in organic agriculture, which had been developing the biodynamic culture of coffee since 1964.[9] Drawing on the knowledge of elder Mam, of other indigenous groups in Mexico, of Guatemalan technicians, and even of Chiapas's plantation owners, one hundred sixty peasants of the municipalities of Siltepec, Motozintla, Chicomuselo, Amatenango de la Frontera, and Bellavista founded the first agro-ecological cooperative society in the Sierra in 1986, thus beginning what would be one of the country's most successful cooperative endeavors.[10]

The cooperative society started to export its coffee first to alternative

Municipal head town of Motozintla. This is where the agro-ecological movement of the Mam region originated. PHOTO BY RICHARD CISNEROS LÓPEZ.

and organic coffee markets that were not subject to the fluctuations of the traditional market and that paid well above New York prices, giving growers incomes that were between 50 and 100 percent higher. By 1991 IS-MAM was exporting its coffee at an average price of 115 cents a pound, in contrast to the New York price of 60 cents. This comparative advantage, together with the low production costs realized by eliminating chemicals, led many small regional producers to turn to organic agriculture.

But both organic and alternative markets have a limited number of consumers and distribution centers and thus are rapidly saturated. Still, IS-MAM's entry into the international market coincided with the emergence of a movement that questioned some of the premises of the alternative market, giving priority to the search for new sales strategies and new markets, and, instead of rejecting capitalism, sought to use it more equitably.[11]

Contrary to the alternative market that rejected commercial networks, the equitable market saw the need to go to large distribution centers and use mass communication to promote products. Thus ISMAM came into the market at the right time, with a solidarity network that supported its conquest of new markets but demanded a number of conditions, not only for production, but also for its functioning and organization.

From the very beginning, discourses and practices born in the peasant agro-ecological movement have been constructed in a constant dialogue with other global discourses, to which we now turn.

Globalization and Organic Markets: Mam Identity and Agro-ecological Discourses [12]

We have seen that Mexican nationalist discourse and agrarian policies have had an important impact on the social construction of Mam identity. Still, direct access of the Mam to a global market and their contact with other cultural discourses and organizational experiences have also had an influence on these processes of social construction. With Roland Robertson (1990), I hold that the present globalization process is only one more step in a long process, which acquires new characteristics with new technological developments. In the first chapter we saw how Mam peasants of the Sierra Madre have been linked through coffee production to a global economy since the beginning of the twentieth century. Thanks to Mam laborers in Soconusco, between 1927 and 1928 plantation owners were able to export 227,040 quintals of coffee to Germany, the United States, England, France, Spain, and Switzerland (information from the German Consulate, 1930, cited in Waibel 1946). We also saw how their everyday lives were strongly affected by an international decline in coffee prices, the recession of the 1930s, and the forfeiture of German plantations during World War II.

In this new stage of capital reorganization (Harvey 1990), we can see that technological change and further developments in communication, the fluidity of information, the deregulation of national markets, and more capital flexibility have had a direct impact on the daily life of the Mam peasant. The Mam have been part of the global market for centuries. What is new about this stage of globalization is that they now have more direct contact with the global community through participation in information and communication structures, such as the organic coffee market and the fair trade solidarity movement. Through promotional trips of the Commercialization Commission, through the telephone, and recently even through electronic mail, the Mam have overcome isolation imposed by traditional, regional, and national political structures. What Jean-François Lyotard (1984) and David Harvey (1990) have called the space-time compression characteristic of globalization has allowed the Mam to establish contact with other indigenous peoples in the world, with European and American ecologists, and with Japanese businessmen. These experiences have, of course, influenced their worldview and the way they have shaped their cultural discourse. Spaces of confluence have been created, where they have been able to share their experience.

> I went through Holland, Germany, and Switzerland; I got to know these countries. . . . [W]e exchanged, well, experiences, about how they did things over there and how we do them here; and they liked the project we have here very much. Then we are thinking that they buy from us a healthy product and it is well worth it for them; they pay at a slightly higher price, but they are buying a good thing. For them it is an advantage, because this uneasiness has emerged in them, they are also in favor of the environment, in favor of development through land; then they tell me, if we buy your product, we are also sharing your effort, not only for you but for the environment, and this way you can develop a project for people to live.[13]

This encounter with European alternative markets has represented an important effort for peasants who have never been out of the Sierra. IS-MAM's secretary, who has only three years of primary school education, pointed out:

> To commercialize we went in search of markets; we went to lose the fear of going into new countries to find other possibilities to sell our product to just markets, to fair markets. Possibly we are now exporting our product to alternative markets, at a price above that of the New York exchange; we are selling to these markets. . . . We are exporting to several countries, such as Holland, Germany, France, Switzerland, Belgium, Sweden, Austria, the United States, and Japan. . . . It was difficult for me to stand up in front of my peasant brothers and to go abroad; there was also the fear of going out; many things we suffered on the way; suffering but also tomorrow [there will be] a benefit.[14]

Some who have theorized the consequences for cultural identities of this new stage of globalization have proposed that the homogenizing force of the capitalist market will overcome the power of resistance and reconstruction of local cultures, thus creating a worldwide "postmodern condition," which would tend to erase cultural specificities (e.g., Jameson 1989, 1990). Others have analyzed resistance strategies developed to face global capitalism, which include the reinforcement of ethnic identities (Kearney 1991; Rouse 1991). Although many of these authors have focused on diasporas to the "first world," or on so-called migratory circuits (Gilroy

1987; Rouse 1991; Glick-Schiller, Basch, and Blanc-Szanton 1992), they still help us to understand the new hybrid cultures emerging among those who did not choose to migrate.

Cultural hybridization has occurred through historical appropriation. For example, ISMAM members brought back from one of their trips to the United States what they called the "Chief Seattle Manifesto," written in 1854 "by the head of a native North American tribe to the President of the United States." [15] The document, with drawings added by the members of ISMAM, was mimeographed and now circulates in Sierra communities. The mimeographed document begins with the question, "What is the relation between what American Indians thought and the destruction the Motozintla Sierra is suffering today?" and then describes the defense of nature made more than one hundred years ago in distant lands by a Native American: "How can the sky be bought or sold, or even the heat of the earth? Such an idea is unknown to us. If you do not own the freshness of the air, or the sparkle of waters, how could you then buy them? Each parcel of this land is sacred to my people" (mimeograph n.d.). The members of the cooperatives have not only adopted some elements of the worldviews of Canadian and North American native people, but they have also learned from new Native American businesspeople about commercialization, production, and the formulation of a corporate image, among other things. The Indigenous Free Trade Agreement is about to be signed, which will allow North American Indians to invest in an ecotourism and fishing project ISMAM is planning to develop in Chiapas's coastal region (Nigh 1997). Other spheres of communication have enabled contact with other social groups—North American Indians, European cooperativist groups, American organic farmers, certification agencies, and so on—that constitute global information structures in which they now participate (Lash and Urry 1994:64). Aspects of these structures have been appropriated and integrated into a new Mam identity that is then projected back as an image, both corporate and ethnic, through the same global information structures.

Although defense of the earth, nature, and culture is central to ISMAM and Nan Choch discourse and practice, their ideology and practices have been shaped by the demands of the alternative and equitable markets. A clear example of this is the certification that is a prerequisite for entering the equitable trade market. ISMAM sells 57 percent of its coffee through Max Havelaar-Trans Fair, an association that supports the sale of products in equitable markets and certifies "socially responsible" production and distribution (Renard 1999). The Max Havelaar label is not

Alternative and equitable markets are a very important commercial niche for
ISMAM. PHOTO BY ANA ALVAREZ VELASCO.

a trademark; it is added to brands that buy their products from cooperative societies of democratically organized small producers, at a price fixed
by the association that guarantees a fair return to the peasants. The Max
Havelaar label justifies the high prices of its products by adding the symbolic value of justice and solidarity. To have access to this market niche,
ISMAM partners agreed to use only family labor and not paid workers, to
work in solidarity with members, and to organize its cooperative society
on democratic principles, guaranteeing participation to all members, including women; political independence; no political, religious, or gender discrimination; crop diversification; and an administrative and control
structure that minimizes the risk of embezzlement (Renard 1999:199). If
any of these conditions is not fulfilled, the equitable market will be closed
to the cooperative society.

The cooperative society is governed by a general assembly composed
of all its members. Representatives of the twenty-eight member regions
meet once a month to discuss problems specific to each region and to make
decisions on the use of the common fund, special courses, infrastructure acquisition, and so on. The organization has become even stronger
through its agreements with the equitable market. Similarly, women's participation has been the result not only of Mam women's activism in the
cooperative society but also of the demands of the new market niche.

If the Max Havelaar label adds symbolic value to ISMAM coffee by alluding to its democratic structure and its philosophy of solidarity, the use of a corporate image claiming the Maya roots of its producers makes Café Mam a product with meaning that goes well beyond its quality and organic origin. Thus reinvention of a utopian past of harmony with nature has been used by members of ISMAM as cultural capital on the global market. The use of historical narratives to give "authenticity" to a product in a competitive market has been analyzed by Robert C. Ulin (1995) for the case of Bordeaux wines, illustrating the dialectical connection between commodity production and invention of tradition. Similar to Bordeaux wine producers, who by inventing a particular historical narrative created the *grand crus* (elite wines) for an elite market and enhanced their competitiveness, ISMAM invented an advertising image to meet the demands of a select organic market. The past has became symbolic capital in their effort to enhance the international marketability of their product.

Equitable and organic markets in Europe, the United States, and Japan are now particularly interested in supporting and buying products from "authentically indigenous" cultivators. Consequently, the cultural task of rescuing Mam identity now coincides with a marketing effort to construct a corporate image that can respond to the symbolic demand of "first world" ecologists and "Greens." Thus ISMAM has responded to

Café Mam destined for the international market. PHOTO BY ANA ALVAREZ VELASCO.

the demand for organic coffee produced by "genuine indigenous people" with "Mam Coffee: Organically Grown and Socially Responsible"; and the international market is told that "Mam organic coffee is cultivated and produced by the last descendants of the Mayan people." Perhaps, together with an expanded ecological consciousness, these alternative and equitable markets have been influenced by what some researchers have called "imperialist nostalgia" (e.g., Rosaldo 1989), that is, the desire to renew contact with "the noble savage" once ravaged by colonialism. The consumption of Café Mam becomes one way to support "the last descendants of the Mayan people."

New Cultural Discourses and the Reinvention of Mam Utopia

The cultural discourses that Mam organic producers have constructed in the framework of global information and communication structures are not only market strategies to reach a certain type of selected consumers, they have also given new meaning to their lives and new structure to their everyday dynamics. The cooperative has become a very important space of productive organization for many Mam peasants and at the same time has allowed the construction of a new sense of identity that is expressed in a new discourse claiming not only their rights as peasants, but also as indigenous peoples. For cooperative members, being Mam did not necessarily mean speaking the Mam language or using the costumes financed by the INI but rather recovering a common history and trying to relate harmoniously with Mother Earth.

This claim for ethnic identity is reflected in the names of the two main organic growers' cooperative societies. Lowland coffee producers named their organization Indígenas de la Sierra Madre de Motozintla, or Motozintla Sierra Madre Indigenous People, and highland potato and vegetable producers called themselves Nan Choch, meaning "Our Mother Earth" in the Mam language. The need to revalue Mam identity was integral to the need to recover respect for the earth.

> We saw the need to begin organizing ourselves and recovering our culture. We had to know who we were, to find out where we wanted to go. Then we got organized to recover the culture, recover the traditions, recover the earth, recover the life of animals. Thus Nan Choch was born, to recover the culture, the traditions and nature.[16]

The need to recover their own history led to the construction of a discourse on a mythical past of abundance and harmony with nature. Fiction and reality were mixed in the construction of this "Mam Utopia," where the land was fertile, where Mother Earth was respected and provided for every need, where there was equality and work was available, and where laws were not necessary and everybody respected elders' advice (FOCIES 1994:12-16).

This mythically constructed past of respect for nature contrasts sharply with the reality discovered in 1925 by the German geographer Leo Waibel, who described the highland region of the Sierra, inhabited by "Indians of Guatemalan origin foreign to the region":

> The forest is cut down by men with axes, but they seldom cut trees uniformly, although in general they leave standing the largest trees, or at least part of their trunk and always all stumps. Then they burn everything, whether to get rid of all the wood, or to prevent undergrowth. This superficial clearing system is easy to achieve and this is the only explanation for the fact that those beautiful Sierra Madre mountain trees which existed long ago have disappeared completely over large areas in just a few decades. Indigenous peoples are destructive of forests, and their unplanned clearing represents great danger for Sierra hydrology, especially for the future of coffee plantations. (1946: 203)

Although Waibel's testimony may be weakened by racist descriptions of indigenous populations, it is important to note that depredation in the Sierra predates the use of agrochemical substances, as pointed out by many of the documents of the local agro-ecological cooperative societies. Supported by their adviser, Father Jorge Aguilar, these Mam have been able to invite historians who specialize in Chiapas pre-Hispanic and colonial history to help in the collective reconstruction of this forgotten history. Concrete data have little importance, however, as the aim is to reconstruct a common past that will give them strength and help them build a future. Descriptions of a mythical past continue to mix historical times of the recent past, as remembered by old people, with the remote past, often reconstructed on the basis of information from mass media. Thus we find references to life in caves, where people slept on straw and skins, where "tribes" communicated with smoke and horns, wrote in signs, and counted with pebbles (FOCIES 1994:12-16).

Not all ISMAM and Nan Choch members have the same attitude toward this "rescue of the past." For some, it is only the beginning of an "introductory discourse" that is very useful when dealing with international clients but that has little to do with everyday life in their communities. Others have substantially altered their way of life on joining co-operative societies. Such is the case for members of the new community Unión Fuerza Liberadora (Liberating Force Union), an agro-ecological village founded in 1988 in the municipality of Motozintla whose organizing principle is "cultural rescue."

Coming originally from Colonia Zaragoza, in the highlands of the municipality of Motozintla, just a few steps from the Guatemalan border, founders of this "utopian community" were landless people who had received several organic agriculture courses from Maderas del Pueblo (Woods of the People), an NGO linked to the Catholic church. In 1988, after purchasing twelve hectares of land from indebted peasants in the lowlands near Colonia Belisario Domínguez, sixty-five persons formed this new community, started to collectively grow organic coffee, and became members of ISMAM. But Liberating Force Union's project went beyond organic farming, and, without leaving ISMAM, they decided to constitute themselves as a Society of Social Solidarity (SSS) in order to obtain legal recognition that would allow them to promote their own cultural rescue projects.

After deciding that the curriculum did not serve the needs of peasant children, the community expelled teachers sent by the Ministry of Education (Secretaría de Educación Pública). They then founded their own "agro-ecological" school, so that all children could learn to relate with nature in a different manner, recover their Mam language, and practice handicraft techniques used by "the elders."

> For pottery we still do not have a teacher. This has been women's preoccupation, a person comes, but just like that gives a few clues. But for weaving we do have a person who gave training for several days; most people are already involved in this course. We are also trying to recover the Mam language for our children. . . . [I]t is part of a new future we are trying to recover, together with the organic technique, and we want to carry everything on in a parallel development to stop what comes from outside.[17]

Commissions have been established to teach organic agriculture, traditional medicine, cooperative societies (which also address administrative and organizational issues), pottery, waist-loom weaving, and the Mam language. These commissions are made up of five persons, each of whom teaches one day a month. This system of taking turns has remedied the lack of teachers and involved the whole community in educational projects.

In the new agro-ecological schools, parents are involved in teaching children organic agriculture. PHOTO BY RICHARD CISNEROS LÓPEZ.

For waist-loom weaving, a refugee Mam woman was invited to train community women.

All members of the community talk about the need to end their foreign dependency and achieve a truly self-sustaining community through the production of food, clothing, and tools, yet their coffee, like that of other ISMAM members, is being sold in the United States, Europe, and Canada. The construction of a building for the agro-ecological school has been financed by the Interamerican Foundation through a Mexican nonprofit organization whose aim is to support "native cultures."

Liberating Force Union members see "cultural rescue" as a means of survival and oppose agrarian development based on agrochemical products, which has so far benefited them little. There is a clear awareness of the need to rescue their culture, which has been denied by integrationist policies.

> We must not lose what is ours; it is our duty to recover our native language; it is the conception that our forefathers had in them. . . . [W]ith courage we must take it seriously; we must not only recover the language, but everything integrated, to return to what was before.[18]

This discourse is considered too extreme even by other ISMAM members, although it is not secessionist or fundamentalist but reflects a new hybrid identity, in which historical memory and ecological ideology serve as the foundation for the construction of new traditions. For Liberating Force Union members, the rescue of traditions goes hand in hand with training courses to improve cattle handling, knowledge of new potential markets, and even trips to Europe when commercialization demands it.

By pointing out the hybrid character of Mam ecologists, I do not want to delegitimize it for other "more authentic" identities. Rather, I hold that the Mam case illustrates with particular clarity the process by which all ethnic identities are constructed, as changing, situational, historical products and not as millenarian identities that have survived internal or external colonialism.

Collective Reflection and New Spaces of Organization

Agro-ecological cooperative societies have meant for these indigenous peasants not only the possibility of recovering a denied identity while attaining better living conditions but also new spaces for political learning. Both cooperative societies have provided a special place for the ongoing education of their members, with two axes for reflection: on the one hand, the importance of collective work, with its advantages and problems, and, on the other, the peasant-ecological path as an alternative for sustainable development.

Among the requirements for joining the cooperative societies is a workshop called Organized Communal Work (Trabajo Común Organizado [TCO]), which, while analyzing the capitalist system, emphasizes the capacity of peasants themselves to change their circumstances through collective work. This workshop, designed by the Center for Community Production (Centro de Producción Comunitaria [CEPROCOM]), linked to the Diocese of Tehuantepec, has become a significant political learning experience. Beyond the workshop's educational content, which is centered on the relationship between local problems and global causes, participants experience the possibility of sharing opinions, discussing, reflecting, and being listened to, which results in a reappraisal of their own knowledge and enhances their capacity for analysis. Such learning dynamics as psychodrama, used in the TCO, have been used by Mam peasants in their communities as a form of social critique and analysis. This educational influence has reached "cultural rescue" groups linked to official indigenism, which are starting to include in their publications scenes representing plantation labor and the consequences of the use of agrochemicals.

Through discussion, reflection, and consensus developed in cooperative societies, Mam peasants have acquired access to a new language that has enriched other organizational spaces. On this point, Levine (1992:13), in his analysis of *comunidades eclesiales de base* (ecclesial base communities) in Venezuela and Colombia, points out that "apart from the achievement of proximate objectives like building a school, laying a water line, or founding a cooperative, experience in groups also furthers the construction of languages, universes of discourse, and expectation."

Yet the experience of collective reflection has not necessarily produced ideological homogenization. For some, political struggle takes place only through the control of processes of production and commercialization, by achieving self-sufficiency and engaging in development based on agrochemical products; while for others, political struggle includes wresting municipal power from the authorities and resisting the official government party. Such ideological differences have become evident in the new political conjuncture created in Chiapas since January 1, 1994, with the armed uprising of the Ejército Zapatista de Liberación Nacional.

From the beginning, clergy who have supported the formation of agroecological cooperative societies have supported organic agriculture not only as a technological option but also as a political alternative. From their perspective, the resulting dependency of the producer on conventional agricultural techniques exacerbates authoritarian structures and *caciquismo* (rule by political bosses). Dependency on external inputs and nonlocal markets makes peasants more vulnerable to strategies of control by the state. From this perspective, their regional priority should not be conventional political struggle but rather the development of an economy of self-subsistence. Father Aguilar Reina points out:

> For us, the priority is food self-sufficiency; we cannot build political independence if we have not solved the problem of our stomachs, and solving it without falling into dependency or becoming slaves. This question about the technological package proposed by the state, which many organizations have taken as workable, is nothing but technological pseudoslavery; whoever has the fertilizer holds the power, for there is the power to produce corn, and corn is the basis of life sustenance. The point is to find a way to produce food without falling into this type of dependency, then it will benefit us in the long run as stronger political independence.[19]

What was once merely a political rift over means became a chasm in the context of war. In support of the EZLN and in rejection of an election process considered to be fraudulent, the Peaceful Civil Resistance (Resistencia Civil Pacífica) emerged in August 1995. This movement included invading several plantations, taking municipal presidencies, closing roads, and establishing a parallel government "in resistance," headed by the leftist candidate Amado Avendaño, from the Partido de la Revolución Democrática (PRD). In their official discourse, both Nan Choch and ISMAM remained outside the Civil Resistance movement. However, many of their members independently supported the struggle, causing frequent friction with other members but especially with authorities of the Catholic church. The bishop of Tapachula, Felipe Arzimendi, urged all catechists and members of the congregation to stay out of the Civil Resistance and publicly supported the legitimacy of the electoral process, thus denying the legitimacy of claims of fraud made by a large segment of society. ISMAM and Nan Choch advisers seem to have decided to align themselves with the bishop and have dissociated themselves from PRD's political demands.

Conflicting political perspectives during this present conjuncture have prevented the formation of a common front, a situation that I analyze in the next chapter.

Mam Women and Gender Demands

Women have played a key role in ISMAM and Nan Choch cooperative societies, not only as laborers but also as active and participating members in general assemblies. In contrast to the Mam women who participate in the dance groups, the women members of ISMAM and Nan Choch have struggled to have active participation in their organizations. This is in part the result of their critical reflection in TCO workshops. Although gender inequality is not discussed in the TCO workshops, discussions of other inequalities has helped them to question the limits of the democratic patriarchy.

However, many Mam women have been forced to leave the domestic sphere and undertake agricultural labor or look for economic support elsewhere, in part because male migration to urban regions during the last two decades has been much greater in the Sierra than in other regions of the state. This has left many women as heads of households and in charge of coffee production, sales, and so on. Managing these new responsibilities, together with the high level of bilingualism resulting from the aggressive Hispanicizing campaigns of the 1930s, has given Sierra women more experience with dealing with state representatives. This change in women's roles contrasts sharply with the situation of Tzotzil and Tzeltal women in the highlands, who until very recently have had very little participation in the political sphere (Garza Caligaris and Ruíz Ortíz 1992; Rosenbaum 1993; Eber 1995).

The right of fathers to decide whom their daughters must marry, which has been denounced very recently by some indigenous women of the highlands as forced marriage and a violation of their rights, was already being questioned by many Mam women at the beginning of the twentieth century. Although this practice still exists among some families, more and more women are questioning their parents' authority to make decisions about their lives. Old women's testimonies tell us that already as girls they had won the right to decide whom and when to marry.

> I had left the corte for about a year when he spoke to me. Let him continue speaking if he is patient. . . . When he asked me to marry him I told him: You want to sleep with a woman, but I do not know how to work, I do not know. And who knows how they are in your house. Perhaps they are evil, perhaps you drink and are mad in your house, who knows how you are. If you are a good man you have to show it to me, have patience. . . . He spoke with my father and I accepted in the third year. But I never married, only open union.[20]

Open unions were formalized through the "hand petition," or formal engagement. Today this petition usually takes place after the young couple has reached an agreement.

With greater control over domestic decision making, women have moved toward greater public participation since the peasant mobilizations of the 1970s. Particularly in the lowlands of Motozintla, Mazapa de Madero, Amatenango de la Frontera, and Frontera Comalapa, women have been active in the peasant movement. Hundreds of Mam and mestizo women mobilized with men to demand, among other things, more just land distribution. Land has been one of the main demands of peasant organizations such as OCEZ or OPEZ, but in several historic moments, local peasants have also mobilized against labor conditions akin to serfdom, in favor of better conditions for the commercialization of their products, and against an extremely discriminatory judicial system. In all of these mobilizations, peasant women have been present to support the political and economic demands of their communities.

What is absolutely new in the present participation of local indigenous women, particularly within the agro-ecological movement, is the fact that they have become more vocal, not only in supporting the demands of their companions or in representing their communities, but also in demanding respect for their specific rights as women. Mam indigenous women have begun demanding more significant participation in decision making in their communities and organizations. In conjunction with their participation in agro-ecological cooperative societies and in promoting respect for earth and nature, large numbers of Mam women have insisted on more democratic relations within the family, the community, and the social organization. The Proposals of Mam and Mochó Peoples (Propuestas de los Pueblos Mam y Mochós), written by men and women of Nan Choch, ISMAM, and the Grupos de Trabajo Común of the Sierra Foranía, included a point on women's rights, signaling the need to

> respect women's dignity in the different aspects; participate with the same rights in meetings; take into consideration women's voices in all aspects of community life; establish relations with other women's organizations in ejidal juntas; promote encounters with other organizations and exchange experiences.

The inclusion of these demands in the documents of agro-ecological organizations is the result of many years of struggle by Mam women to have their needs recognized as priorities. It is worth noting that in the forum where these demands were discussed, the greatest opposition did not come from Mam peasants but from several agronomist advisers, who found them irrelevant, compared to the ecological problems facing the region.

In spite of the patriarchal character of the Catholic church, the new social ministry promoted by liberation theologians has endorsed greater participation of women in community development and has supported their service as pastoral agents. The reflection promoted by liberation theology is colored by a class perspective, which does not usually include a critique of gender inequality. Yet their training in organic agriculture and resource administration, as well as the new spaces for participation, has allowed many women to consider anew their place in their communities. Doña Cedema, one of the leaders of Nan Choch, exemplifies this "new consciousness":

> I like to analyze, to see things that are wrong, because my conscience tells me it is not right; that I was born for a purpose, to do something for our future. God gives us life to do something; we did not come to the world simply to take up space; we must do something to have a better life. . . . I think that if we contribute something our daughters will be better, more respected, with more rights in life and not like us. We are working for their future, so that they can have a better future, and also so that our country can have women who know how to fight, defend our rights. If I stay all alone in my corner I can do nothing, because I would be busy only with my housework and would not think of others; it is very good to think about others.[21]

This wish to "do something" led Doña Cedema to promote a women's project, as part of Nan Choch, called A New Dawn in the Sierra (Nuevo Amanecer en la Sierra). She and forty other women of Zaragoza, Tonincaque, Berriozábal, Belem, Granados Tacanque, Tonischihuán, and Aquiles Serdán, in the municipality of Motozintla, have begun to meet to discuss "women's dignity." They have planned collective poultry and cattle farms managed by women using agro-ecological techniques. For this purpose, they made contact with the Belisario Domínguez Women's Group (Grupo de Mujeres Campesinas de Belisario Domínguez), the Grupo de Mujeres de San Cristóbal de las Casas, and the Women's Commission of NGO Coordination for Peace (Comisión de Mujeres de la Coordinadora de Organizaciones No Gubernamentales por la Paz [CONPAZ]). The collective farms are not yet operating, but with the support of the above organizations, they have developed several workshops on women's rights, reproductive rights and sexuality, and democracy and political participation. As a result of these workshops, women of

A New Dawn in the Sierra have developed a proposal and sent it to several international funding agencies that are interested in supporting peasant women.

> After receiving this training [training in organic agriculture provided by Nan Choch] we started to carry out small collective jobs in horticulture, growing corn, wheat, and beans. To do this, at the beginning about sixty men and women from thirteen communities got together. Our achievement at that time was to have a common fund, from the sale of half of our crop, since the other half was for self-consumption; we also gained knowledge in organic horticulture. . . . Then there was a split, and forty of us remained in the organization, all women, and our present objective is to find possible solutions for our economic problems through productive projects, and to obtain training in resource administration. We think that it is important to find alternatives for our situation as women. That is why we have also received support to reflect on our situation and propose actions as women to achieve a change in our lives, in the family as well as in the community. We want our capacity and dignity as women to be valued.[22]

Acknowledging as unfair social relations that had been accepted as "normal" or even "natural," and verbalizing what had been silent by making the doxa into a discourse (Bourdieu 1977), has represented an important step in confronting the patriarchal discourse, used by official sectors as well as by cooperative societies themselves. These new discourses are starting to influence everyday practice and to modify, however slightly, gender relations.

> As for me, the organization has given me much. For example, at home inequality has been prevented; for I have seen many couples in which husbands oppress women very much. Here there are small talks, and men are beginning to understand that we are all human, that we have the same dignity, and this is already shared at home, at work and all that. That is what the struggle has given, this has been achieved and has helped me to be happy.[23]

At present executive positions in the cooperative societies are held exclusively by men, and domestic violence is still a problem in the region, even among members of the organic growers' movement. Nevertheless, the fact that gender demands are included in the platforms of cooperative societies and are always present in assemblies, forums, workshops, and regional encounters is a new phenomenon in the peasant movement in Chiapas.

One cannot generalize about the success of ISMAM as an organic cooperative society, because several unique elements contributed to its growth into the coffee firm it is today. Its success as a cooperative society was partially determined by the historical moment of its birth. In the mid-1980s European Social Democrats, in an effort to counteract political-military movements in Latin America, channeled much of their development resources into countries of the ill-defined "third world." Agro-ecological societies such as UCIRI and ISMAM benefited from competition between North American and European agencies for influence in Latin America. German financing through the German Environmental Protection Agency (GEPA) and American financing through the Agency for International Development and the Interamerican Foundation supported and promoted local organic agriculture. Coincidentally, the birth of the equitable market, with its new commercialization strategies that use mass media and have access to large trade groups, allowed ISMAM coffee producers to leave the restricted niche of the alternative market and widen their trade networks.

Such conditions, together with the efforts of its members, have made ISMAM one of the most successful organic coffee cooperative societies in all of Latin America. The cooperative is exporting organic coffee to Japan, Germany, Austria, Sweden, Switzerland, Holland, Belgium, France, Spain, and the United States, with profits now up to $7 million a year. Its area of influence has extended beyond the Mam region, including Tojolabal, Tzeltal, and Mochó indigenous peoples, from approximately one hundred communities distributed in twenty municipalities in Chiapas. In 1995 ISMAM members cultivated five thousand hectares of organic coffee, bought their own processing plant in the town of Tapachula, and established eighteen rural laboratories for biological pest control (Ramos Solórzano 1995).

Still, in the last few years ISMAM has had to face two main problems. First, the political and ideological differences between its members increased after the Zapatista uprising and drove some producers of the rain forest region out of the cooperative, thus preventing the formation of a unified organization of organic producers. Second, because of the rise in the international price of coffee, the solidarity network has stopped offering a bonus, or the bonus has become very small, so that the price difference between regular and organic coffee has decreased. This has led several members to place their own economic interests above their agro-ecological principles, and they have formed another association that markets nonorganic as well as organic coffee.

In spite of the present political and production problems faced by IS-MAM, the important role that the agro-ecological movement has played in the emergence of new cultural discourses, the creation of spaces for organization, and the improvement of living standards for an important sector of Mam population cannot be denied.

The political choices of Mam organic growers in the near future will depend not only on ideology and organizational structure; they will be mediated by class and gender differences, by regional situation—whether inside or outside the conflict zone, in coffee-growing zones or in the highlands—by specific histories, and by relations with the state and previous political experience, among many other factors. For the moment, the voices of the agro-ecological Mam have begun to be heard by the peasant movement in Chiapas, and their experience has had an impact, still unpredictable, on the contemporary history of Chiapas indigenous peoples. Almost ten years after the birth of the agro-ecological movement, we can say that it has achieved one of its main aims: improving the living conditions of an important sector of Sierra Madre inhabitants. This economic success does not imply the absence of internal problems. The history of Nan Choch and ISMAM members has been filled with contradictions, conflicts, encounters, and disencounters, which this chapter could not fully explore. Nan Choch organic vegetable producers have not had the same opportunities in the international markets as ISMAM, because they have been competing against U.S.-subsidized agriculture and also because many of their products are perishable and thus they have had to sell them in local markets. Their relations with the state have been characterized at times by negotiation and at times by confrontation; the cooperative has not always been a harmonious space of collective growth but one where political, gender, and class differences have manifested themselves. Nevertheless, with all their shortcomings, these two experiences have represented an opening in the Mam peasants' universe of possibilities. In the face of predatory technology, a global economy, and the homogenizing tendencies of transnational capitalism, these agro-ecological cooperative societies have given Sierra Madre Mam peasants new fighting strategies. Pointing out and analyzing the processes of historical construction of cultural identities, without mystifying them, is a fruitful way to recognize Mam peasants as social subjects, with their contradictions, aspirations, and internal struggles, and not as ahistorical myths, responding to the needs of an Occidental utopia.

Chapter

7

FROM PRONASOL TO THE
ZAPATISTA UPRISING

One February morning in 1992 the indigenist radio station XEVFS, "the Voice of the Southern Border," announced that Congress had approved constitutional amendments to Article 27 recommended by the administration of Carlos Salinas de Gortari. The amendments would establish the legal basis for the ejido to become private property. The broadcast explained that, among other things, this new Agrarian Law would allow peasants to sell or rent out their lands; and private companies would be able to buy ejidal lands from ejidatarios and investors for private use or to incorporate them into agribusinesses. Finally, the broadcast announced that this agrarian reform meant that dispossessed peasants would no longer be able to apply for land.[1] This was depressing news for Miguel, a resident of Ejido Vega del Rosario, who had been waiting eight years for a decision on his application for land. His was one of 3,483 applications from Chiapas peasants filed at the Ministry of Agrarian Reform (Secretaría de la Reforma Agraria [SRA]) that were awaiting examination by Mexico City civil servants. *Rezago agrario* (agrarian lag) is the official term used to describe the official limbo of many thousands of files like Miguel's. Miguel, who had been helping his father on a coffee plantation, for several months had considered seeking employment in the United States, but his hope of obtaining a piece of land in Siltepec had made him reject the idea. Now his dreams of land had evaporated.

The rumor that land distribution had ended spread rapidly throughout the Sierra Madre. No one knew the details of the constitutional amendments. People now spoke of a return to the "time of the fincas" and feared the arrival of foreigners who would get hold of ejidal lands.

> We found out that the president had changed the law and that now the rich could take our ejido, that gringos, Germans, and people from everywhere would come to start large companies and take our land. That is what we heard. Then my son and I went down to Motozintla to talk with the priest so that he could explain to us what was happening with the Agrarian Law.[2]

Even the head of the Confederation of Mexican Peasants (Confederación Nacional Campesina [CNC]), the official peasant organization in the Sierra region, Jorge Velázquez Escobar, declared in Motozintla a few days after the news about the new Agrarian Law: "With amendments to Article 27, peasants will sell their lands and will be once more enslaved as *jornaleros* [agricultural workers]. That is why I ask my party for enough information and counseling to know what is going on."[3]

In view of the fear and uncertainty occasioned by the news among Sierra peasants, some cooperative societies, such as ISMAM and Nan Choch, organized workshops to analyze the implications of the new law. Although it was not actually as dramatic as rumors made it, the amendments became a symbol of Salinas de Gortari's antipeasant policies. Sierra inhabitants were once again receiving a double message: on the one hand, indigenist officials, through PRONASOL and its Regional Funds, were now explaining to the peasants the importance of *concertación* (agreement), of the right to decide on their own projects and on governmental financing; on the other, the government was making decisions at the national level that directly affected them without asking their opinion. Thus, at the national level, with the writing of the new Agrarian Law, concertación had played no role, which would become a key issue in the Zapatista uprising.

Salinismo: The Administration's Two-faced Policy

The two constitutional amendments enacted at the beginning of 1992 are parallel, yet contradictory, policies that characterized the administration of Salinas de Gortari. A month before the changes to Article 27 were published, Congress had approved an amendment to Article 4 acknowledging the multicultural nature of the Mexican nation.[4] By amending Article 4, Congress acknowledged the right of indigenous peoples to have a different culture. However, the amendment to Article 27 signaled the end of land distribution.[5] While acknowledging the cultural rights of indigenous peoples, the Salinista administration had at the same time denied them their agrarian rights. The Chiapas Sierra Madre communities first heard of the existence of "cultural rights" in those legal terms when an INI anthropologist spoke of the Solidarity Funds for the Promotion of the Culture of Indigenous Peoples, which would finance "cultural rescue" projects. For Mam peasants, as for most Chiapas indigenous peoples, the right to own land has always been integral to demands for cultural rights. The representations seen in the performances of Danzas Mames and the testimonies of its members (see Chapter 5), as well as the discourse on Mother Earth by organic producers (see Chapter 6), refer to this wider definition of "indigenous culture." The new Agrarian Law made the legal acknowledgment of the multicultural nature of the Mexican nation a mere demagogic measure, which, as denounced by some independent indigenous organizations, "came five hundred years too late."[6]

The main goals of the amendments to Article 27 were to modernize the agrarian world and to promote private investment in agriculture, substituting small-scale agriculture with agroexporting companies. Once more it was argued that there was no more land to be distributed and a new agrarian law was needed to provide security for future investors. Such amendments were part of the so-called economic restructuring policy that Salinas de Gortari's administration carried out following the direction of the International Monetary Fund. This restructuring included the privatization of state-controlled companies, the removal of guaranteed prices for agricultural products, the end of subsidies, and the opening of markets to imported goods. Economists described these changes as a transition from the import-substitution industrialization model, prevailing generally between 1940 and 1980, to the export-oriented industrialization model. This new model gave priority to the opening of markets, leaving local producers to face "freely" the global market (Alvarez Béjar 1992).

For Mexican staple cereal producers, the end of guaranteed prices meant competing against highly technologized and subsidized American agriculture, whose low-cost products easily displaced local production. Promoters of economic liberation argued that this situation would only affect medium-sized producers and would benefit the poorest peasants who were not self-sufficient in corn production, such as Sierra Madre inhabitants. According to the 1994 census, of 686 communities in the Sierra region, only 92 produced corn, yielding 56,811.6 tons on 33,939 cultivated hectares. Although the staple food in the region is corn, only 28 percent of all arable land (115,818 hectares) is dedicated to this crop.[7] The municipalities of Mazapa de Madero, El Porvenir, Bejucal de Ocampo, and La Grandeza produce small amounts that are not sufficient for their own consumption; because of the rough hilly land and periodic frosts (some of these communities are located at more than 12,000 feet above sea level), during the last decades, residents have depended on subsidized corn distributed by CONASUPO stores (CCI Mazapa de Madero 1994). Contrary to what is argued by defenders of economic liberation, the end of guaranteed prices did not lower the prices of staple products. New prices have not been determined by an "international free market" but by local monopolizers, and Sierra peasants have been charged for transporting corn from the Comalapa prairies or corn-producing plains of La Frailesca. The discourse favoring a free market economy has not adequately taken into consideration the way in which the lack of roads, efficient transportation, and warehouses has affected the price of staple products.

Sierra coffee growers also faced serious problems as a result of Salinas de Gortari's restructuration. Since the end of the 1970s, coffee has become the main crop of ejidatarios in the Sierra lowlands. By 1994 the CCI Mazapa de Madero reported 6,914 coffee growers cultivating 30,413 hectares with an annual yield of 21,309 tons. For coffee-growing ejidatarios, economic restructuring meant the end of INMECAFE and fewer agrarian credits, which together with the international decline in coffee prices and the end of subsidies for staple cereals made many consider migrating to the towns.

> Look, it was in 1989 that I went to the North for the first time. That year our coffee was paid half of what we expected, because I did not know what happened at the international scale and that was that. I had two hectares I cultivated together with my two brothers, and that year it just did not yield enough for the three families. It was then that the Guatemalan coyotes went through the ejido; they were Mam also and knew the way well. Other cousins had already gone with them to North Carolina. They were already working at a ranch growing cabbage and there they took me. I paid them N$2,800 to take me to the very place where my cousins were. The ranch was called Warsaw and several Mam persons from San Marcos and many people from the Sierra were working there.[8]

Others found in collective organization and organic agriculture a creative way out of the coffee crisis.

As a result of protests by coffee-growing peasants, the state decided to promote an emergency plan to support this sector, as part of a wider social policy being promoted by PRONASOL (Harvey 1994, 1998). The Support Program for Coffee Producers (Programa de Apoyo a los Productores de Café) began to operate in twelve coffee-growing states, including Chiapas.

In the Sierra region, the Support Program started during the production cycle of 1990–1991 with the existing organizations of coffee producers while supporting the formation or legal recognition of other such organizations. Coffee producers' organizations formed the Regional Operative Group (Grupo Operativo Regional), which determined the way the Support Program's aid would be distributed. By 1994 in the region there were already 177 Local Solidarity Committees (Comités Locales de Solidaridad), as the organizations participating in the program were called, which included 8,287 producers. PRONASOL offered support in the amount of N$400, interest-free (*recurso fresco*), per cultivated hectare (US$53 per hectare), which would be returned to the Local Solidarity Committee's revolving fund when the coffee was sold. By that time, the total amount of recovered resources, plus the newly granted resources, amounted to N$10,524,970 (roughly US$1,403,329; CCI Mazapa de Madero 1994). Although the Support Program helped Sierra coffee producers to survive the decline in the international price of coffee and face economic restructuring, the opposition insisted that PRONASOL had not attained its aim, namely, to improve the living standard of small-scale coffee growers (60 percent of whom live in extreme poverty). According to the critics, in 1989 a small-scale coffee grower with a minimum of two hectares (the average for Mam peasants) that yielded a crop of five hundred pounds would obtain in the market a sum equivalent to 369 days of minimum-wage labor. By 1995 the same producers obtained only 195 days of minimum-wage labor. This situation drew criticism.

> Small coffee producers are poorer today than when Solidarity began. Clearly PRONASOL is not to blame for this situation, though it did not prevent it either. It is true, given the withdrawal of INMECAFE, without PRONASOL things would be worse. But the situation is, nevertheless, far from good. (Hernández Navarro and Celis Callejas 1994:229)

In spite of such limitations, the Support Program, together with the Regional Funds for the Development of Indigenous Peoples (Fondo Regional para el Desarrollo de los Pueblos Indígenas), helped the "reformist" sector within the state to cushion, albeit minimally, the impact that neoliberal economic restructuring was having on indigenous communities throughout the country. PRONASOL, which in 1992 became the Ministry for Social Development (Secretaría de Desarrollo Social [SEDESOL]), was the key element in the political strategy for such sectors. In the new political context "modernizing reformists," many of whom had been trained by COPLAMAR in the 1970s, allied themselves with neoliberal technocrats, who advocated modernization of the state apparatus along with economic restructuring. This political alliance between two such seemingly different sectors has been analyzed from several perspectives. For some, such as Denise Dresser (1994), PRONASOL is but another governmental strategy to control the popular sector: it was not born out of opposition to the state's neoliberal policies but was a response to the neoliberal program's need for legitimation. According to Dresser, PRONASOL does not address the needs of workers and peasants, but those of an emerging political class within the official party:

> PRONASOL provides the political conditions necessary to sustain the neoliberal model. By redefining the members of the old corporatist coalitions as consumers of PRONASOL benefits, the program has helped rebuild the state's constituencies. By incorporating social reformers into the ranks of bureaucracy, PRONASOL has enhanced the representativeness of the political elite and reinforced its ties with autonomous social groups. (1994:144)

For other researchers, the governmental program has not only been part of the state's hegemonic strategies but has also created opportunities for popular representation. For Jonathan Fox (1993), PRONASOL, like COPLAMAR, is the result of a "sandwich strategy," which opens possibilities for social change by combining popular pressure from below with reformist concessions from above. Fox points out,

> Through waves of mobilization and partial reforms, representatives of society's most oppressed groups—rural indigenous movements—increased their capacity to bargain with the state while retaining an important degree of autonomy. (1994:216)

This reading of PRONASOL underscores its organizational achievements more than its effectiveness at countering neoliberal economic measures.

Through PRONASOL, Salinas de Gortari's administration appropriated many of the political strategies of the Mexican political left by encouraging grassroots participation through Municipal and Regional Committees (Comités Municipales y Regionales). Many old left militants—particularly Maoists—joined the state through PRONASOL, promoting, with the new governmental program, a work style that gave priority to popular meetings and to the formation of more participatory, horizontally organized networks (Moguel 1994). Through these new work strategies, the administration confronted the old PRI's corporatist model, which had relied on guild political organizations to control rural and urban workers (see Chapter 4), while competing for the sympathy of the popular sectors in regions where the left and independent peasant movements had progressed.

Salinas de Gortari wanted to break with the old-style corporatist state that during the 1930s had created guild organizations such as the Confederation of Mexican Workers (Confederación de Trabajadores Mexicanos [CTM]), created in 1936 to include workers in the official party; the Confederation of Mexican Peasants, created in 1938; and the Federation for State Workers (Federación de Trabajadores al Servicio del Estado [FSTSE]), for civil servants.

With the creation of new and more horizontal networks, such as Solidaridad's Municipal and Regional Committees, Salinas de Gortari's administration wanted to renew old client relationships between the state and the popular sectors. The loss of prestige of official organizations such as the CTM and the CNC made it a priority to create a new "mass policy," before independent popular organizations could mobilize.

Although viewing power as a dialectical process will help us see PRONASOL neither solely as a control strategy used by ruling elites nor solely as a response to the demands of popular sectors, but as an arena of negotiation where the Mexican state and popular sectors mutually constitute each other, Dresser's and Fox's perspectives help us to understand relations between the state and the popular sectors as ones of shifting power, in which hegemony and counterhegemony permanently construct and reconstruct themselves. What emerges as a control strategy can be appropriated by peasants in their struggle, as in the case of the Indigenous Supreme Councils and that of many social organizations formed to obtain PRONASOL funds. In other contexts, such arenas of struggle are institutionalized anew.

The participative indigenism of the late 1970s was seen as the predecessor to PRONASOL, and once more anthropologists were instrumental in the emergence of this new social program in another six-year term (*sexenio*). Arturo Warman, who for decades had been criticizing the links between anthropologists and the state, was placed at the head of the INI and later in charge of promoting the "counterreform" as secretary of agrarian reform.[9]

In the Sierra Madre, the INI took the reins of PRONASOL programs in indigenous communities, creating through the Regional Funds spaces for administration not monopolized by the official party, where they finally managed to achieve some of the goals defined years before by participative indigenism. At the same time, however, PRONASOL Municipal Funds, administered by PRIista mayors, finally strengthened local cacicazgos and enriched mestizo elites, fomenting popular discontent that would become a municipal insurrection with the Zapatista rebellion.

PRONASOL Indigenismo

The most significant change that the INI underwent when Salinas de Gortari took power was its link with PRONASOL. Since Luis Echeverrías's administration (1970–1976), there have been attempts to construct a social network that would allow the state to find new interlocutors beyond the ineffective official peasant organizations. These attempts were continued by PRONASOL indigenism. By creating the Solidarity Regional Funds (Fondos Regionales de Solidaridad), Salinas de Gortari promoted the creation of new spaces for political management apart from traditional guild organizations.

Contrary to past practices, the neoliberal state sought to use product-oriented and cultural organizations to consolidate its power. For the new elite, politics, productivity, and culture were conceived as belonging to separate spheres. Measures for economic restructuring, directly linked to national and transnational power relations, were presented as benign technical adaptations in the new economic context. In the same way, relations with popular sectors, marked by inequality in the handling of resources and in decision making, were nonetheless represented as technical or cultural counseling.

It was mainly through two INI-PRONASO programs—Regional Funds for the Development of Indigenous Peoples and Solidarity Funds for the Promotion of the Cultural Patrimony, also known as Cultural Funds—that the state established a new dialogue with Mam peasants. Rather than depart from preceding indigenist policies, such as had occurred in 1976 with the removal of Gonzalo Aguirre Beltrán, the appointment of Arturo Warman as head of the INI represented consolidation of participative indigenism. The challenge was to attain what the Community Committees, created by INI in 1976, had not achieved: true direct participation of indigenous peoples in indigenist programs. The new management established as its goal the transfer of functions to indigenous communities and organizations. This goal was in line with participative indigenism, as well as with similar neoliberal proposals to reduce the state apparatus to a minimum. Warman described the basic guidelines for the INI:

1) The participation of indigenous peoples and communities in the planning and execution of this institution's programs.

2) This participation must finally hand over institutional functions to indigenous organizations and collectivities, as well as to other public institutions and social groups involved with and committed to indigenist action.

3) The coordination with federal, state and municipal institutions of society as well as international agencies will be a permanent characteristic of every single action of this Institute. (1989:1)

The Solidarity Regional Funds were created to transfer responsibility to peasant organizations. The General Assembly of Representatives of the Solidarity Funds, composed of members of the Local Committee of Solidarity, became responsible for the discussion and approval of proposals presented by peasants to PRONASOL. Contrary to other PRONASOL programs, the Regional Funds did not necessarily create new organizations but worked with already existing product-oriented organizations.

Through PRONASOL, the INI was strengthened, shifting from an intermediary with other state institutions to a development agency. In the case of the CCI Mazapa de Madero, its development projects had been limited to the sheep improvement program, the distribution of fertilizers and pesticides, and support of a small fruit canning factory in the municipality of La Grandeza. In 1990 the Regional Funds for the Development of Indigenous Peoples and the General Assembly of Representatives of the Solidarity Funds were established with the participation of thirteen indigenous and peasant organizations. Among these thirteen organizations were the smaller groups such as Societies of Social Solidarity (SSS), which included a single ejido; official organizations linked to Workers, Peasants and Teachers Solidarity (Solidaridad Obrero Campesino Magisterial [SOCAMA]), and independent organizations such as ISMAM. Six projects were supported in 1990: potato culture, technical aid for cattle breeding, corn culture, technical apicultural assistance, rehabilitation of coffee plantations, and rehabilitation of orchards. These six projects obtained a total sum of N\$500,000 (US\$177,935), which was distributed by the CCI Mazapa de Madero (CCI Mazapa de Madero 1994).

Four years later thirty-six organizations received Regional Funds, benefiting 198 Sierra settlements, with a total amount of N\$3,554,424

(US$1,110,757; CCI Mazapa de Madero 1994). Among them were a trans-porters' organization with only fifteen members, the SSS CECEISTAS de Motozintla, and cooperative societies of more than one thousand mem-bers, such as ISMAM (1,878) and the Unión de Ejidos Profesor Otilio Montaño (1,115). Projects obtaining financing ranged from coffee com-mercialization at the international level to the acquisition of a corn mill or a dozen chickens. In spite of the immediate importance of such funds for Sierra inhabitants, they cannot be considered as actually replacing loans granted by the State Bank for Rural Credit (BANRURAL) before eco-nomic restructuring. Opponents of the Regional Funds have pointed out that they amount to between just one-third and one-fourth of all moneys granted by BANRURAL and other commercial banks for similar agri-cultural projects; in addition, critics have pointed out that they are not generally handed over on time and do not include any relevant technical counseling (Myhre 1996:136).

Political independence and the management of PRONASOL Regional Funds depend greatly on the development of social organizations in the regions where they are established. As Jonathan Fox points out:

> The potential distribution of pluralistic leadership consuls de-pended fundamentally on the varying "thickness" of Mexico's orga-nized indigenous civil society. This "accumulation of forces" was very uneven and many regions still lacked autonomous groups with the bargaining power or organizational capacity needed to handle development projects. In these regions officials continued to control the Regional Funds. (1994:196)

In the case of the Sierra Madre, more than half of the organizations that were supported by the Regional Funds were created specifically to participate in the PRONASOL program. In spite of the participative op-portunities this program afforded, it is important to acknowledge that, due to the complex process of obtaining the funds, only a very small sec-tor of Mam peasants has been able to benefit from them. The first con-dition for obtaining support from the Regional Funds program is to be registered as a social organization with the Ministry of Foreign Affairs (Secretaría de Relaciones Exteriores). To this end, new types of organiza-tions have been created for different responsibilities and fiscal rights, such as Social Solidarity Societies, Rural Production Societies (Sociedades de Producción Rural), Nonprofit Associations (Asociaciones Civiles), and Cooperative Societies (Sociedades Cooperativas). An understanding of the differences between such organizations, in order to choose the most appropriate one, requires at least an information and training workshop. Preparing the legal documents for registration at the Ministry of Foreign Affairs, sending them to Mexico City, paying the necessary fees, and being registered turn this process into a bureaucratic circus, which very few organizations can handle. Independent social organizations created in the Sierra for participation in the Regional Funds have usually been advised by the Catholic church or by an NGO called Chiltak A.C., located in San Cristóbal de las Casas, whose goal is to support and promote collective organization among Chiapas peasants. Those communities that have had no technical counseling for obtaining legal registration have been excluded from PRONASOL benefits.

For sectors that have obtained legal registration, the bureaucratic nightmare has continued, for they have had to learn how to write projects and justifications and prepare budgets and present them in a document acceptable to PRONASOL officials. Similarly, representatives from the various organizations who sit on the evaluation committees for PRONASOL funds are not compensated for the loss of time or the cost of transportation to Motozintla to attend committee meetings. Self-administration for indigenous groups becomes stifled with so much red tape. These bureaucratic procedures are preventing the broad-scale participation that was originally intended.

Parallel to their support for productive projects, INI-PRONASOL instituted its Cultural Funds program. The Area of Cultural Patrimony, which since the creation of the CCI Mazapa de Madero had been limited to administrative work for other areas, or to writing "regional diagnoses," was finally responsible for the development of a more structured program.

The creation of the Solidarity Funds for the Promotion of the Culture of Indigenous Peoples was announced on August 8, 1990, in San Felipe del Progreso, in the state of Mexico, when President Salinas de Gortari met for the first time with the National Council of Indigenous Peoples (CNPI). On that occasion, the president announced the constitutional amendments to Article 4 and described indigenous cultures as part of "the national heritage":

> Our indigenous fellow citizens also demand respect for their culture and their tradition, for their identity and social organization. They have in them the deepest roots of our nationality, which is plural but always one, and solidarity with our common country. We cannot allow something that basic, as simple as respect, to be denied to indigenous people, or to any of our fellow citizens. . . . Their culture must be untouchable. It is one of the essential parts of our national

heritage, of our collective wealth. Their rights as Mexicans protect it, but we shall try to make such protection even better defined, by promoting it to the rank of our highest law. (INI 1992:4)

This discourse on Multicultural Mexico, which was first articulated in official indigenism at the end of the 1970s, was institutionalized by the constitutional amendments. Legal acknowledgment of the right to cultural difference was accompanied by a number of cultural policies, which, while representing and legitimizing certain identities, also created new subjectivities (Hernández Castillo and Ortíz Elizondo 1996).

The Cultural Funds were part of the new cultural policies aiming at the support and promotion of "Mexico's indigenous cultures." Unlike the Regional Funds, the Cultural Funds cannot be recovered, and their goals are as follows:

1) To contribute to a community's greater understanding of its own culture.
2) To strengthen and develop diverse forms of cultural expression.
3) To reinforce elements and traits of their own culture.
4) To promote those initiatives of cultural appropriation and innovation within the framework of their own culture. (INI 1992:6)

Unlike the Regional Funds, whose interlocutors were legally constituted social organizations, the Cultural Funds used a web of relations that were developed by the Mam Supreme Councils to promote the new indigenist program. As a result, PRONASOL programs prompted a new social network through the legalization and support of product-oriented organizations while legitimizing the Supreme Councils as "cultural" representatives of the Mam people. Danzas Mames received financial support from the new PRONASOL program for their project to reinvent tradition, an effort that had begun in the late 1980s. The Supreme Councils and the representatives of Danzas Mames became negotiators for the new funds that were available for cultural promotion. Obtaining economic support, however small, strengthened the position of Mam representatives in Danzas Mames.

The awarding of Cultural Funds is not accomplished by a composite council with the participation of indigenous organizations but by the Coordination Commission for the Support of State Indigenous Cultures in which municipal authorities, officials of the local Cultural Centers (Casas de la Cultura), and a representative of the National Council for Culture

and Art (Consejo Nacional para la Cultura y las Artes [CONACULTA])
and of the INI. Once more, the principles of participative indigenism are
disregarded and the decision on whether to finance projects is in the hands
of bureaucrats.

In the Mam region, the Cultural Funds began to be used in 1991, when
fourteen of the seventeen proposals submitted were approved for a sum
of N$71,400 (US$23,800; CCI Mazapa de Madero 1994). Of these fourteen proposals, half were requests by various Danzas Mames groups for
support to buy marimbas or traditional costumes; of the others, four
concerned the development of handicrafts and workshops for weaving
and woodworking, and the remaining three concerned the teaching of
the Mam language. By 1994 the Cultural Funds had financed fifty-eight
projects, benefiting 2,286 persons, with a total of N$488,110 (US$152,534;
CCI Mazapa de Madero 1994). More than half of these projects were requests by Danzas Mames to buy musical instruments and "traditional"
costumes for their performances.

The proposals submitted to PRONASOL were written by the INI-
CCI anthropologist at the request of Danzas representatives. The anthropologist would usually include the group's history and testimonies he had
obtained on the importance of their culture. For example, a project presented by the Danzas group from Ejido Payacal in Amatenango de la Frontera, argued the following:

> We Mam are indigenous people, who, like any human beings, have
> feelings, so we have had the need to express them through music.
> The marimba as a native instrument from our land has been a
> medium to express such feelings. Yet the influence of mass media
> [radio and television] and the great amount of modern music have
> begun to undermine the sentimental quality of our people, so much
> so that some young people who ignore the cultural value of such
> traditions make fun of those who practice them.[10]

Usually, such projects that underline the break between tradition and
modernity—defending the former and attacking the latter—are those
financed by the PRONASOL Cultural Funds. While agrarian policies
were aimed at modernizing indigenous peoples, by turning ejidos into private lands and promoting export crops, cultural policies wanted to "take
care of the national heritage" by maintaining "tradition."

Although the goal of the Cultural Funds is to "promote those initiatives of cultural appropriation and innovation within the framework of
their own tradition," nonetheless, indigenist officials and bureaucrats from

other institutions determine whether an innovation should belong to their "own" culture. In the Sierra region, where Presbyterianism has played a very important role in the preservation of the Mam language, religious music, nevertheless, has not been considered "indigenous," and the cultural project proposals of Protestant groups have usually been rejected. The state assumes the right to recognize and legitimize some cultural manifestations while rejecting others. The yearly assessment report of the CCI Mazapa de Madero specifies that the Cultural Funds cannot be used to promote "noncultural" activities (i.e., non-Catholic rituals and music):

> In the selection and priority of applications sent to this Centro Coordinador [Coordinator Center] we have been very careful, for many ask for electric instruments. We know beforehand that they are "popular" cultural manifestations, but they are closely linked to religious sects, and our rules do not accept this type of support. That is why they are rejected. Rather, we try to support groups or community organizations interested in rescuing authentic music and dance. (CCI Mazapa de Madero 1994)

Despite such regulations, once funds are released, indigenist officials have no control over the cultural products of "rescue groups," and cultural hybridization characterizes the process of reinventing tradition among groups of Danzas Mames and organic growers (see Chapters 5 and 6).

In spite of bureaucratic limitations on the Regional and Cultural Funds, it must be acknowledged that in the Sierra region INI-PRONASOL has supported sectors linked both to the official party and to independent groups. In the Evaluation Committee, administered by the CCI Mam-Mochó-Cakchiquel, two organic cooperative societies, ISMAM and Unión de Ejidos Profesor Otilio Montaño, became the two most influential organizations. Because of their numerical importance and their effective internal organization, they have influenced the decisions of other committee members. ISMAM is a relatively moderate cooperative in the spectrum of peasant organizations, but compared to the Unión de Ejidos Profesor Otilio Montaño, which is openly linked to the official party, this Mam cooperative has become a counterweight to the PRONASOL PRIist committees.

At the state level, most indigenous and peasant organizations have received some financing from the PRONASOL Regional Funds. When in January 1994 the Council of Indigenous and Peasant Organizations (Consejo Estatal de Organizaciones Indígenas y Campesinas [CEOIC]) was formed, which originally supported Zapatistas' demands, 240 of its

280 social organizations had already received moneys from the Regional Funds. Margarito Ruíz, Tojolabal leader and founder of the Independent Front of Indigenous Peoples (Frente Independiente de Pueblos Indígenas [FIPI]), acknowledged this situation in 1993:

> The situation in Chiapas is exceptional, since the majority of the so-called "independent" and "political" organizations are in the Regional Funds. This has been achieved because of the maturity of the Chiapas independent movement, and a certain separation between the INI's political clientele and governor clientele, which have set up parallel indigenismos. . . . When indigenous organizations are able to effectively take the Regional Funds into their own hands, they can become an important space for participation and decision making and can facilitate the creation of a phase of "transitions"— not transfer—from indigenismo to post-indigenismo. (Quoted in Fox 1994:212)

Yet the political pluralism of indigenist officials was rejected by local PRIists, such as the state governor, Patrocinio González Garrido (1988–1993). With a much less conciliatory attitude than that of "modernizing reformists," González Garrido dealt harshly with independent movements. By modifying the state penal code, this PRIist governor legalized the repression of certain independent movements (Collier 1994). Freedom of the press, demonstrations, and public criticism of the government were restricted on the grounds that such activities threatened authority (Articles 13, 120, 135). Any act considered as disrupting "public order" or as "obstructing state functions" could be penalized as "rebellion" (*Periódico Oficial*, Tuxtla Gutiérrez Chiapas, No. 99, January 1988:31–36). Such organizations as the Independent Organization of Agrarian Workers and Peasants (Central Independiente de Obreros Agrícolas y Campesinos [CIOAC]) and the Emiliano Zapata Peasant Organization (OCEZ) were targets of the new governor's repressive measures, and two of their leaders, Sebastián Pérez and Arturo Albores, were "mysteriously murdered" (Harvey 1994). Discourses on "cultural plurality" and on "agreement and political plurality," promoted by some indigenist officials, were rejected by conservative sectors of Chiapas. In 1994 David Velasco, the INI state representative, pointed out the pervasiveness of this resistance:

> There is evidently much resistance at the level of local power to promote this vision of multiculturalism and respect for plurality. This resistance is at all levels, I cannot say only in the government,

in all of them, cattle breeders, middle classes, in the streets. Those sectors cannot acknowledge that indigenous groups are valuable by themselves and are quite capable of deciding their own future. There is evidently much resistance of every kind. The INI, like many organizations and institutions working in marginal regions, faces this type of resistance.[11]

That INI-PRONASOL financed the very organizations that the state governor and the ruling elites tried to control has turned indigenist officials into the political enemies of local power. The INI, for example, had suffered several acts of harassment that included the threat of closing the indigenist radio station of Las Margaritas, and three of its top officials were accused of fraud in March 1992 and imprisoned for several months. The alleged reason for this imprisonment was the acquisition of cattle different from that specified in the PRONASOL budget. Peasant organizations denounced this action as a reprimand by local officials for the support INI was giving to their organizations through the Regional Funds (*La Jornada*, March 21, 1992). Among those imprisoned was Dr. Ricardo Paniagua, a native of Motozintla and grandson of Don Ricardo Alfonso Paniagua, who, in 1920, had founded in the Mariscal District the Chiapas Socialist Party (Partido Socialista Chiapaneco) and, in 1927, was murdered by order of President Plutarco Elías Calles (Spenser 1988; Benjamin 1990). In the Sierra region, this local history has marked people's perceptions of the conflict between the federal and the local government. The INI gained legitimacy in the region, and for the people the diverging interests of various sectors within the state became even clearer.

A very different experience was that of the PRONASOL Municipal Funds, whose administration was completely in the hands of local mayors. To strengthen municipal governments and promote decentralization, PRONASOL decided to divert part of its budget for public works, which was previously used by several ministries, to the Municipal Funds. Municipal mayors were responsible for the distribution of the Municipal Funds for public investment as well as for the handling of the so-called Credits by Word (Créditos a la Palabra), which were small credits for production granted individually and requiring only the "producer's word of honor." Between 1989 and 1993 the World Bank granted a loan of US$350 million to the Mexican government in support of rural development in the country's four poorest states: Oaxaca, Guerrero, Chiapas, and Hidalgo. Out of this loan about $100 million were given to the Municipal Funds (Cornelius, Craig, and Fox 1994:16). In the case of the Sierra Madre, the administration of such funds was under the absolute control of PRIist mayors. In 1992 and 1993 several sectors of society denounced the corruption and cronyism with which these "credits by word" were being dispensed to the municipalities of Siltepec, Mazapa de Madero, Motozintla, El Porvenir, and Bella Vista. Also, on several occasions the state government was asked to audit the administration of the PRONASOL Municipal Funds that were to be invested in public works. These petitions went unanswered (see News Summary from the Center of Analysis and Information of Chiapas [CIACH] 1992, 1993).

While the federal government, through INI-PRONASOL, was promoting the new multicultural discourse and the creation of new opportunities for participation, the state and municipal governments revealed their repressive and authoritarian strategies. Such contradictory messages and actions influenced how Mam peasants in different sectors perceived the state. For those benefiting from PRONASOL funds, the state was still a site for negotiation, and they accepted the terms of the dialogue by constituting themselves as social organizations. In this sense, the state exerted its hegemony through its capacity to define the rules of the game. The most marginal sectors, which had no organizational support for fulfilling the bureaucratic requirements of PRONASOL and did not receive the Regional Funds, confronted the state's most exclusionary and authoritarian face. These were the sectors that participated most actively in the Peaceful Civil Resistance movement after August 1994 in support of the demands of the EZLN. The emergence of this armed organization revealed the crisis of hegemony under Salinas de Gortari's administration. PRONASOL's mediating efforts were not enough to cushion the effects that the economic restructuring was having on the most marginal sectors of Chiapas's society. Indigenous Zapatistas claimed as theirs the "power to name" in mapping out spaces for daily participation (Roseberry 1994). The Zapatista uprising signaled the beginning of a new dialogue between indigenous people and the state in which Mam peasants would actively participate.

The Impact of the Zapatista Rebellion on the Life of Mam Peasants

On January 1, 1994, rumors of war traveled throughout the Sierra Madre. It was said that "indigenous brothers" had taken over the municipal capitals of Altamirano, Chanal, Huixtán, Las Margaritas, Oxchuc, Ocosingo, and San Cristóbal. Some linked this uprising with the so-called Mazapa de Madero war, which began on January 1, 1973, when villagers occupied their municipal office to oppose an imposed candidate, leading to violent eviction by the army. That New Year's confrontation between unarmed peasants and the federal army was the most recent memory of a "war" in the region.

When Motozintla merchants shut their stores it became the first New Year's Day in many years on which the streets of the town were deserted. Many well-to-do families left for Tapachula, for fear that the Sierra Indians would also rebel. When the private television chain Televisa mistakenly broadcast in its newscast "24 Horas" that the village of Huixtla had been overtaken by Zapatista commandos, fear overtook those who had remained. In fact, the Tzotzil community of Huixtán had been mistaken by television broadcasters for Huixtla, a mestizo village just forty-five minutes from Motozintla.

That day XEVFS did not broadcast. People would later learn that the indigenist radio station had been occupied by Zapatista troops and that technical problems had prevented them from broadcasting to borderland inhabitants "The First Declaration of the Lacandon Rain Forest." In this document they had declared war against the National Army and called on all Mexicans to participate in the overthrow of President Salinas de Gortari's illegitimate government. Four days after the uprising, photocopies of "Despertador Mexicano," an EZLN pamphlet, began circulating in the Sierra Madre communities. It justified the Zapatista action as a rebellion against seventy years of PRI dictatorship on the basis of Article 39 of the Mexican Constitution, which asserts "the unalienable right of the people to alter or modify their form of government." National symbols were now being appropriated by indigenous people from the rain forest and the highlands to demand the construction of a Mexican nation under new terms, which may be seen in the language of the now-historic "First Declaration of the Lacandon Rain Forest":

> We have the Mexican people on our side. We have our country and the tricolor flag is loved and respected by INSURGENT troops. We use the colors red and black in our uniform as symbols of the working people's strikes and struggles. Our flag displays the letters EZLN, Ejército Zapatista de Liberación Nacional, and with it we shall always go to combat. We reject right now any attempt to disparage the just cause of our struggle by accusing us of drug trafficking, narcoguerrilla, banditry or any adjective that might be used by our enemies. Our struggle follows our constitutional law and lives under the flag of justice and equality. ("El Despertador Mexicano," January 1994, vol. 1, no. 1)

After ineffectual attempts by the Mexican government to deny the indigenous nature of this rebellion in the face of Zapatista images broadcast by the mass media, the EZLN had to be officially recognized as made
up primarily by Chiapas indigenous people.[12] The EZLN would later
announce that their high command as well as their troops were Tzotzil, Tzeltal, Chol, Tojolabal, and mestizo peasants. Mam peasants, such
as Zoque, Lacandon, Chuj, K'anjobal, Jacalteco, Mochó, and Cakchiquel
indigenous peoples, did not participate directly in the EZLN. Notwithstanding, the Zapatista uprising has had a radical influence on their everyday life and perspectives for the future.

The Rain Forest

Many Zapatista troops are rain forest colonizers who, like Las Ceibas
dwellers, had left their native communities in the 1960s and 1970s in search
of land to cultivate. Following the colonization campaigns promoted by
the government and the earlier spontaneous colonization, the rain forest became a meeting place for indigenous peoples from all over the state
and even the country. Just in the border region from Vértice de Santiago
to Marqués de Comillas, Chuj, K'anjobal, Mam, Tzotzil, Tzeltal, Tojolabal, Chol, Zoque, Nahuatl, and Chinanteco settlements were found,
together with mestizos from Veracruz, Hidalgo, Tabasco, Oaxaca, Guerrero, Campeche, Durango, and the Distrito Federal; there were also camps
of Guatemalan refugees who spoke Mam, Chuj, K'anjobal, Quiché' Ixil,
Cakchiquel, and Jacalteco. In addition to cultural exchange, evident in
linguistic loans and the strengthening of indigenous languages that had
almost vanished, such as Chuj and K'anjobal, there was sharing of organizational experiences. The community was no longer the main reference point for these settlers, and new social spaces were created through
peasant organizations, religious groups, and commercial networks (Collier 1994; Harvey 1998; Leyva Solano and Ascencio 1996). In Las Margaritas rain forest the ejidal assembly made it possible for Mexican ejidatarios
and Guatemalan refugees to discuss the political situation of Chiapas and
Guatemala (Hernández Castillo et al. 1993). At Marqués de Comillas, indigenous peasants and urban workers shared experiences and worldviews
(González Ponciano 1991). Community borders expanded with the rain
forest diaspora, and Chiapas indigenous peoples learned about and discussed national problems, listened to Central American radio stations, and
began to sell their products beyond the national border.

It was in one of these multilingual and multicultural sites that during the 1970s a political movement began to take shape, and in it indige-

nous colonizers and militants from a Maoist organization called Popular Politics (Política Popular) converged. Several versions of this meeting have been released since the Zapatista uprising, primarily based on official sources rather than scholarly ones (Tello 1995), some focused on the history of peasant organizations (Harvey 1994, 1998; Hernández Navarro 1995) and others an anthropological analysis of the new configuration of peasant organizations (Collier 1994; Leyva Solano and Ascencio 1996). All versions agree on the "hybrid" character of the Zapatista movement. The exchange of experiences between indigenous and mestizo people from several regions of the state and the country has allowed many global perspectives and political and religious ideologies to coalesce into a political-military movement, which evidenced how "neoliberal utopianism" had been a failure.

Mam rain forest colonizers were silent witnesses to this encounter. After the Zapatista uprising, they informed me that since the late 1970s they had known of the existence of a political-military organization, which had had no name. The antimilitary religious principles of the Mam Jehovah's Witnesses had kept them away from the emerging rebel organization for several years. It was their objection, however, to the presence of the Federal Army, or any armed organization, in the rain forest that had kept this a secret shared by all its inhabitants. The peaceful coexistence ended when Zapatista militants decided to go public and challenged the Federal Army.

At the end of December 1993, a group of Zapatista troops had visited Las Ceibas and in an ejidal meeting had informed the residents that the armed struggle would begin in a few days. They invited them to join the EZLN troops or the civilian militias. Jehovah's Witnesses at that meeting expressed their antimilitary feelings and were, therefore, told that if they remained in the ejido, the EZLN could not hold themselves responsible for their security, for there might be violence in the region.[13] The ejidatarios were divided; some wanted to leave their community and seek shelter with their families and "brothers" in the town of Comitán and the Comalapa plains; others saw the uprising as a "sign of the times" and as a sign of the coming of Armageddon and wanted to witness the end of "the things of this world":

> After all these men arrived and told us there would be war, we were all afraid. But some wanted to go away and leave everything behind: the coffee plantation, the corn fields, and the Kingdom Hall. Others suggested we stay and wait for the end of the things of this world,

since that was what we had come to the rain forest for, to wait for the coming of Armageddon.[14]

Las Ceibas dwellers waited together for the coming events of January 1. In spite of their rejection of armed struggle and their unhappiness at being forced to migrate again, they would not denounce the Zapatista militants or support the state in its campaigns to discredit them. One week after the violent confrontation began, Las Ceibas was deserted. Some would return weeks later, while others would decide to leave forever the piece of land that had taken them so many years to obtain. The difficulties of surviving in disputed territory and the coffee crisis turned this Paradise on Earth into an inhospitable place for many Mam Jehovah's Witness peasants. Seven families returned to the Sierra and lived with relatives or friends; three decided to stay in Comitán and take up commerce; others chose to leave the state and follow the example of other Mam peasants who had become construction workers or laborers in Cancún or Villahermosa. More than half of the former community of Las Ceibas, at the time of this writing, awaits the outcome of the peace talks and experience daily the tensions of the "armed truce."

After the Zapatista uprising, the Federal Army established a huge military base just a few kilometers from the ejidal limits of Las Ceibas. On the San Quintin military base, multistory buildings that house the soldiers rise above the rain forest vegetation, creating a surreal landscape. The massive presence of troops in the region has upset the everyday lives of its inhabitants, and prostitution, alcohol, and drugs have been denounced by several sectors of the indigenous population as corollary to the presence of the army in their communities. On March 8, 1996, about five thousand indigenous women from all over the state took to the streets of San Cristóbal de las Casas, demanding that soldiers leave their communities. One of the women said,

> We want the army to leave. Our houses are used as brothels, the few classrooms available for our children are occupied by soldiers, sport fields are used as parking lots for war tanks and helicopters of that bad government. (*La Jornada*, April 9, 1996:12)

Mam people from Las Ceibas have decided once more to take shelter within their religious group and isolate themselves from the "life of sin" that has come to the rain forest with the soldiers. They find themselves once more silent witnesses, but now of the militarization of the rain forest by the Federal Army.

The Sierra

While the Zapatista forces and the army were fighting in the highlands, other army troops arrived at the military base of Motozintla, in the heart of the Sierra Madre. A report by state government advisers released to the national press classified the Sierra region as one of those in danger of being "influenced" by the Zapatista rebellion (*La Jornada*, January 17, 1996).

After the first twelve days of battle, during which the Federal Army put under siege and harassed indigenous communities considered EZLN sympathizers, President Salinas de Gortari responded to national and international pressure by declaring a unilateral ceasefire on January 12, 1994. The president's decision to seek a negotiated outcome of the armed conflict was seen by some analysts as a victory for the "reformist" sectors in the state. The removal of Patrocinio González Garrido, former Chiapas governor and then secretary of the interior, was an indication of the temporary weakening of the hard line within the state party.

The Zapatista uprising became a catalyst for a number of expressions of discontent by Chiapas peasants, which included taking over land and town halls and demanding fairer land distribution and democratization of municipal government.

On January 27, 1994, the Mam Supreme Council of the lowlands led a demonstration in front of the local office of the Ministry of Agrarian Reform in the city of Tapachula, demanding the restitution of the lands of the Finca La Patria, whose ejidal rights had been granted to fifty Mam families in November 1978. According to the Mam supreme councillor, Ancelmo Pérez, after the secretary negotiated with the former owners — Juan Heidegeith, Carlos Bracamontes, and Juan Dorantes — 440 out of the 661 hectares that had been distributed to the Mam peasants were confiscated again. Of the lands left to them, 182 hectares belonged to an ecological reserve that could not be cultivated. In a letter addressed to the president and released to the local press, the Mam supreme councillor spoke to the irony of this injustice:

> If you are not going to grant us the rights over our ancestral lands, then make the necessary formalities so that our fifty families can have passports to go work in the United States, for we are already foreigners in our own territory, being displaced by finqueros from other countries who have become lords of the Soconusco. (*El Sureste de Chiapas*, Tapachula, January 28, 1994)

We thus see how the right to land remains inextricably linked to the Mames' idea of citizens' rights. Denunciation of their historical exclusion from the nation remains integral to their claims as Mam people.

At the same time, the corrupt and authoritarian attitude of municipal governments, which had been denounced for months in the local press, was openly rejected by peasant occupations of municipal presidencies in the Sierra. On February 25, the occupations of town halls began, the first being that of Bella Vista. This occupation was led by the OCEZ-CNPA, demanding the removal of Fortino de León Roblero, who was accused of embezzling PRONASOL Municipal Funds. This occupation would last for more than nine months, until the mayor's removal was achieved on September 25 of the same year.

On March 3, Mam peasants of the Sierra Indigenous and Peasant Organization (Coordinadora Indígena y Campesina de la Sierra [COICS]), a group created after the Zapatista uprising, occupied the Siltepec town hall. Though these peasants would be evicted by the police, they would return to occupy municipal buildings three more times until they had achieved the discharge of the corrupt mayor.

In Mazapa de Madero, Motozintla, and El Porvenir, peasants mobilized and demanded changes in municipal authorities. At the same time, throughout the Sierra a movement challenged electric energy rates, and whole communities refused to pay the fees until a lower fixed rate was established for each peasant. To achieve this, they formed the Peoples' Commission of Electricity (Comisión Popular de Electricidad). The state responded to all these mobilizations in two ways: first, the Sierra was militarized and the number of troops in the region was doubled; and second, independent and official organizations were invited by the government to form a common front.

By the end of January, ISMAM and Nan Choch directors received an invitation from the state government to meet with other indigenous and peasant organizations in the city of San Cristóbal de las Casas to discuss the need for a peaceful solution to the conflict. Other local organizations were also invited, such as official organizations like the regional CNC, the Unión de Ejidos Profesor Otilio Montaño, and SOCAMA and the independent organizations OPEZ and OCEZ-CNPA.

On January 24 and 25, 280 indigenous organizations met in the warehouses of the Pakal Cooperative Society on the outskirts of San Cristóbal. This meeting, which had been organized originally by the government to show the "world" that thousands of Chiapas indigenous persons had not chosen to take up arms, would instead become a site for the confluence of indigenous and peasant movements to express their support for Zapatista demands. Out of this meeting would be formed the CEOIC, to be joined immediately by Mam agro-ecological cooperative societies.

Also at this meeting, Zapatista demands were analyzed and regional experiences shared. Some government officials had argued that the Zapatista rebellion could not possibly have an indigenous character as it had begun by rejecting NAFTA and, moreover, that their demands did not seem to have the local nature of Indian riots. The level of the discussion challenged these ahistorical perceptions of the indigenous population by officials:

> In relation to the Free Trade Agreement, it should be reviewed to suggest changes during the next international meeting that will be held during the next six months. It should also consider salaries equivalent to those of the United States or Canada. . . . There must be a real popular consultation of all sectors involved, since up to now they have only taken into consideration the opinion of the financial, industrial, and commercial sectors. (Group Three: Toward a New Constitutional Agreement, January 25, 1994)

While indigenist officials still talked about the "spontaneity of Indian riots," Chiapas indigenous peoples were not only placing their struggle in the framework of the nation, they were also beginning to reflect on the consequences of economic globalization on their lives.

Mam peasants brought to the first two CEOIC meetings their experience in organic agriculture and suggested that discussion groups include the topic of alternative development based on sustainable agriculture. In later meetings, the differences between official and independent sectors would become more evident. "Bilingual teachers" at the meeting, many of them linked to official organizations such as SOCAMA, being the more effective speakers, would sometimes monopolize the discussion. A few weeks after the CEOIC was formed, ISMAM released to the press its decision to leave the council as a protest against the position of some official organizations. Months later, after some organizations had negotiated their land demands with the government outside the council, the CEOIC broke into independent official factions (Harvey 1994). In spite of the departure of official sectors, ISMAM remained outside the independent CEOIC and decided to take up the issue of sustainable development separately.

Negotiations between the EZLN and the government began on February 21, 1994, and as of this writing, there have been unsuccessful attempts

to initiate talks and there has been no real commitment by the government. Nevertheless, through this process, the indigenous population has
been able to consider the ramifications of several of the key issues put forward by Zapatistas and government representatives.

The need to discuss an alternative means of development has become
more pressing for Sierra Madre organic growers since the beginning of
the peace talks. The Zapatistas had not questioned the technological program that the Green Revolution had brought to Sierra communities,
which from the point of view of organic growers had had very negative
consequences for the land and the life of indigenous peasants. To open
the debate on the need for new avenues of development, ISMAM and
Nan Choch members, together with technical advisers from the Agro-
ecological Center San Francisco de Asís and other Sierra Madre TCOs,
organized the Regional Forum of Mam and Mochó Communities on Proposals for Alternative Ways of Agricultural Production for Facing Poverty
in Chiapas, which took place March 1 to 13, 1994. Some members of peasant organizations saw this forum as an expression of the "productivist"
character of agro-ecological organizations, which did not consider land
claims relevant to their concerns. An ISMAM member pointed out, "I do
not think they are opposite demands, but different. They recover land on
the sides, and we recover it from above." Conciliating these two positions
has been the challenge of independent organizations over the past several
years.

In their invitations to the forum, agro-ecological peasants stated:

> As a contribution to the search for new alternatives to the difficult
> situation undergone by the state of Chiapas, we, Mam and Mo-
> chó organizations, working with agro-ecological methods based on
> the protection of the environment and popular wisdom, have our
> word to say. While we are brothers in our struggle for the defense
> of human rights that the whole civil society is carrying out with
> all passion and intensity, we feel the need to go deeper into this
> problem that we live in the countryside and to contribute with our
> experience.[15]

The forum was attended by some one hundred Sierra peasants, representing several communities, as well as special guests from NGOs linked
to organic agriculture. Papers presented by "experts" were followed by
discussions on specific subjects: land, production and commercialization,
knowledge of the ancients, education and housing, and indigenous law and
women's rights. The conclusions of the forum were used to write a docu-

ment titled "Proposals from the Mam and Mochó Peoples to Strengthen the Autonomy of Indigenous Peoples." This document summarized two days of discussion in the following terms:

1. Land: We must have our right to land, to the territory and its natural resources. The property of our lands must be secure and guaranteed. We want to care for and protect our Mother Earth to be able to enjoy her generous fruits and not allow her to be destroyed by inappropriate (deadly) techniques.

2. Production: We are trying to find a form of production that can yield abundant riches and is at the same time fair, that does not destroy nature or permit exploitation among human beings. Production must be able to satisfy self-consumption and local needs and must be based on traditional techniques and the wisdom of our ancestors to achieve integration of the community and the peoples.

3. Commercialization: We want to find a fair exchange that can strengthen everyone and commercialization favoring the production of organic crops. We seek the promotion of direct relations with consumers and fair prices.

4. Credit: We struggle for credits that can really give strength to our communities, used according to the needs of each group and handled by ourselves. We want credits to respect the autonomy of peoples or groups, to support productive processes, not input credits, such as pesticides and pumps, and we want seeds not to be conditioned on monoculture.

5. Housing: We want proper housing that can give us strength and keep us healthy, built with material not harmful to Mother Nature.

6. Education: We want to promote education responding to the needs we have as indigenous peoples. We want this education to respect and preserve traditional values and promote the rescue of indigenous language.

7. Health: We want our people to obtain health with dignity, in a way in which we can produce our healthy food and natural medicine. We want traditional medicine to be respected and traditional doctors to be recognized.

8. Our own law: We want democracy, justice, and peace, based on respect for the dignity and culture of our people; and to promote a democratic culture. We want to propose the community law to solve our problems, but not on the idea that we all have a good community tradition, but that we must create it.

9. Women's rights: We seek for women the same rights of participation, dignity, and decision as for men.

10. Organization: We want a broad organization through common work, which can help us live together peacefully with other peoples and with nature. (FOCIES 1994)

This document made public the new organization that was born out of this forum—Front of Indigenous Communities and Organizations of the Sierra (Frente de Organizaciones y Comunidades Indígenas de la Sierra [FOCIES]). It expresses the experience of many years of collective reflection in the TCO groups (see Chapter 6) and in many forums and assemblies where organic growers discussed local problems. The difference between the demands presented in the 1974 and 1975 Indigenous Congresses and those made by CEOIC twenty years later is the inclusion of an agro-ecological perspective and the search for less destructive development alternatives. Their critical perspective on community law is also interesting. In contrast to the Indianist discourse of some organizations defending "Indigenous Law" as essentially democratic, agro-ecological Mam point to the need to work on the construction of a democratic community culture. Such a critical perspective stems in part from the struggle of Mam women within their communities for the recognition of their right to participate equally with men, thus rejecting those elements of "tradition" that exclude them. Copies of the "Proposals from the Mam and Mochó Peoples to Strengthen the Autonomy of Indigenous Peoples" were sent to the EZLN as well as to government representatives. In later meetings, the Zapatistas would include among their negotiation points the need to develop sustainable agriculture.

Other sectors of the Mam population expressed their sympathy for the Zapatista struggle more openly, by participating in Peaceful Civil Resistance in 1994 and 1995 and in the struggle for the construction of pluriethnic autonomous regions after 1996. During the Civil Resistance movement of 1994, forty-four fincas were occupied in Soconusco and the Sierra by organized indigenous and mestizo peasants. Most of them were later violently evicted by the police. Among the organizations claiming responsibility for such land occupations were the Soconusco Regional Council of Indigenous and Peasant Organizations (Consejo Regional de Organizaciones Indígenas y Campesinas del Soconusco), the Mam Supreme Council (Consejo Supremo Mam), OCEZ, OPEZ, and CEOIC.[16]

Members from twelve of the twenty-two Danzas Mames groups supported the parallel government and gave their land taxes and electricity fees to the Resistance governor, Lic. Amado Avendaño. The close friendship of Don Eugenio, the coordinator of Danzas Mames, with the PRIist governor Eduardo Robledo Rincón led the dance groups supporting the Resistance governor to decide to form a separate organization. After lengthy discussions, however, they agreed to work together, with each having the freedom to determine the content of their performances and whether to participate in official events.

Publicly, ISMAM and Nan Choch disassociated themselves from Peaceful Civil Resistance, but many of their members supported the struggle, causing frequent friction with other members, especially the Catholic authorities. Conflicting political perspectives and strategies thwarted the Sierra peasants' attempt to form a common front with all agro-ecological growers. FOCIES disappeared three months after its birth, when some of its members decided to join the Civil Resistance.

Zapatismo has allowed a segment of Mam peasants to strengthen their links with a broader indigenous movement through the new opportunities for political discussion that have been opened in Chiapas. In this sense, it has fostered cohesion and a sense of identity that extends beyond the community and the linguistic group to a community of the indigenous peoples of Mexico. Yet, at the same time, it has deepened the differences between those sectors opposing the government and those linked to the official party. The organization, the religious group, the community, and even the family are now crossed over by a line dividing those who favor the Zapatistas and those who favor the government. Divisions that already existed within communities are now marked by the presence of two armies: the Federal Army and the Zapatistas.

Claiming the Power to Name: The Struggle for Autonomy

The discourses on autonomy that have developed in the framework of the peace dialogue have challenged the official discourse on Multicultural Mexico, demonstrating the need for indigenous peoples to define the terms of their own collective recognition, including control and governance of their own territory. The Zapatista political proposal on autonomy was well received by a peasant movement that for decades had been struggling for land and municipal power and helped to articulate these demands in terms that now included the concept of autonomy. One of the leaders of the CEOIC describes this process:

> In 1992, after analyzing that municipal presidencies had been acting as a refuge for landowners, that they still controlled from there— with politicians in their hands—the regional economic processes,

we joined the struggle for municipal power. Now, with the uprising of the Ejército Zapatista de Liberación Nacional (EZLN), we gave a public name to our decision to govern ourselves: autonomy. (Rojas 1996:219)

Zapatistas, and later the indigenous movement at the state level, have claimed the right to "name," and they struggle to establish new terms in the construction of the nation. Contrary to other resistance spaces in which Mam peasants had participated, in the struggle for the construction of autonomy the terms of the "dialogue" have not been set by the state; it is a proposal that breaks the hegemonic discourse on the nation. The concept of autonomy has become the center of the political debate in Mexico, and the state has been forced to accept the terms of the dialogue, whether to disqualify, redefine, or reject them. The struggle to define the meaning of autonomy has become an arena in which to confront and negotiate several definitions of nation, tradition, modernity, ethnic identity, and citizenship. Different points of view have been developed, inside the state as well as among the indigenous population.

Although the concept of autonomy had been essential to the struggle of Mam organic producers, it was conceived in productive and political terms and contained no wider project of territorial control and restructuring of municipal organization. When the Zapatista movement claimed the construction of multiethnic autonomous regions, some Mam and mestizo peasants from the municipalities of Bella Vista, Amatenango de la Frontera, and Frontera Comalapa decided to take such proposals to their organizations, and on March 5, 1997, they declared publicly that sixty-six of their communities would become part of the newly established autonomous municipality of Tierra y Libertad (Land and Freedom).[17]

The seat of the municipality is in Ejido Amparo Aguatinta, in the rain forest region. It is the largest of the autonomous municipalities created since 1996 under Zapatista influence, for it contains the old municipalities of Las Margaritas, La Independencia, La Trinitaria, Frontera Comalapa, Bella Vista, Motozintla, and Amatenango de la Frontera. Because of the distance between the border region of the Sierra and the municipal seat of the rain forest, additional seats of the autonomous municipality were established in the communities of Paso Hondo, in Frontera Comalapa, and Belizario Domínguez, in Motozintla. Although up to this time the only Sierra communities that have joined the autonomous municipality are Bella Vista and Motozintla, many communities of Siltepec, La Grandeza, and Mazapa de Madero have discussed the possibility of joining and have maintained a close relationship with the auxiliary offices.

Thus a new geographic arrangement, imposed on official municipalities, has been created with no governmental acknowledgment. The new autonomous municipalities whose creation has been declared in the mass media are San Pedro Michoacán, Tierra y Libertad, San Juan de la Libertad, San Juan Cancuc, Zona Autonónoma de Tenejapa, Moisés Gandhi, Nuevo Bochil, Santa Catarina, Magdalena de la Paz, Ernesto Che Guevara, San Andrés Sac'amché de los Pobres, Tzot Choj, Pohló, Sitalá, Amatenango del Valle, Nuevo Venustiano Carranza, Nicolás Ruiz and Socoltenango. These rebel municipalities encompass whole regions and include several communities, many of them belonging to different official municipalities.[18]

Recognition of the autonomous municipalities and the inclusion of the right to autonomy in the Constitution have been the main points of contention in the dialogue between the EZLN and the government. The Panel on Indigenous Culture and Rights (Mesa de Derechos y Cultura Indígenas), composed of advisers and guests invited by both sides, was set up to discuss, among other things, indigenous peoples' right to autonomy. Among the governmental representatives there were two main positions, the "hard line," led by officials from the Ministry of the Interior, and the "negotiating line," led by INI officials. The INI proposed communal autonomy, claimed particularly by Oaxaca indigenous peoples, as a middle solution—between the more radical demand of regional autonomy by a sector of the indigenous movement and the total rejection of any kind of autonomy by the government. Some researchers have suggested that the INI's proposal was a strategy to divide the indigenous movement and to weaken the demands for autonomy (e.g., Díaz Polanco 1997). Their proposal can be seen also as an expression of the hegemonic process of the Mexican state, which, as we have seen, has been clever enough to include in its discourses and policies some of the demands of the subordinate sectors as a way to legitimate its power.

The "negotiating line" seemed to prevail when on February 16, 1996, the first agreements were signed—known as the San Andrés Agreements, a reference to San Andrés Larráizar, now San Andrés Sac'amche de los Pobres, where the meetings were held—which recognized the right of indigenous peoples to self-determination and communal autonomy. But this was only the beginning of a long process. The president of Mexico, Ernesto Zedillo, had remained on the sidelines during the negotiations, and only ten months later, when the agreements passed into law, he decided to consult his legal advisers. To the surprise of many, he stated that he knew nothing about the agreements his representatives had signed.

Starting from this "revision," the government disowned the San Andrés Agreements and issued a new proposal that omitted the right of indigenous peoples to self-government, the use and enjoyment of their natural resources, and their own normative systems.[19]

The rejection of the peoples' demands for autonomy centered on two arguments, the danger of national disintegration and the total disqualification of indigenous culture and forms of organization by "legal advisers." The ever-present racism in Mexican society became evident during the public debate that followed the presidential rejection of the San Andrés Agreements.

Ignacio Burgoa Orihuela, a legal expert and one of the advisers consulted by President Zedillo, was the first to speak against autonomy:

> Which are the lands that the indigenous peoples use and occupy? Can such lands contain private properties, federal or municipal properties? To solve these questions, we need geographical, historical, and economic studies. . . . If this law were approved by the Congress, there would be "indigenous sovereignty" or an "indigenous power" independent of the municipal, state, and federal power, against the Constitution itself . . . and what means of communication do they refer to? Will it be donkeys, carts, or tamemes—[that is,] human beings dedicated to the transportation of merchandise or human beings?[20]

The answer from the indigenous movement was not long in coming. Disowning any secessionist intention, Mixteco leader Adelfo Regino Montes, representing the Indigenous National Congress, pointed out:

> There is no reason to fear. There are no reasons to enter the realm of mistrust or technical confusion; politically, the concepts of autonomy and sovereignty are radically different. Traditionally, it has been said that autonomy is an attribute of the state. . . . [O]n the contrary, autonomy is the faculty that peoples have within the framework of the state—and not out of it—to determine their living conditions in coordination with state and federal governments. When we Mexican indigenous peoples claim our right to self-determination concretely in indigenous autonomy, we are not upsetting sovereignty.[21]

In spite of the declarations of legal experts, indigenous leaders, and the EZLN itself, the danger of the fragmentation of the country was declared by its president as an argument against autonomy in his visits to Tenek,

Pame, Tepehuan, Nahuatl and Otomí peoples in January and February 1997.

Burgoa Orihuela spoke of the danger that indigenous peoples would go back to "human sacrifices" if autonomy were granted to them (*La Jornada*, March 4, 1997). And some anthropologists, such as Roger Bartra, pointed to the colonial origin of indigenous cultures and warned against "the seeds of violence and antidemocracy" that the recognition of the "uses and customs" would entail (*La Jornada Semanal*, August 31, 1997).

Before the threat of decentralization, the redistribution of power, and discussion of the need for a new national project, sectors of the government, of the Mexican intelligentsia, and of local power groups forgot their old "folklorisms" and their interest in indigenous cultures and set out to disqualify them as "primitive," "violent," and "antidemocratic." Nineteenth-century discourses reappear before the danger of indigenous autonomy.

The positions within the indigenous movement are not homogeneous either. Historical and regional differences have created different proposals: for the Lacandon rain forest colonizers, who came from different parts of the country and the state, autonomy has to be multiethnic, while Sonora Yaquis demand the creation of a Yaqui autonomous region; as for Oaxaca indigenous peoples, they still seek communal autonomy. Overcoming these differences and joining forces to demand the recognition of the different projects by the state has been one of the main challenges of the Indigenous National Congress.[22]

The new discourse on autonomy opens the space for the formation of new subjectivities that are barely visible in the current political scene. As yet there is no assurance that these new spaces will be more democratic or egalitarian than the community or the nation.

For the moment, we can see that the proposals for political autonomy by a sector of the indigenous movement, the Asamblea Nacional Indígena Plural por la Autonomía (ANIPA), as well as by Oaxaca's communalist movement and by the EZLN itself, represent a rupture in the hegemonic discourse on the nation and make possible new relationships between indigenous peoples and the state, and also with Mexican society in general. For example, to achieve recognition of their indigenous languages and cultural forms, there needs to be reorganization of the educational and health systems nationwide. Most of the autonomous municipalities have adopted the proposals of the agro-ecological peasant movement and express the need for sustainable growth that recovers traditional indigenous agriculture and organic agriculture; in this sense, they are against the agrochemical transnational corporations, and they call for economic autonomy so that they can dispense with middlemen and control the means of production and marketing. The claim for their own normative systems and forms of government questions electoral democracy as the only way to achieve broader political participation.[23]

The struggle for autonomy goes well beyond a confrontation with the state, for it is the construction of a new project of an all-inclusive, plural nation. It is a struggle against Mexican society's racism, against the centralism of the federal government, against transnational corporations that promote agrochemical products, against political parties that deny other forms of constructing democracy, against local middlemen who steal the profits of indigenous peoples. It is a struggle against many fronts, and thus it is full of complications and obstacles.

One obstacle is the idealization of the indigenous past, partly as a reaction against racism. The absolute denial of their cultural forms has led indigenous leaders and their advisers to present an idealized vision of their communities, which underlines the conciliatory character of their normative systems, the ecological purity of their worldview, and the democratic character of their forms of government.[24]

Both the racist view and the ideal view are ahistorical, in that they deny the complexity of cultural identities. It seems that there are only two possible representations, the nineteenth-century perspective, which sees indigenous culture as primitive and thus easily destroyed, and the essentialist perspective, which sees it as millenarian, ecological, and democratic.

Organized indigenous women have confronted both representations and have played a very important role in the development of a critical vision from the indigenous movement itself.

The Voices of Women

The active participation of women has been especially noticeable since the emergence of the Zapatista movement. Mam women in agro-ecological cooperative societies have brought to many of these forums their interest in alternative development. They have also taken back to their communities and organizations new ideas about their rights as women and as indigenous people.

Along with their participation in FOCIES and in local mobilizations, a group of Mam women has traveled to San Cristóbal de las Casas to discuss with other indigenous women proposals for legislative changes on cultural rights and indigenous autonomy, the formation of a state women's convention, and, since 1995, their participation as guests of the EZLN in the peace talks panel "Indigenous Rights and Culture."

As a result of the demands for autonomy by the EZLN, the government sought to add a "regulatory law" to the recently amended Article 4 of the Constitution that formalized its previous legal acknowledgment of a multicultural nation. Conferences on the regulatory law were quickly convened, in which the INI proposed revisions. In addition, the government organized regional conferences at the national level, which were mostly attended by indigenous people linked to the official party. Indigenous women were not invited. When questioned about this, INI officials answered that indigenous women were not interested in participating and wanted nothing to do with laws or political matters.

In May 1994 a group of Chiapas indigenous women belied this image of political passivity by participating in the "Workshop-Meeting on the Rights of Women in Our Customs and Traditions" (Encuentro-Taller Los Derechos de las Mujeres en Nuestras Costumbres y Tradiciones). The workshop was organized by indigenous and ladino (nonindigenous) women from several NGOs in the Chiapas highlands in order to reflect broadly on women's rights and specifically on the implications for their lives of the amendments to Article 4 and the proposed "Regulatory Law."[25] It was attended by seventy indigenous women—Mam, Tzotzil, Tzeltal, and Tojolabal—of different backgrounds: artisans, midwives, merchants, and growers. They discussed the discrimination they experienced in the workplace, in state institutions, and in the home. Catholics, traditionalists, and Protestants, all shared their experiences as women in the community, in the town, and in peasant organizations. By means of dramatizations and discussions, they presented the different forms of discrimination occurring in the Sierra, the rain forest, and the highlands. The Zapatistas' "Law of Women" was a constant subject in all of the work groups. This law, published by the *Despertador Mexicano* and later broadcast by other media, expressed the feeling of Zapatistas on their rights as women and as indigenous people.[26] Most of the women at the meeting knew of the law and suggested that the discussion on Article 4 be linked to the demands of Zapatista women.

The different ways of "being a woman" have been marked by regional, cultural, and organizational differences, and by discovering their commonalities and comparing experiences, a bridge has been built between participating women. Sierra Mam women were represented by eight Nan Choch members, who, like the Nan Choch men, brought to the debate the agro-ecological perspective. These women have been fighting on two

Zapatista women, with their Revolutionary Law of Women, have had symbolic importance in the struggle of Mam women for their rights. PHOTO BY ANA ALVAREZ VELASCO.

fronts: they have been insisting that women's rights be discussed within their cooperative societies, and they have insisted that organized indigenous women from other parts of the state consider the need to think about an alternative model of agrarian development with more respect for Mother Earth.

During the workshop-meeting, Sierra women explained to the others their grandparents' experiences, when the Law of Government had forbidden the Mam language, so they would not be mistaken for Guatemalan, and demanded that their costumes be burned in public squares in order to "civilize" them. Unlike Tzotzil and Tzeltal women, who spoke about discrimination by *cashlanes* (non-Indians) or ladinos and about repression by finqueros, Mam women used more abstract concepts, partly as a result of the reflection encouraged in workshops in their organizations: "But that is only what is seen. In fact, what mistreats us all is the capitalist system."[27]

The women prepared a document that was sent to the press and the Congress expressing the tension between the need to acknowledge the cultural rights of indigenous peoples and the demand that exclusionary customs be changed. The right to choose one's partner, to inherit land, and to hold office are among their demands:

We had better have documents where we women say that there are customs that do not respect us and we want them changed. Violence is not right. It is not fair we can be sold for money. Neither is it fair when "by custom" we are not allowed to be representatives or have land rights. We do not want bad customs.[28]

The document also refers to the beneficial aspects of "custom." Tzotzil midwives wanted recognition of traditional medical practices, Tzeltal women spoke of the need for bilingual education respecting culture, and Mam Sierra women spoke of the importance of recovering respect for nature and Mother Earth, which their ancestors had had before the arrival of pesticides and fertilizers.

The workshop was followed by a number of meetings that strengthened the links of Nan Choch Mam women with members of indigenous and peasant organizations from other parts of the state. On July 28 and 29, 1994, the First Convention of Chiapas Women (Convención Estatal Mujeres Chiapanecas) was held to discuss the proposals indigenous and mestizo women would take to the meeting between civil society and the EZLN, which was held August 6 through 9 in Aguascalientes, Chiapas. From then on, the voices of indigenous women have been heard in all political forums throughout the state that have been held to discuss the conditions of a "peace with social justice."

The EZLN and the government agreed to organize four discussion groups, one of which would be on women's rights. The EZLN has invited organized indigenous women to each of the discussion groups so that their specific demands could be taken into consideration in the negotiations. In the first discussion group on indigenous rights and culture, Mam women of A New Dawn in the Sierra cooperative society were invited by the EZLN to share the experience of their double struggle as women and as indigenous people.

Although ethnic, class, and political differences caused the dissolution of the State Convention of Chiapas Women, in which Mam women participated actively (Hernández Castillo 1998b), the convention was successful in ensuring that women's demands would remain in the forefront in subsequent discussions. For example, CNI and ANIPA, under pressure from women members, had to convoke the National Encounters of Indigenous Women. Women have demanded from the state the right to cultural difference and from their communities the right to change the customs they deem unfair. In documents generated at various meetings, indigenous women have demanded the right to national citizenship and have supported the national indigenous demand that their traditions must be maintained, but they have done so through a discourse that allows the possibility of "changing while staying and staying by changing."

Women have been the main defenders of autonomous regions, facing the army or paramilitary groups and in many cases risking their own lives. But theirs has not been an "acritical" defense of autonomy. In fact, while they defend the new projects in territories under Zapatista influence, some of them have participated in the political debate to influence the terms in which autonomy is understood. A sector of organized women, including Mam women of the agro-ecological movement, have fought not to let the project of autonomy start from an idealized vision of indigenous communities that does not acknowledge the need for democratization of many traditional political practices.

At the same time, in the ANIPA, Chiapas women, together with indigenous peasant women from all over the country, have fought to make projects for autonomy all-inclusive and to open new spaces of participation for women. On this subject, the report of one of their meetings points out:

> We women are the majority of the inhabitants of our villages, and we do not want to stay as the shadows of what men do. . . . We want an autonomy with a woman's voice, face, and conscience so that we can reconstruct the female part of our community that has been forgotten. We demand our right to the land; even when marriages split, we want an equal share for husband and wife.[29]

Among the new encounter spaces created since Zapatismo is the Seminar on Constitutional Changes to Article 4 (Seminario sobre las Reformas del 4⁰. Constitucional), which continued discussions that began in the workshop "Women's Rights in Our Customs and Traditions," in which indigenous women from throughout the country met periodically in 1996 in Mexico City to discuss legal reforms with regard to the rights of indigenous peoples. The meetings led to a document that supports the demand for autonomy but extends its definition and interprets it from a gender perspective. The document refers to economic autonomy, which is defined as the right of indigenous women to access to and equal control over the means of production; to political autonomy, which entails basic political rights; to physical autonomy, which is the right to make decisions about their own bodies and to live free of violence; and to sociocultural autonomy, defined as the right to claim their specific identities as indigenous.[30]

Opportunities for organization by women have increased since the Zapatista uprising. PHOTO BY ANA ALVAREZ VELASCO.

Yet this new political activism has met with violence and repression. For the most conservative sectors of mestizo and indigenous society, the existence of organized women in some community or region has become almost a synonym for Zapatista influence, although this is not always the case. Organized women, whether Zapatista or not, have become a symbol of resistance and subversion and thus the focus of political violence.

Again a Two-faced Policy: Economic Aid and Paramilitarization

From the beginning of the conflict in 1994, governmental reports pointed to the Sierra region as a zone "that could be influenced by the Zapatista uprising." The government has increased social expenditures in this region, building roads, schools, and health centers while injecting money into agricultural production organizations through loans at low interest or interest-free and support for infrastructure acquisition. Yet this social investment policy has come with repression against indigenous and peasant organizations that have openly supported the Zapatista uprising. Although the presence of the Federal Army has considerably increased since 1994, especially at the military base at Motozintla, in the heart of the Sierra, repression against the indigenous and peasant movement has come primarily from the police and paramilitary groups that defend the interests of local finqueros.[31]

This two-faced policy is intended to divide the indigenous and peasant movement. It is an attempt to prevent agricultural production organizations from participating in the struggle for autonomy while demobilizing organizations close to the EZLN by giving paramilitary groups free rein to attack those who have occupied the fincas and to terrorize the people of the Sierra.

Coffee producer organizations, such as ISMAM and the Cooperativa Otilio Montaño, have been given credits through BANRURAL and other economic aid from the Support Program for Coffee Producers. At the same time, the Fondo Nacional de Empresas de Solidaridad has given about 6 million pesos a year to smaller social organizations.

Although the government has previously shown little interest in organic agriculture, since 1994 it has supported the agro-ecological cooperative societies. Scarcely five months after the beginning of the conflict, in a public ceremony ISMAM received from the Ministry of Social Development one million pesos from the Solidaridad program and the promise to legalize the Tapachula processing plant that ISMAM had been renting since 1990. A year later, in November 1995, President Zedillo granted ISMAM the National Exports Award, offering them a larger credit line than any other cooperative society in Mexico. In August 1998 the Ministry of Agrarian Reform helped ISMAM to buy the 286-hectare Finca Belén in the municipality of Motozintla, paying 60 percent of the total cost while the remaining 40 percent was paid by the cooperative society.

Government support has bought the loyalty of ISMAM directors, and the political independence that they had proclaimed seems to be in danger. Although ISMAM had maintained a critical but respectful position toward the EZLN, in 1995 the administrator of the cooperative society published press inserts criticizing the Zapatista movement for its influence on the decline of coffee production in the region of conflict. This position is not shared by all members, and many of them were not even aware of this initiative by the administrator. Because of such incidents, and the lack of communication between the executive committee and its members in the rain forest and the municipalities of Simojovel and Jaltenango, in 1995 these three regions, which accounted for 30 percent of its production and 35 percent of its members, decided to leave ISMAM and form the Federación Indígena Ecológica de Chiapas (Indigenous Ecological Federation of Chiapas [FIECH]) (Renard 1999:286). Together with the internal divisions that have reduced its sphere of influence, the rise in the price of conventional coffee and natural disasters have placed ISMAM in a crisis situation.

Strangely enough, while organic agriculture was a solution for the crisis caused by the fall in the price of coffee in 1989, the 1994–1995 price increase placed organic producers in a dilemma: lose the comparative market advantages or renounce their agro-ecological principles and return to nonorganic coffee production, which entails less labor. At the same time, equitable markets were no longer attractive, since they could not raise their prices excessively and remain competitive.

Besides the loss of principles entailed in leaving the agro-ecological way, abandoning the integrated technological package had practical ramifications. They would lose their organic coffee certification, closing the doors to that market forever, and by turning their backs on the equitable market, they might endanger their place in this preferential niche, which had given them strength as an organization. Before this situation, an important sector of ISMAM led by the members of the executive committee decided to incorporate under the name San Jerónimo S.A. ISMAM is a Social Solidarity Society, a legal entity that has low fiscal charges, but if it is dissolved, it must leave its assets to a charity. To avoid endangering the credibility of ISMAM as an organic producer, the promoters of the new company decided to retain membership in both organizations. The new company buys nonorganic coffee from small independent producers and processes it in ISMAM's processing plant.

This initiative has aroused criticism and mistrust in an important sector of ISMAM, which decided not to participate in the project, which they considered a betrayal of the principles of respect for Mother Earth, as well as a new form of *coyotaje* (middleman practices), which the cooperative society had been founded originally to combat. ISMAM has survived, in spite of these differences, but the struggle between those ready to explore nonorganic markets and those that remain loyal to agro-ecological principles has endangered the democratic and solidary space created years ago.

In addition to their internal problems, organic producers have had to face the violence of nature, which destroyed almost all their crops in 1997–1998. In September 1998 Chiapas, and especially the Sierra and coastal regions, suffered one of the worst natural disasters of the last twenty-five years. According to President Zedillo, it was a natural disaster as terrible as the earthquake that struck Mexico City in 1985. Rains caused more than fifty rivers to overflow, flooding ten towns, among them Motozintla, whose main buildings were almost completely destroyed by avalanches of mud. About eighty communities were covered by mud, leaving four hundred thousand inhabitants homeless and, in the Sierra region alone, killing between three hundred and four hundred people, according to different official sources. The media reported that two billion dollars would be required to rebuild the infrastructure in both regions.[32] The rain destroyed almost 80 percent of the coffee crop that year, and although the government sent emergency aid to reconstruct roads, schools, and health centers, by 1999 local people were still suffering the consequences of the natural disaster.

Mam indigenous people who supported Peaceful Civil Resistance and autonomy movements have had to face not only the violence of nature but also that of security corps and paramilitary groups who have imprisoned, repressed, and even murdered them. Although paramilitary groups in this region are not as well known to the public as Paz y Justicia in the Chol region, or Mascara Roja in the Tzotzil area in the highlands, since the Peaceful Civil Resistance movement began in 1994, several of the invaded fincas were repossessed by heavily armed civilians, often dressed in black and wearing military boots, who were accused by peasant organizations of being members of paramilitary groups.[33]

By mid-1996 a guerrilla group that had carried out armed actions in Guerrero and Oaxaca appeared in Chiapas. At this time the Ejército Popular Revolucionario (Revolutionary Popular Army [EPR]) carried out propaganda actions near Motozintla and other Sierra communities, which served as an excuse to increase the police presence in the region and search the houses of organized peasants.

There has also been selective repression against the leaders of indigenous and peasant organizations. In February 1996 Maximiliano Hernández, local leader of OPEZ, was tortured and murdered by four "unknown heavily armed" men (CONPAZ 1996). In 1995 a member of ISMAM was murdered by PRIista peasants during an electoral dispute in the municipality of Chicomuselo. In October 1997 autonomous authorities of Paso Hondo were held and beaten by a group of armed peasants, supported by local authorities, who accused them of destroying water pipes and having a clandestine jail. In November of the same year, Eusebio Sánchez Bartolón, a Nan Choch technical adviser, was kidnapped and murdered in the town of Motozintla by "armed men." Also, since the creation of autonomous municipalities, the presence of governmental armed corps has increased. Independent peasant organizations, such as OPEZ and the Frente Amplio de Organizaciones (FAO-LN), have withstood threats and aggression by paramilitary groups named Los Carrancistas and Justicia Social. Autonomous Paso Hondo authorities have denounced the establishment of a paramilitary training center in the border town of Ciudad Cuauhtémoc, where young recruits are paid six hundred pesos a fortnight and are trained by Paso Hondo police.[34]

These stories have been confirmed by Mam supreme councillor Ancelmo Pérez Mejía, who has played an important role in denouncing paramilitary groups in the Sierra and coastal regions. According to Pérez, these groups are paid by coffee landlords and trained by military personnel.[35]

Present paramilitary groups are a new version of the so-called *guardias blancas* (white guards), which for decades have defended the interests of Chiapas's finqueros. The existence of armed civilian groups at the service of local power groups has been legalized by state governments in different historical times. From 1952 to 1958 Efraín Arana Osorio's government authorized the creation of the Cattle Breeding Auxiliary Police Forces (Cuerpos de Policía Auxiliar Ganadera), and in the 1960s Gov. Samuel León Brindis signed the Cattle Breeding Law (Ley de Ganadería) supporting the existence of the Cattle Breeding Honorary Police (Policía Honoraria Ganadera), paid by finquero associations. These armed groups exist to this day in several forms, serving the interests of finqueros and cattle breeders or indigenous caciques, or even serving the alliance between both sectors, depending on the region.

The strategy of making indigenous people fight against each other was used as part of the counterinsurgent wars in Guatemala, with the creation of the Civilian Self-Defense Patrols (Patrullas de Autodefensa Civil [PAC]), in which all males over the age of fifteen were forced to participate. The unraveling of the social fabric that this strategy caused is one of the high costs of the war that is still being paid in Guatemala (Le Bott 1995). Unlike the PAC, paramilitary groups in Chiapas are not openly financed by the government, but their links with the official party and local power groups have been denounced by human rights agencies (Centro de Derechos Humanos Fray Bartolomé de Las Casas 1996; Human Rights Watch 1997). Among the most clearly documented cases are PRI deputies Samuel Sánchez Sánchez and Norberto Sántiz López, the former of the paramilitary group Paz y Justicia and the latter of the Indigenous Revolutionary Anti-Zapatista Movement (Movimiento Indígena Revolucionario Antizapatista [MIRA]); the former governor, Elmar Setzer Marseille, linked to the Chinchulines; and the PRI municipal president of El Bosque,

Sebastián López, linked to the paramilitary group Los Plátanos (Centro de Derechos Humanos Fray Bartolomé de Las Casas 1996; Human Rights Watch 1997).

Two factors have contributed significantly to the paramilitarization of Chiapas. The first is the existence of a large group of unemployed young indigenous men, who have neither land nor expectations and have found in paramilitary groups a source of economic resources and power in their community. The second is the existence of indigenous cacicazgos linked to local power groups who have seen their own power threatened by the Zapatista uprising and by the creation of autonomous municipalities and so have decided to ally themselves with the most conservative sectors of the official party.

In many cases, paramilitary groups have used sexual rape as an instrument of repression and intimidation against communities that attempt to establish autonomous governments or those they consider close to the EZLN. For example, mass rape was used as part of the repression in repossessions of fincas in the Soconusco region, and in April 1996 land invaders led by OPEZ in the municipality of Suchiate were violently evicted by forty men wearing black uniforms and covering their faces, who used high-powered guns and raped ten women, leaving fifteen men gravely wounded (CONPAZ 1996).

The political use of sexual rape was one of the points in the first stage of the dialogue between EZLN and the government, in the discussion group on Culture and Indigenous Rights, which took place October 18–23, 1995, in San Cristóbal de las Casas. In the women's discussion group, women invited both by the federal government and the EZLN, in spite of their political differences, agreed that rape should be treated as a war crime, in accordance with international agreements. Yet, up to this time, there has been no initiative to put into practice agreements reached in those discussion groups.

Gender analyses in other militarized regions, such as Diane Nelson's in Guatemala (1995), Davida Wood's in Palestine (1995), and Dette Denich's in Sarajevo (1995), point out that in contexts of political and military conflict, women's sexuality becomes a symbolic space of political struggle, and rape is used to demonstrate power and domination over the enemy. Chiapas has been no exception, and militarization and paramilitarization have affected women in a specific way in this undeclared dirty war. In a patriarchal ideology—which still considers women sexual objects and the symbols of family honor—rape, sexual torture, and body mutilations are an attack against all men of the enemy group. Just like Serbian soldiers, paramilitary groups in Chiapas "appropriated women simultaneously as objects of sexual violence and as symbols in a contest with rival males that replicated the traditional forms of patriarchy, in which men's inability to protect 'their women' and to control their sexuality is perceived as a critical symptom of weakness" (Denich 1994:16).

Violence against organized women in Chiapas is at the same time a "punishment" for their political participation and a message to men in their families and organizations. That most of the members of the thirty-two paramilitary groups presently existing in Chiapas are also indigenous has led the public to speak of a "fratricidal war." The Acteal mass murders on December 22, 1997, have been the most violent and denounced of all paramilitary actions. After the murder of thirty-two women and thirteen men in a Tzotzil community, government officials and mass media have repeated over and over that it is a war between brothers, made more violent by the Zapatista uprising. Explanations have placed the origin of this mass murder in "interfamily disputes," reaching the conclusion that all indigenous peoples tend to solve their disputes through violence. This "naturalization" of violence has been used in several contexts as a discursive strategy to orientalize indigenous peoples and hides a racist point of view that still sees these societies as "violent and irrational." The state responsibility in the formation of local cacicazgos (see Rus 1994; Garza Caligaris and Hernández Castillo 1998), as well as its indirect or direct support of the paramilitarization of indigenous society (Centro de Derechos Humanos Fray Bartolomé de las Casas 1996; Human Rights Watch 1997) has been documented by researchers and human rights organizations to contradict the official versions of "intercommunity disputes."

The cruelty of the Acteal murders, the mutilation of the bodies of pregnant women, and the fact that the majority of the victims are women and children have led several women researchers to analyze the gendered forms that the low-intensity war is taking in Chiapas (Hernández Castillo 1998b).

To understand how gender marks the specific forms of violence in Chiapas today, it is important to remember the symbolic and political roles that women have played in recent struggles for democratization and autonomy. The participation of indigenous women has become a threat to the structures of community power, as well as to the hegemonic project of a nation that has been constructed with no consideration for the indigenous population.

The use of similar practices of war in different parts of the world, in which women become the center of violence, has been analyzed by several researchers specializing in what is presently known as the anthropology of war. Carolyn Nordstrom, who focuses on military violence, has found in different parts of the world the local impact of a global war industry, whose activities range from arms sales to training in low-intensity warfare. In her most recent book on Mozambique, she says something that we might well consider in our analysis of violence in Chiapas:

> Having conducted on-site research at the epicenters of wars over three continents and a decade and a half, I have learned that the whole concept of local wars, whether central or peripheral, is largely a fiction.
>
> Massive interlinked and very international war-related industries make war possible in any location in the world. I have seen the same weapons vendors, mercenaries, military advisors, supplies and military training manuals—both illicit and formal—circle the globe, moving from one war to the next. Politicians, military and paramilitary troops, and diplomats meet and talk across virtually all boundaries of nation and state. . . . This global flux of information, tactics, weapons, money, and personnel brokers tremendous power throughout the warzones of the world. The examples supporting this are legion. To give but one, when a torture technique is introduced into a country, that same technique can be found throughout the world in several day's time. Obviously transmitted with the physical techniques of harming bodies is a complex culture that specifies who can and should be targeted for torture, how and for what reasons and to what end. (Nordstrom 1997:5)

The relationship among what is local, national, and global is a basic methodological premise for any analysis attempting an explanation of the complexity of violence in Chiapas. Anthropological functionalism that presents indigenous communities as closed corporate communities has been questioned and disclaimed by the critical anthropology of the last decades. This is a good moment to retake what history and anthropology have taught us about contextualizing indigenous cultures in the framework of national and global economy. Only by placing "interfamily" and "intercommunity" disputes in wider contexts, and in the light of the relations between the state and indigenous peoples, can we explain the vast complexity of violence in Chiapas.

Perhaps the militarization and paramilitarization described here are the darkest part of the recent history of the relationship between the state and Mam peasants. As this process is taking place as I am finishing this book, I cannot explore its complexity here. The impact of paramilitarization on everyday life in Mam communities remains to be studied.

Yet the progress of paramilitarization in Chiapas and the priority given to strategies of control over the construction of consensus tell us of the success of the "hard line" over the "negotiating line" within the government and are one more expression of the hegemony crisis in the present Mexican state.

CONCLUSION

The voices of the Mam peasants of Chiapas tell us about the way in which the nation is lived and conceived on the "other border," the southern border of Mexico and the cultural border of changing and contextual identities that have been constructed in dialogue with official discourses and in a context of global markets. This case study helps us to approach the way in which "indigenous cultures" have been historically produced in a dialectical relation of resistance and domination with the Mexican nation-state. The extreme experiences of rapid change and cultural reinvention help us to reflect on the wider processes of ethnic identity construction that are taking place in contemporary Mexico. As I have been pointing out throughout this book, cultural identities cannot be seen apart from power relations.

Assimilationist campaigns in the 1930s imposed a Mexican identity on southern border inhabitants and forbade cultural practices identified as "backward" by a national modernizing project. At the same time, the National Presbyterian church offered Sierra peasants the feeling of belonging to a religious transnational community. The coexistence of multiple identities, recently theorized by postmodern anthropology, is reflected by testimonies of converts, who define themselves as "Mam, Presbyterian, and Mexican."

The historical relations of Mam peasants with coffee plantations, their constant migrations, and their scattered settlements question the existence of a "closed corporate community" that has only recently been "hit" by capitalist development. It is equally difficult to state that before the development of means of communication and a greater exchange of information, ethnic identities were unified and homogeneous, that is, that there was only one way to imagine themselves as Mam. Only a historical reconstruction of the pre-Hispanic and colonial experience of Sierra and Soconusco inhabitants might provide us with the necessary elements to understand the way in which collective identities were imagined. What we can indeed state is that a greater flow of information and the widening of social, political, and religious links beyond the community, the region, and even the nation has helped Mam indigenous peoples to imagine themselves as part of other collectivities, which does not necessarily mean that they cease to identify themselves as "Mam."

Some nostalgic perspectives on "peasant community" mourn the way economic globalization has "destroyed" indigenous cultures. Independent of my own feeling about the disappearance of "isolated communities" (if they ever existed), the reality is that Mam peasants, the readers of this book, and I share the experience of being inserted into an increasingly globalized economy and are part of what some have called the "global village." To avoid ahistorical descriptions of Mexico's indigenous peoples, it is important to acknowledge that "all of us inhabit an interdependent late-twentieth-century world marked by borrowing and lending across porous national and cultural boundaries that are saturated with inequality, power and domination" (Rosaldo 1987:217). Yet, in this historical context, the Mam have not only been the victims of national projects and capitalist development, but also historical subjects who have accepted, negotiated with, or challenged many such forces.

During the 1940s, Mam indigenous peoples became ejidatarios who were incorporated by postrevolutionary governments into their peasant organizations. Land distribution and corporative policies contributed to the configuration of a new peasant identity that replaced indigenous identity. Mam identity has not had a linear historic continuity and for decades has been replaced by other identities, to appear again under new historical conditions. In this sense, we might state in relation to Mam peasants what James Clifford (1988:342) pointed out for the New England Mashpee: "Their history was a series of cultural and political transactions, not all-or-nothing conversions or resistances. Indians in Mashpee lived and acted between cultures in a series of ad hoc engagements."

Since the 1980s we find Jehovah's Witnesses in Las Margaritas rain forest, Presbyterians in the Sierra, and members of Danzas Mames and of organic cooperative societies who in different social contexts have begun

to identify themselves again as Mam, often parallel to other, broader iden-
tifications. Through the reconstruction of a narrative about a common
origin and a past of shared suffering, links of belonging were established
within a collectivity. Rain forest and Sierra Mam, in spite of their religious
and political differences, reconstructed through their oral tradition, and
later by means of radio programs, the memories of the times of the "Law
of Government" and "the burning of costumes," of work at the fincas and
the dangers of the "purple disease," of the struggle for land and the acquisition of ejido plots. The Mam constitute a textual community, in the
sense that Joanne Rappaport (1990) refers to the Páez of Colombia, that is
to say, a community whose sense of belonging is constructed around one
or several narratives (texts) of a shared past. Although the "texts" of the
Mam are not written but oral, they fulfill the same function as the indigenous documents analyzed by Rappaport (1990:120): "Their contents are
most frequently experienced through practical activity and through ritual,
frequently tied to the legitimization of political power, and are primarily
communicated through narrative performance. Thus, they bind together
a peculiar Páez [or Mam] community."

Yet it is important to acknowledge that the adoption of a Mam identity has not been "a totally free and rational choice" but rather the result
of wider social and political processes in the framework of relations of
domination. During the transition from a mestizo Mexico to a multicultural Mexico in the late 1970s, the state once more assumed the right to
legitimize certain indigenous identities while denying others. Although
the spaces created by the state, such as the Indigenous Supreme Councils,
were accepted by Mam peasants, much of the official discourse was either
challenged or rejected by means of several strategies.

In the analysis of participative indigenism and PRONASOL indigenism, we found once more that the hegemony of the state is not something
achieved but a process in constant renegotiation. Through these hegemonic processes, the Mexican state created new spaces of control, for
example, the Indigenous Supreme Councils during the 1970s or the
PRONASOL Regional Funds during the 1990s. Yet meanings and symbols promoted by the Mexican state were not mechanically reproduced by
Sierra peasants but were reformulated or challenged through the representations of Danzas Mames, the religious utopia of the Jehovah's Witnesses, or the productive and cultural practices of organic growers.

The terms in which "Multicultural Mexico" was being officially defined
were challenged by several sectors of the Mam population, who pointed
to their right to land as part of their cultural rights. Through Danzas per-

formances and texts made public by organic cooperative societies, Mam peasants revealed that the state's recognition of their right to (abstract) culture was not enough, stressing instead that to expand the sense of citizenship to sectors of the indigenous population who had been excluded until then, their agrarian claims also had to be addressed as part of their cultural claims. By pointing to the close link between the productive, political, and cultural spheres, Mam peasants have challenged the technocratic visions of neoliberalism, which wants to promote agrarian development from a technical perspective of "productivity" and "feasibility," disregarding the political and cultural implications.

Mam women have also played an important role in challenging the official discourse on cultural rights. As a result of extensive organizational experience and collective reflection, they have developed a gender analysis that has been included in the platforms of their organizations. The importance of not mythifying cultural traditions as naturally democratic has been pointed out by several of them in their discussions on customary law. From this perspective, the "cultures" composing Multicultural Mexico are not static and achieved cultures but rather cultures in constant change that must also be democratized. In spite of the contestatory nature of these discourses, they were not born totally isolated from official discourses but have taken over many of their premises, expressing what some researchers have called "contradictory consciousness" (e.g., Hale 1994).

In their performances members of Danzas Mames have confronted the narratives of the past that have been legitimized by official history and have challenged official indigenism's limited perspective on "culture." Yet, at the same time, they have accepted the idea that the state should establish the terms of the "dialogue" by forming Supreme Councils and by participating in the indigenist projects devised by and planned from the nation's center.

The Jehovah's Witnesses have developed an antistate discourse linking the Mexican state to the forces of evil, reinterpreting much of this group's religious ideology through their own experience. In their antistate and antimodernizing narratives they have developed a symbolic resistance before a national project that has excluded them throughout history. Yet they have reproduced the conformist premises of this transnational religion, which sees "worldly problems" as an unavoidable and necessary evil, a view that has limited the possibility of alliance with other sectors of the Mam population. In the contemporary political context, the rejection of organizational processes has placed them outside the movement for autonomy that is taking place in the rain forest.

Organic growers have broadened their opposition beyond the nation-state and have challenged a whole mode of development, which they consider predatory and ethnocentric. Through collective organization they have struggled for the appropriation, not only of the productive, but also of the commercialization process. At the same time, in their wish to break the ties of dependency on the state, they have accepted, and even backed, many of the neoliberal premises on the need to reduce the state apparatus and on the development of free trade. And the struggle for reform of the state and municipal control has not been seen as a priority in the agro-ecological perspective. Strangely enough, their success as an economic project has awakened the interest of the state, especially since the Zapatista uprising, and they have enjoyed privileged treatment by governmental, banking, and development agencies, which has led them to strengthen their links with the state and limit the possibilities of political alliances with independent organizations.

The contradictory consciousness of these different sectors of the Mam population have challenged a "homogeneous project of a nation" from different perspectives, but they have often done so within the terms established by the state itself. Rather than analyze the way cultural differences have been "used" or "deepened" by the state, I have tried to address the productive capacity of power. By means of its institutions, its political organizations, its ritual practices, its repressive measures, or its conciliatory spaces, the Mexican state has contributed to the creation of new collective identities.

The importance of colonial or postcolonial relations of domination in the formation of ethnic identities has been pointed out by several anthropologists as an argument to deny the "authenticity" or "value" of Mesoamerican indigenous cultures (see Aguirre Beltrán 1967; Martínez Peláez 1970; Friedlander 1975). Although these points of view were already confronting essentialist visions of ethnic identity in the 1950s, they assumed that there was a "utopian identity" space outside power relations, often identified with the nation. The aim of this book has not been to mark some identities as less "authentic" than others but rather to historicize the way in which power relations have marked the construction of the nation as well as that of the "Mam ethnic group." In this sense, I must acknowledge that my analytic approach has been influenced by my own border crossings, by retaking propositions from the theoretical debate on identity in both the Anglo-Saxon and the Latin American anthropological traditions. My last thoughts are a product of almost ten years of dialogue with Mam peasants, but also of the many dialogues in both anthropological traditions.

In both traditions there has been a tension among three points of view, which some have called primordialist-instrumentalist-historicist (e.g., Bentley 1987).[1] Both traditions have debated whether being indigenous is linked to primordial or essential traits of a pre-Hispanic origin (primordialist/essentialist), or whether they are resistance strategies of differentiation developed within colonial or postcolonial contexts (instrumentalist), or whether indigenous identity is a historical product in constant transformation, influenced by the contexts of inequality (historicist/constructivist). Yet what has changed has been the historical moment in which each of these perspectives has been hegemonic among Latin American and Anglo-Saxon anthropologists.

While American culturalism in the 1950s and 1960s searched in indigenous practices and rituals for the survival of ancient Mesoamerican civilizations,[2] the Mexican anthropologist Gonzalo Aguirre Beltrán, in his classic work *Regiones de refugio* (1967), pointed out that indigenous identity was a historical product born from colonial and postcolonial social relations. This antiessentialist position coincided with contemporary constructivism by positing identity as a relational historical product, and yet it inferred from this premise that indigenous cultures, because they were influenced by domination relations, had no validity and had to be transformed through acculturation (Aguirre Beltrán 1967, 1970).[3]

Strangely, thirty years later, when Aguirre Beltrán's works have been rejected by the so-called Mexican critical anthropology, because of the ideological support they provided to official indigenism, American and English neo-Marxist and poststructuralist social scientists are beginning to use historical constructivism as a way to explain how all identities are socially and culturally constructed in contexts of domination (Gilroy 1987; Clifford 1988; Rosaldo 1993; Hale 1994). In Latin America, meanwhile, because of the political struggle for the acknowledgment of indigenous rights, many anthropologists and indigenous leaders have used a strategic essentialism to claim the right to cultural difference (Cojti 1991; FIPI 1988; Bartolomé and Barabás 1996; León Portilla 1997).[4]

Strategic essentialisms cannot be disqualified without taking into account the historical and political contexts in which they are born and the open or hidden racism to which they respond (see Chapter 7). Yet indigenous organizations themselves are beginning to see the need to separate the utopic impulse of these primordialist representations from the limitations they impose on the construction of an alternative project of a nation (see Gutiérrez and Palomo 1999). I acknowledge that in the current Mexican political context, in which the deconstruction of indigenous cultures has been used to disqualify their "authenticity" and delegitimize their claims for autonomy, recovering Aguirre Beltrán's historical constructivisms is particularly debatable. Yet this book wants to give new meaning to these interpretations, rejecting the existence of a utopic space apart from power, which helps us to see the challenges and limitations any type of identity politics has to face. Contrary to those who have pointed to the internal contradictions in the everyday life of indigenous communities as an argument for denying the feasibility of autonomic projects (Viqueira 1999), I think that the acknowledgment of the way in which power relations influence our subjectivities does not deny the possibility of constructing, on the basis of this contradictory consciousness, new collective imaginaries.

The real question behind this debate is whether it is possible to point at the historical, changing, and contextual character of identities and yet support claims for the right to cultural difference. My answer is yes, as I have shown throughout this book. Mam indigenous women, together with women from other Mesoamerican regions, have undertaken this double fight: demanding from the state the right to cultural difference and trying to change within their communities traditions that deny their rights. It is not a struggle for the acknowledgment of an essential culture but for the right to reconstruct, confront, or reproduce their culture, not in the terms established by the state, but in those defined by the indigenous peoples themselves, within the framework of their own internal pluralisms.

The emergence of these new discourses confronting official definitions of the nation, as well as essentialist conceptions of culture and tradition, has come in a moment of rupture, in which indigenous peoples have claimed the right to "name," to establish the terms of the "dialogue." In these moments, which some have named "points of rupture" (Roseberry 1994) or "penetrations" (Willis 1981; Foley 1990), common sense (Comaroff and Comaroff 1991) or doxa (Bourdieu 1977), is challenged; what had been formerly assumed as natural becomes subject to debate or challenge, thus creating a crisis in the hegemony of the state.

The Zapatista uprising and the movements for autonomy that followed represent one of these moments of rupture. Zapatista peasants established the terms of the "dialogue," and a new language on "autonomy" and territorial control was claimed as their own by EZLN peasants. For some Mam peasants, this moment has represented the unification with a wider community made up of the "indigenous peoples of Mexico" and the appropriation of a new discourse on political and cultural rights.

Yet the coexistence of indigenous identity with other political and religious identities cannot be denied without the danger of imposing another cultural fundamentalism. The Zapatistas seem to be conscious of this danger, as reflected in their constant references to respect for religious and political pluralism. Contrary to Central American avant-garde political movements, the EZLN does not assume itself to be the carrier of the "correct political project," and its objective is not taking power. In its attempt to form alliances, it has called for a plural front in which popular movements can struggle in different ways for a true democracy. Neil Harvey (1996, 1998) refers to this pluralist project as an indigenous version of radical democracy. Taking up Chantal Mouffe's and Ernesto Laclau's proposals for liberal democracies (Laclau and Mouffe 1985; Mouffe 1996), Harvey points out that the proliferation of collective identities in peripheral countries has made possible the idea of a radical indigenous democracy in which the struggles of different social movements against different "enemies" can be articulated without losing their political specificity, through what they call a "chain of equivalences."

With regard to a radical postmodernism that in the name of respect for "the individual" denies the possibility of collective mobilization, Mouffe says,

> The kind of pluralism I am advocating requires the establishment of a common bond, so that the multiplicity of democratic identities and differences does not explode into a separatism that would lead to the negation of the political community; for without any reference to the political community, democratic politics cannot exist. Therefore, those of us who are committed to a radicalization and extension of the principles of liberty and equality should envisage a type of political community that is created through a chain of equivalence among democratic struggles and identities. (1996:44)

Achieving a sense of community based on respect for difference is the political challenge currently faced by the EZLN. Yet, now that the military siege is closing on Zapatista communities and the paramilitarization of Chiapas is increasing the differences between the sectors of indigenous society, Zapatista pluralism seems to be on trial.

The Zapatista command is calling on civil society to discuss different strategies for carrying on the struggle, trying to construct a "chain of equivalences" to articulate the struggles of different popular sectors. At the same time, local power groups are betting on internal differences among communities to develop their own "low-intensity war." From the Chiapas Sierra Madre to Las Margaritas rain forest, "unknown" groups, linked to local landowners, are beginning to distribute weapons in communities, trying to polarize internal differences. The success of one of these two strategies will determine the near future of Mam peasants and of all Chiapas indigenous peoples, as well as the possibilities of imagining a new type of nation.

NOTES

Preface

1. The term *neoliberalism* is used in the Mexican context to refer to a set of policies based on the diminished importance of the state and on privatization and economic and financial deregulation, together with the promotion of the export of manufactured goods. This economic model replaced the statist model, which prevailed from the 1930s to the beginning of the 1980s and was protectionist and based on import-substitution industrialization. In the economic terminology of international organisms, these policies have also been called "structural adjustment programs" and became widespread in the third world at the beginning of the 1980s.

2. NAFTA, known in Mexico as TLC (Tratado de Libre Comercio), is one of the main initiatives promoted by Salinas de Gortari's government to lock in economic reforms, especially with regard to commercial and financial programs. It is the first open trade agreement in the world signed by two developed countries, the United States and Canada, and a developing country, Mexico.

3. *Salinismo* is the term used in Mexico to refer to the government programs and administration of Carlos Salinas de Gortari.

4. Arturo Warman, "Chiapas Hoy," *La Jornada*, January 16, 1994.

Introduction

1. In the state of Chiapas, the 1990 General Census of Population and Housing (Censo General de Vivienda) reports 8,725 persons who identify themselves as Mam. This number includes refugees settled in the municipalities of Frontera Comalapa (629), La Trinitaria (132), Las Margaritas (1,068), Ocosingo (117), and Venustiano Carranza (108). As the Mam refugee population falls outside the scope of this book, their border experience is not discussed.

2. *Ejidos* were communal lands divided into small lots and given to peasants for their individual use. These lots could not be sold or mortaged. They could be inherited but not subdivided, and if a peasant moved away, his land remained with the communal governing body. Ejido lands were privatized by Salinas de Gortari's government at the beginning of 1992 (see Chapter 7). For the historical origin of the ejido, see Chapter 1.

3. The term *Mames* is the plural of *Mam.*

4. Throughout I use the pseudonym Las Ceibas to refer to this community.

5. The term *mestizo* is used in the Mexican context to designate a descendant of mixed Indian-white parentage, used more generally to refer to the Mexican population, which does not identify itself culturally as Indian.

6. For a critique of the conception of culture as cultural difference, see Rosaldo 1987:201.

7. During their first years as refugees, Guatemalan peasants received many demonstrations of solidarity from Mexican peasants, who allowed them to live on ejidal lands and supported them in emergencies. Mexicans gave refugees a piece of land on which to build their huts and cultivate their milpas, while in return the Mexicans could rely on a cheap and ready workforce for coffee harvesting. Over the years, the support the Guatemalans received from UNHCR and other international organizations began to cause unrest among the Mexican population. For an analysis of relations between Guatemalan refugees and Mexican peasants, see Hernández Castillo et al. 1992.

8. *Idiomista* is a local term that derives from *idioma,* "language"; a closer translation would be the neologism "languagist." It is used to refer to those people who speak an Indian language. The Spanish term is used throughout this book.

9. The term *antiguos,* or ancients, is used as a substantive to refer to ancestors.

10. *Indigenistas* refers to those anthropologists who theoretically justified the acculturation of indigenous peoples in the name of "progress." The terms *campesinista* and *descampesinista* refer to two lines of thought within Latin American Marxism. The campesinistas, influenced by Maoism, underline the importance of the peasantry as a political avant-garde in countries where productive forces are not well developed. Descampesinistas posit the necessary disappearance of the peasantry as a consequence of the development of productive forces and as a prerequisite for the formation of a proletarian avant-garde. For an analysis of these two positions, see Foladori 1981.

11. *Coyotes* are guides for hire for Mexican workers wishing to cross illegally into the United States. Some coyotes have become notorious for accepting money and then abandoning their "clients" in difficult or dangerous situations.

12. "Because I am in all cultures at the same time, soul between two worlds, three, four, my head buzzes with contradictions. I am disoriented by all the voices talking to me at the same time."

13. Andrés Medina, field diary, December 4, 1967.

14. Throughout, I use the words *finca* and *finquero* for coffee plantations and large landowners, respectively, because of the special meaning they carry in the historical memory of the Sierra Madre inhabitants.

15. The term *indigenismo* is used in the Mexican context to refer to a state policy, and this is the way it is used in this book, in contrast to Indianismo, used to refer to political ideologies having ethnic identity as their core claim.

First Border Crossing. Don Roberto

1. To respect the narrators' privacy, in the personal testimonies of the four Border Crossings I have taken the liberty of changing some details that might make possible their identification. Except for Don Eugenio Roblero, who asked explicitly to include his name and story in this book, all other names are pseudonyms. In several cases, I have completed individuals' stories by referring to the testimonies of relatives or friends.

2. The language that has been classified linguistically as Mam is also identified by speakers as Mame or Tokiol, and all three terms are currently used.

3. *Tata* is a term for "father." "Tata Lázaro" was the nickname used by popular sectors to refer to President Lázaro Cárdenas.

I. The Postrevolutionary National Project and the Mexicanization of the Mam People

1. The 1910 Mexican Revolution has been described as a "populist revolution" that did not target private property or the class structure of Mexican society and was characterized by following "the will of the masses whose aim was to ward off the social revolution by manipulating popular classes through the satisfaction of limited demands. . . . [L]ater, between 1929 and 1938, the masses were embedded in a corporatist system promoted by the official party and the semiofficial union organization" (Córdova 1974:33–34).

2. The term "popular sectors" is used in the Mexican context to refer to all members of the lower and (to a varying extent) lower middle classes, whether Indian or mestizo.

3. Striving to appease the popular sectors, Cárdenas made many changes in presidential protocol, for example, prohibiting tuxedos at official ceremonies and turning the Chapultepec Castle, which had been the residence of presidents, into a museum and living in his own home. In addition, he cut official incomes by half, allotting the rest to social projects, and created a free telegraph service so that peasants and workers could send him their complaints and opinions (see Córdova 1974; Anguiano 1975).

4. Interview with G.M., municipality of Mazapa de Madero, November 1994.

5. Interview with L.V., municipality of El Porvenir, September 1994.

6. Interview with L.V., municipality of El Porvenir, September 1994.

7. Interview with M.R., municipality of La Grandeza, October 1994.

8. Interview with S.V., municipality of El Porvenir, September 1994.

9. Following Benedict Anderson, I am referring to the nation as an imagined community, "because even the members of the smallest nation will never get to know their fellow-citizens, will never meet them, or even hear of them, still in their mind each of them lives the image of their communion" (Anderson 1983:15).

10. Interview with J.M., municipality of La Grandeza, February 1995.

11. Interview with A.M., municipality of Las Margaritas, January 1990.

12. Interview with N.V., municipality of El Porvenir, September 1994.

13. Interview with E.T., municipality of Tapachula, May 1995.

14. Interview with G.M., municipality of Mazapa de Madero, December 1994.

15. Interview with J.M., municipality of El Porvenir, May 1990. J.M. is sixty years old, so the events he is referring to probably took place at the end of the nineteenth century.

16. Coffee is a crop that requires intensive labor at harvest time but very little during the rest of the year.

17. Interview with E.R., municipality of El Porvenir, August 1994.

18. Interview with A.S., municipality of La Grandeza, February 1995.

19. Approximately 25 pounds.

20. Interview with F.M., municipality of Las Margaritas, October 1989. Based on his age (about sixty), we can estimate that these are three generations of workers, one at the end of the nineteenth century, another at the beginning of the twentieth century, and a third between the 1940s and 1950s.

21. Interview with F.S., municipality Bejucal de Ocampo, January 1990.

22. Interview with E.R., municipality El Porvenir, August 20, 1994.

23. Interview with E.R., municipality El Porvenir, August 20, 1994.

24. The PNR was the predecessor of the Partido Revolucionario Institucional (PRI), which has been in power in Mexico for more than sixty years.

25. Interview with N.M., municipality of El Porvenir, January 1990.

26. Interview with U.L., municipality of Las Margaritas, July 1990.

27. Interview with H.L., governor of the Presbyterian church of Mazapa de Madero, June 1990.

28. Testimonies collected in the municipalities of La Grandeza, El Porvenir, and Mazapa de Madero.

29. Interview with H.L., municipality of Mazapa de Madero, June 1990.

30. Interview with J.F., municipality of Mazapa de Madero, June 12, 1990.

31. Interview with H.L., municipality of Mazapa de Madero, June 1990.

32. Interview with M.H., municipality of Mazapa de Madero, September 1994.

33. Ibid.

2. The Modernizing Project

1. Onchocercosis has not been completely eradicated in Chiapas, although the number of cases has decreased considerably.

2. Data from the Documentation Center and Agrarian Information, Secretary of Agrarian Reform, Mexico 1988.

3. The INI's predecessors were the Department of Education and Culture for the Indigenous Race (Departamento de Educación y Cultura para la Raza Indígena), directed by José Vasconcelos, established in 1921; Houses for the Indian Student (Casas del Estudiante Indígena), directed by Moisés Sáenz, 1926; the Autonomous Department for Indigenous Matters (Departamento Autónomo de Asuntos Indígenas) 1936; and General Office for Indigenous Matters (Dirección General de Asuntos Indígenas), 1947.

4. The first CCI was founded at San Cristóbal de las Casas, under the direction of Aguirre Beltrán himself in March 1951, attempting to cover both the Tzotzil and Tzeltal regions. The Tzotzil CCI of Bochil and the Tzeltal CCI of Ocosingo were created in November 1971, the Chol of Salto del Agua in January 1973, the Tojolabal-Tzeltal of Las Margaritas in June 1974, and the Zoque of Copainalá in July 1975.

5. For a review of works by geographers and travelers to the Sierra Madre, see Fernández Galán 1995.

6. The anthropologist Manuel Gamio headed this study, and the participants in the ethnographic part were Anne Chapman, who wrote a report on economics, Arturo Monzón, who analyzed working conditions on coffee plantations, and Isabel Horcazitas and Ricardo Pozas, who studied aspects of the cultural life of the indigenous peoples in the infected region (Pozas 1952a, 1952b).

7. Ten years later, based on this same field experience, Pozas wrote a museographic script, having many of the characteristics of an anthropological essay.

8. Interview with G.H., municipality of El Porvenir, December 1994. As this man is sixty years old, he is telling about his experience in the fincas during the 1950s.

9. Interview with A.S., municipality of La Grandeza, February 1995.

10. His wish to contribute to the improvement of living conditions of indigenous peoples led Pozas to become director of the Indigenist Coordinator Center Tzeltal-Tzotzil (Centro Coordinador Indigenista Tzeltal-Tzotzil) in 1953; yet his critical views made him break off with official indigenism, a position he maintained until his death in 1993.

11. Interview with Andrés Medina, March 16, 1995.

12. Ibid.

13. Interview with Otto Schumann, March 21, 1995.

14. According to Otto Schumann, Tectiteco is not related to Cakchiquel, which is spoken by a large percentage of Guatemalan indigenous groups and was mistakenly used by indigenist officials (personal communication).

15. Interview with Otto Schumann, March 18, 1995.

16. Interview with Andrés Medina, March 16, 1995.

17. Ibid.

18. Ibid.

19. This trip included visits to the settlements of Tuzantán, Motozintla, Mazapa de Madero, Tierra Blanca, Valle Obregón, Amatenango de la Frontera, Chimalapa, Malé, Nueva Independencia, Revolución, El Porvenir, and Bejucal de Ocampo.

20. Interview with Andrés Medina, March 16, 1995.

21. Testimony of A.E., Ejido Las Ceibas, municipality of Las Margaritas, June 1989.

22. Testimony of U.R., municipality of Las Margaritas, November 1989.

23. Ibid.

24. Ibid.

Second Border Crossing. Pedro

1. "Publisher" (*publicador*) refers to a Jehovah's Witnesses preacher.

2. He is referring to the "civilizing through clothing" campaigns that were promoted under Governor Victorico Grajales's administration.

3. Interview in Ejido Las Ceibas, municipality of Las Margaritas, November 1989.

3. Mam Jehovah's Witnesses

1. For the history of the colonization of the Lacandon rain forest, see Paz Salinas 1989; Acevedo 1992; Hernández Castillo 1994.

2. Official censuses bundle together under the generic term "Protestant" all non-

Catholic religious groups, which for the Sierra municipalities and Las Margaritas totals 67,730 people representing 25 percent of the population included in the census (Chiapas XI Censo General de Población y Vivienda 1990, I:215–220). Yet at the national level these groups have grown surprisingly in recent years, becoming the second-largest community of Jehovah's Witnesses after the United States. By 1994 there were 9,574 congregations with 1.3 million members, representing 1.5 percent of Mexico's total population (Fortuny 1995:169).

3. Among the religious principles that differentiate the Jehovah's Witnesses from other Christian groups are the following. First, they consider that the mystery of the Trinity is a pagan myth that exists in several cultures. There is only one God. Second, Jesus is not God. He is only His son. Third, the soul is mortal and dies with the body but will resuscitate after Armageddon, when evil will be destroyed forever in the world. Fourth, baptism does not cleanse sin; it is only a symbol of dedication to Jehovah. It should be done by immersion and after special preparation. Fifth, they deny the virginity of Mary and affirm that if Jesus is not God, then Mary is not the Mother of God. She was a virgin when she conceived Jesus, but after Him she had other sons. For an in-depth analysis of the doctrinal principles of Jehovah's Witnesses, see Beckford 1975; Penton 1985.

4. This idea of a millennium was developed by the religious group's founder, Charles Taze Russell, who announced that God would descend to earth to rule for one thousand years from 1914 to 2914. But since God did not descend to earth in 1914, this prophecy was altered, establishing that God had descended in an imperceptible manner to fight against Satan. At the end of the thousand years, Satan and all sinners would be destroyed forever. The best 144,000 Jehovah's Witnesses would rule with God in Heaven; the others would live happily ever after.

5. During 1988 in the southern border region, I had access to *Watchtower* and *Awake!* magazines announcing the decadence of the national state. In borderland communities, I was able to read such articles as "The Main Victims of Religious Persecution" (*Awake!* 69, no. 11, June 1988); "The Last of the Large World Powers" (*Watchtower* 109, no. 10, May 1988); and "The Long March of Nations Is About to End" (*Watchtower* 109, no. 11, June 1988). For a description of the antinationalist discourse of Jehovah's Witnesses, see Stevenson 1967:160–161; Bottings and Bottings 1984:166–186; Hernández Castillo 1989:162–169; Kaplan 1989:4–7.

6. Interview with M.H., municipality of Las Margaritas, May 1989.

7. Interview with U.R., municipality of Las Margaritas, September 1989.

8. Interview with P.G., municipality of Las Margaritas, September 1989.

9. Interview with M.H., municipality of Las Margaritas, December 1989.

10. Interview with G.P., municipality of Las Margaritas, February 1990.

11. Interview with G.P., municipality of Las Margaritas, September 1989.

12. Interview with M.H., municipality of Las Margaritas, February 1990.

13. The Ceibas-Sur Company meets on Wednesdays, Fridays, and Sundays, the Ceibas-Norte Company on Tuesdays, Thursdays, and Sundays.

14. See "¿Qué ha logrado el movimiento feminista?" (What Has the Feminist Movement Achieved?) in *Awake!* 69, no. 14, June 1988.

15. Interview with U.H., municipality of Las Margaritas, October 1989.

16. Even some six-year-old girls lead the study of girls four or five years old.

17. Case studies of conversions to Jehovah's Witnesses can be found in the analysis of the migration of rural populations to urban areas in Belgium by Johan Leman (1979), of Polish workers to the north of France by Regis Dericquebourg (1977), and of Mexican peasants to the towns of Mérida and Guadalajara by Patricia Fortuny (1995).

18. Interview with U.R., municipality of Las Margaritas, May 1989.

19. Quoted by William Kaplan (1989:7) from J. F. Rutherford's *The Finished Mystery.*

20. Field information provided by the teacher J.C. in Ejido Las Ceibas, municipality of Las Margaritas, September 1989.

21. Interview with U.R., municipality of Las Margaritas, June 1989.

22. Interview with M.H., municipality of Las Margaritas, February 1989.

23. Interview with P.G., municipality of Las Margaritas, September 1989.

24. Interview with Z.L., municipality of Las Margaritas, February 1990.

25. Interview with F.P., Ejido Cuauhtémoc, municipality of La Trinitaria, April 1988.

26. For an analysis of the contents of *Watchtower* and *Awake!* distributed in the border region, see Hernández Castillo 1989.

27. Interview with Z.L., municipality of Las Margaritas, February 1990.

28. The others are the San Cristóbal District, which embraces the northern, central, and highlands regions, and the Tapachula District, comprising the Sierra and the municipalities of the coast.

29. At present, the Jehovah's Witnesses have ninety branches in two hundred countries and islands around the world. All these branches, including the Mexican one, are under the direction of a governing body whose headquarters are in Brooklyn, New York. The governing body is made up of three "anointed Christians" who belong to the 144,000 elected to ascend to Heaven after the battle of Armageddon but who at the moment are living in New York. The president of the governing body is F. W. Franz, who has held this position since 1977.

30. Spanish editions of both magazines are printed in Los Reyes, La Paz, in the state of Mexico. From there they are sent by mail from Mexico City to the municipal capital of La Trinitaria, where they are picked up by the ancients of the various companies established in the region, transported by bus to Ejido Jerusalén in Las Margaritas, and then carried on foot ten kilometers through the forest to Las Ceibas.

31. Interview with L.J., municipality of Las Margaritas, July 1989.

32. Interview with M.H., municipality of Las Margaritas, October 1989.

33. Proyecto de Cabañas y Centro Artesanal, Fondos de Solidaridad para la Promoción del Patrimonio Cultural de los Pueblos Indígenas, October 1991.

4. From Mestizo Mexico to Multicultural Mexico

1. Open criticism of this model can be found in the now-classic anthology *De eso que llaman Antropología Mexicana* (Warman et al. 1970) and in several articles in Instituto Nacional Indigenista, *INI treinta años después: Revisión crítica* (1978).

2. The Tarahumara Supreme Councils are also a recent creation whose origins date

from the 1930s. They represent a local appropriation of a government initiative to organize indigenous communities dispersed throughout the Sierra.

3. Interview with Don Gregorio Morales, first Mam supreme councillor, Mazapa de Madero, December 1994.

4. Interview with Mauricio Rosas Kifuri, October 27, 1995.

5. Interview with Carlos Saldívar, CCI director at Las Margaritas, Chiapas, October 1994.

6. Interview with Mauricio Rosas Kifuri, October 27, 1995.

7. Ibid.

8. Ibid.

9. Proyecto de Albergues Escolares, January 1981 ms., CCI Mam-Mochó-Cakchiquel, Mazapa de Madero.

10. Sección de Investigaciones Antropológicas, Oficio 025, October 13, 1978, CCI Mam-Mochó-Cakchiquel, Mazapa de Madero.

11. Reports of the CCI Mam-Mochó-Cakchiquel, 1979–1983.

Third Border Crossing. Don Eugenio

1. The Mam supreme councillor of the lowlands was elected first and was a man of Mazapa de Madero.

2. The term *gringo* is used in Chiapas to refer to any foreigner, regardless of his nationality.

3. The *cuerda* is a land measure used in Chiapas and Guatemala that is equivalent to approximately five hundred square meters.

4. He is referring to a cultural World Fair that took place in Europe in 1993.

5. Mam Dance Groups

1. Neither do I consider pertinent the distinction made by some authors between hegemonic process and hegemonic outcome (see Roseberry 1994; Mallon 1995). Mallon (1995:6–7) defines hegemonic processes as "a set of nested, continuous processes through which power and meaning are contested, legitimated and redefined in all levels of society," and states that "hegemonic processes become hegemonic outcome only when leaders partially deliver their promises and control the terms of political discourse through incorporation as well as repression." If we consider that even in those moments in which "leaders" seem to control political discourse it is being contested openly or subtly (Scott 1985), then it is necessary to consider hegemonic outcome only as an important stage in the hegemonic process.

2. Interview with Don Gregorio Morales, first Mam supreme councillor, Mazapa de Madero, December 1994.

3. Interview with Don Eugenio Roblero, second Mam supreme councillor, El Porvenir, August 1994.

4. Interview with Nicolás Páez, municipality of La Grandeza, June 1990.

5. Project "Rescate y Fortalecimiento de Leyes y Tradiciones, Memoria Histórica y Crónica del Pasado" (Rescue and Reinforcement of Laws and Traditions, Historical Memory and Chronicle of the Past) presented before the Solidarity Funds for the Promotion of the Cultural Heritage of Indigenous Peoples, January 1994.

6. Interview with Don Eugenio Roblero, second Mam supreme councillor, El Porvenir, August 1994.

7. *Ilol* is the term used among the Tzotzil to refer to traditional healers; in the Mam region, the term *chiman* is used.

8. The performances of "The Child's Baptism," "The Washing of the Head," and "The Planting of the Child" all refer to various rites of passage performed when a child is born. The first refers to the traditional baptism of the Catholic church, the second to a purification rite performed by the parents of the newborn, and the third to the burying of the child's umbilical cord, which is still done, to create a link between the newborn and Mother Earth. For a description of the third ceremony, see Gutiérrez 1996:112–113.

9. Interview with Don Eugenio Roblero, second Mam supreme councillor, El Porvenir, August 1994.

10. The National Solidarity Program (Programa Nacional de Solidaridad [PRONASOL]) was created by Carlos Salinas de Gortari's government (1988–1994) to carry out social programs designed for marginalized regions. PRONASOL is analyzed in Chapter 7.

11. Interview with E.M., municipality of El Porvenir, October 1994.

12. Interview with M.P., municipality of El Porvenir, October 1994.

13. For a critique of "communitarian democracy" from the perspective of indigenous women, see Grupo de Mujeres de San Cristóbal, "Memorias del Encuentro-Taller: Los Derechos de las Mujeres en Nuestras Costumbres y Tradiciones," May 1994. For a critical view of "indigenous consensus" from a gender perspective, see Collier 1995a, 1995b; Hernández Castillo and Ortíz Elizondo 1996.

14. For a critical analysis of the impact of the XEVFS radio programs, see Vargas 1994; for the specific experience of the Mam region, see Gutiérrez Alfonzo 1996.

15. Radio recording in Ejido El Rodeo, municipality of Siltepec, June 1990.

16. He is referring to a soap made with pork fat.

17. F.M.'s speech, Barrio Banderas, municipality of Siltepec, May 1994.

18. M.J.'s speech, Barrio Banderas, municipality of Siltepec, May 1994.

19. S.F.'s speech, Barrio Banderas, municipality of Siltepec, May 1994.

20. Interview with M.M., municipality of El Porvenir, November 1994.

21. Interview with Lic. Juan Armando Becerril, Coordinator of the Sierra Region from the Department of Ethnic Cultures (ICHC), November 24, 1994.

Fourth Border Crossing. Doña Luz

1. She is referring to Trabajo Común Organizado, Common Organized Labor, a workshop taught by the Catholic church to reflect on the importance of collective work. Its content is discussed in Chapter 6.

6. Organic Growers

1. The term *organic growers* or *organic agriculture* does not refer only to agriculture that does not use chemical products but requires the use of an integrated technological program. In the case of organic coffee, this program includes the use of shadow trees, organic fertilizer, and nonchemical pesticides, construction of terraces to avoid

erosion, and the growing of other crops to assure a balanced diet. International organizations need to certify the produce as organic. The term *agro-ecological* refers to a broad movement that promotes new forms of agricultural production that respect and preserve the environment.

2. By "communality," I mean a community feeling historically constructed through social practice, not Weber's meaning, infracommunity.

3. The term *Foranía* used by the Catholic church refers to a parochial geographic division created to organize pastoral work.

4. Prelacies possess the same organizational structure as dioceses, but they are more dependent on the Vatican and are usually under the care of religious orders, that of the Mixes being the Josephines and that of the Huaves, the Salesians.

5. Interview with Father Jorge Aguilar Reina, May 23, 1995, Tapachula, Chiapas.

6. Ibid.

7. In 1989 the International Coffee Agreement was suspended, and prices collapsed, reducing the revenue of the producers by 60 percent. For an analysis of this crisis, see Renard 1999:99–115.

8. Interview with Father Jorge Aguilar Reina, May 23, 1995, Tapachula, Chiapas.

9. Biodynamics is an approach to agriculture that takes into account the preservation and recycling of the life forces with which the producers are working.

10. This first group had no name yet but was constituted as a Social Solidarity Society (Sociedad de Solidaridad Social), a legal entity, under the name Indígenas de la Sierra Madre de Motozintla (ISMAM) in October 1988.

11. For an analysis of the alternative market and the equitable market, see Renard 1999.

12. For a longer version of this section, see Hernández Castillo and Nigh 1998.

13. Interview with C.P.G., Unión Fuerza Liberadora, October 7, 1994.

14. Paper presented by Ciro Pérez at the regional Forum of Mam and Mochó Communities on Alternative Production Proposals to Face Poverty in Chiapas (Foro Regional de Comunidades Mames y Mochós sobre Propuestas de Producción Alternativa ante la Pobreza en Chiapas), March 1–3, 1993.

15. Chief Seattle's speech has become a symbolic document in the agro-ecological movement. The most commonly circulated version of it was actually written in about 1967 by Tom Perry for an environmental film. The only other version was published by a Seattle newspaper editor in 1887, but nobody knows if this publication reproduced Chief Seattle's actual words.

16. Interview with J.S., Motozintla, Chiapas, November 5, 1994.

17. Interview with C.P.G., Unión Fuerza Liberadora, October 7, 1994.

18. Ibid.

19. Interview with Father Jorge Aguilar Reina, May 23, 1995, Tapachula, Chiapas.

20. Testimony collected by Carlos Gutiérrez, municipality of El Porvenir.

21. Interview with Cedema Morales Velázquez, member of the Nan Choch cooperative society, published in "La Doble Jornada," *La Jornada*, September 5, 1994:5.

22. Proyecto de Granjas Colectivas Avícolas y Bovinas de "Nuevo Amanecer de la Sierra," Zaragoza, Motozintla, 1995.

23. Interview with Cedema Morales Velázquez, member of the Nan Choch cooperative society, published in "La Doble Jornada," *La Jornada*, September 5, 1994:5.

7. From PRONASOL to the Zapatista Uprising

1. See *Diario Oficial de la Federación*, February 1992.

2. Interview with P.M., municipality of El Porvenir, April 1994.

3. News Summary from the Center for Analysis and Information of Chiapas (CIACH), February 1992.

4. On January 28, 1992, the *Diario Oficial de México* published a text as an addition to Article 4 in the Constitution. Now, the first paragraph reads as follows: "The Mexican Nation has a multicultural composition originally based on its indigenous peoples. The Law will protect and promote the development of their languages, cultures, habits, customs, resources, specific forms of social organization and will guarantee that their members have effective access to state jurisdiction. In all agrarian trials and procedures in which they are part, their uses and customs will be taken into consideration in the terms established by the Law."

5. This new Agrarian Law states, "Land distribution is no longer possible, since there are no more lands to be distributed; for security in land tenure would not be real, and above all, because it would mean cheating applicants with something that cannot be fulfilled. Reality demands congruence. The reformed Article 27 no longer considers land distribution acts. In accordance, sections X, XI, XII, XIII and XIV, containing this obligation of the state, have been abolished" (Procuraduría Agraria 1993:11–12).

6. Speech by CEOIC representative, October 12, 1995, San Cristóbal de las Casas, Chiapas.

7. Data obtained from the Distrito de Desarrollo Rural No. 07, Ministry of Agriculture, for 1994.

8. Interview with G.C., Col. Belisario Domínguez, Motozintla, November 3, 1993.

9. Critical anthropologists of the 1970s were invited to join the state apparatus in the following two decades. Ironically, in 1979 Arturo Warman criticized the link between Mexican anthropology and the state, pointing out that "anthropological thought has developed within institutions whose goals are not scientific and that establish concrete limits to its development and frequently exert some censorship. Rather than rebel, anthropologists have enthusiastically joined the bureaucratic system. They have strived to establish guild rights by paying with their own independence. They have condemned and persecuted audacity and originality to defend their own corporate rights. Ironically, they have not even conquered their urgent right to retirement" (Warman 1970:30). It looks as if, after joining Salinas de Gortari's administration, Warman has at least conquered his right to retirement.

10. Project "Acquisition of Musical Instruments, Ejido Pacayal," Solidarity Funds for the Promotion of the Culture of Indigenous Peoples, 1992.

11. Interview with David Velasco, Tuxtla Gutiérrez, Chiapas, March 1995.

12. The first official declaration on the uprising was given on January 2, by Socorro Díaz, director of social readaptation and civil protection of the Ministry of the Interior, who pointed out that the rebels were "violent groups with a mixture of interests

and persons from the country as well as from abroad, that have managed to manipulate few indigenous persons." Days later, President Salinas de Gortari again denied that it was an indigenous rebellion.

13. Interview with A.S. in the camp for displaced communities, Comitán, Chiapas, March 12, 1994.

14. Interview with U.R. in the camp for displaced persons, Comitán, Chiapas, March 12, 1994.

15. Invitation to Regional Forum of Mam and Mochó Communities on Proposals for an Alternative Production for Facing Poverty in Chiapas, March 1994.

16. Press review, *El Sureste de Chiapas*, January–December 1994.

17. *La Palabra*, bulletin of the Centro de Información y Análisis de Chiapas (CIACH), March 1997.

18. For a detailed analysis of the way projects for autonomy are functioning in Chiapas and the rest of the country, see Burguete 1999.

19. Modifications in the counterproposal by the government were presented as "changes in form, not in content"; yet a detailed analysis of the document shows that the changes placed limitations on territorial control, the use of resources, and forms of self-government. For a deeper analysis of these documents, see Fernández-Souza, Flota, and Moguel 1997.

20. *La Jornada*, January 10, 1997:13.

21. *La Jornada*, January 19, 1997:10.

22. The differences between communalists, represented by Oaxaca's indigenous movement, and regionalists, led by the Asamblea Nacional Indígena Plural por la Autonomía (ANIPA), have caused the division in the Indigenous National Congress (Congreso Nacional Indígena [CNI]), an organism created after the Zapatista uprising with indigenous organizations throughout the country. These same differences caused a rift between ANIPA and its advisers and the EZLN. For a description of these conflicts, see Díaz Polanco 1997.

23. Concrete proposals on autonomy by the EZLN can be found in the San Andrés Agreements (Ce-Acatl 1996). The proposals of ANIPA, a pioneering organization in the struggle for indigenous autonomy, with great influence in the Tojolabal region, can be found in Burguete 1999; and for an exposition of communalist conceptions, see Regino 1997. An academic analysis of the different positions can be found in Hernández Castillo, Mattiace, and Rus n.d.

24. An example of this idealized point of view is the discourse of some Waxaritaris or Huichol leaders, who during a meeting of the CNI expressed their support for EZLN's demand for autonomy, pointing out, "We are Mexican Waxaritari Indians. We do not want to stop being it. We defend our will to live in the world fulfilling the sacred obligation of planting and giving thanks, so that life may continue. We are survivors of a very far past, and our culture is a message of life, now that the world is in danger of being destroyed by pollution of the seas, the rivers and the air and by the killing of men, plants, and animals" (Speech of the Huichol leader in the Congreso Nacional Indígena, October 12, 1996). In the same sense, the anthropologist and historian Miguel León Portilla defends indigenous autonomy: "Indigenous peoples preserve values that should

be cherished and which in the modern world, in risk of globalization, have been lost. Think of their sense of community and solidarity; their family cohesion; their respect for nature and the knowledge of old age, their rejection of corruption" (*La Jornada*, August 8, 1997:9).

25. The host organizations were the Grupo de Mujeres de San Cristóbal de las Casas A.C.:, the Organización de Médicos Indígenas de los Altos de Chiapas (OMIECH), the Unión de Artesanas S'paz Joloviletik, and the Comisión de Mujeres de CONPAZ.

26. Zapatista women demand, among other things, the right to political participation on equal terms with men, the right to a life free from sexual and domestic violence, the right to decide whom to marry, and the right to decide the number of children they will have. For a wider analysis of the Law of Women, see Hernández Castillo 1994, 1998a.

27. Grupo de Mujeres de San Cristóbal 1994.

28. Ibid.

29. *La Jornada*, December 7, 1995:15.

30. Proposals by indigenous women to the Congreso Nacional Indígena, in the seminar "Reformas al Artículo Cuarto Constitucional," October 8–12, 1996, México, D.F.

31. Paramilitary groups are armed groups that have a direct or indirect relationship with the state apparatus and take specific actions to weaken the actors opposing the present regime; their actions are undertaken in specific political moments, and their goals are clearly defined.

32. *Chiapas al Día*, no. 127, September 19, 1998, CIEPAC, Chiapas, México.

33. The origin and actions of Paz y Justicia have been documented by the Centro de Derechos Humanos Fray Bartolomé de las Casas (1996). For a description of the other thirty-one paramilitary groups in the state, see *Chiapas al Día*, CIEPAC, nos. 139, 140, 144, 154.

34. See *Chiapas al Día*, CIEPAC, no. 140, December 1998.

35. Ibid., nos. 35–36, April 1998.

Conclusion

1. Others have characterized these same tendencies as the School of Cultural Survival, the School of Resistance, and the Processualist School (e.g., Field 1994). Still others have related it to the theory of practice, developed by the French sociologist Pierre Bourdieu (e.g., Bentley 1987).

2. Many pioneering works of the so-called Harvard Project were carried out from this perspective. On this subject, see Vogt 1978.

3. The instrumentalist perspective also became very popular within both traditions under the influence of Fredrik Barth's seminal work (1969), and ethnic identity began to be analyzed as a tool for resistance to be "used" against dominant sectors (Glazer and Moynihan 1975; Varese 1989).

4. Criticism of this essentialism has also come from Latin American anthropologists who have analyzed the way in which collective identities are historically constructed in processes of cultural hybridism (Mato 1994; García Canclini 1995; Sierra

1997) in which regional histories influence the formation of several levels of identity (Lomnitz-Adler 1992). Essentialism has also been criticized by those who claim the validity of the processes of reinvention of traditions (Hernández Castillo 1994; Zarate Hernández 1994).

GLOSSARY

ANIPA: Asamblea Nacional Indígena Plural por la Autonomía (National Plural Assembly for Indigenous Autonomy).

Avecindados: Peasants who live on ejido lands but do not have land rights.

Bolos: Drunkards.

Cacicazgo: Chiefdomship, or the jurisdiction of a *cacique*.

Cacique: During the colonial period, the native ruler of a community; in modern times, the political boss of a community.

Caciquismo: The political system that imposes the rule of the cacique.

Cafetal: Coffee plantation.

Calzón rajado: Short piece of woolen cloth worn by men on top of their cotton trousers.

Caporal: Foreman.

Cashlanes: Local term to refer to nonindigenous peoples living in Mexico.

Castilian: Spanish language, or people who speak Spanish.

CCI: Centro Coordinador Indigenista (Indigenist Coordinator Center).

CEOIC: Consejo Estatal de Organizaciones Indígenas y Campesinas (Council of Indigenous and Peasant Organizations).

CEPROCOM: Centro de Producción Comunitaria (Center for Community Production).

Chamulas: Term for the people of San Juan Chamula (Tzotzil-Maya Indians).

Chapines: Derogatory term for Guatemalans.

Chiman: Sorcerer.

Chuj: Local term to refer to the *temazcal*, or steambath, of pre-Hispanic origin still used in many indigenous communities in Mesoamerica. It is a small room with a low ceiling made of earth and cane, in which there is a small stove with stones that are heated at a very high temperature to produce steam.

CIACH: Centro de Información y Análisis de Chiapas (Chiapas Center for Information and Analysis).

CNC: Confederación Nacional Campesina (National Peasant Confederation).

CNI: Congreso Nacional Indígena (Indigenous National Congress).

COICS: Coordinadora Indígena y Campesina de la Sierra (Sierra Indigenous and Peasant Organization).

Compadre: Kinship relationship between a parent and a godparent.

CONASUPO: Compañía Nacional de Subsistencias Populares (National Company of Popular Basic Products).

CONPAZ: Coodinadora de Organizaciones Gubernamentales por la Paz (Governmental Organizations Coordination for Peace)

Copal: Pungent pine pitch incense used in Maya religious ceremonies.

COPLAMAR: Coordinación Federal del Plan Nacional de Zonas Deprimadas y Grupos Marginados (Federal Coordination of the National Plan for Marginalized Areas and Groups).

Corte: Piece of cotton cloth woven on a foot loom; wrapped around women's waists and tied by a hand-woven belt.

Coyotaje: Corrupt practices of middlemen in which advantage is taken of the lack of market opportunities.

Coyote: Guides for hire for Guatemalan workers wishing to cross illegally into Mexico on their way to the United States. Also used to refer to crooked intermediaries who arrange for the sale of small producers' coffee.

CTM: Confederación de Trabajadores Mexicanos (Confederation of Mexican Workers).

Ejidatario: Owner of ejido lands.

Ejido: Land returned to a community as part of land reform.

ENAH: Escuela Nacional de Antropología e Historia (National School of Anthropology and History).

Enganchadores: Recruiters.

Enganchamiento: System in which recruiters toured indigenous villages, paying workers in advance and forcing them to remain on the plantation until the owner considered that they had worked enough to repay their debts.

EPR: Ejército Popular Revolucionario (Revolutionary Popular Army).

EZLN: Ejército Zapatista de Liberación Nacional (Zapatista National Liberation Army).

Finca: A large farm; in Chiapas usually a commercial plantation growing coffee for sale on the international market.

Finquero: The owner of a finca.

FIPI: Frente Independente de Pueblos Indígenas (Independent Front of Indigenous Peoples).

FOCIES: Frente de Organizaciones y Comunidades Indígenas de la Sierra (Front of Indigenous Organizations and Communities of the Sierra).

Galleras: Plantation living quarters for laborers.

GEPA: German Environmental Protection Agency.

Huipil: Hand-woven blouse worn by indigenous women.

Idiomista: A local term for those who speak an Indian language. The word derives from *idioma,* or language. A closer translation is the neologism "languagist."

Ilol: Practitioner of traditional medicine.

Indigenismo: State policies that promoted integration, designed for indigenous peoples by non-Indians.

INI: Instituto Nacional Indigenista (National Indigenist Institute).

ISMAM: Indígenas de la Sierra Madre de Motozintla (Motozintla Sierra Madre Indigenous Peoples).

Jornaleros: Day laborers.

Mayordomo: Local finca administrator.

Mestizo: Term used to designate a descendant of mixed Indian-white parentage, used more generally to refer to the Mexican population that does not identify itself culturally as Indian.

NAFTA: North American Free Trade Agreement.

Naguales: Witches.

NGO: Nongovernmental organization.

OCEZ: Organización Campesina Emiliano Zapata (Emiliano Zapata Peasant Organization).

Ocote: Pine pitch.

OMIECH: Organización de Médicos Indígenas de los Altos de Chiapas (Organization of Indigenous Doctors of the Chiapas Highlands).

OPEZ: Organización Proletaria Emiliano Zapata (Emiliano Zapata Proletariat Organization).

Peones acasillados: Workers who live on a plantation. They usually work for free in exchange for a place to live or a piece of land on which to grow their corn.

PIDER: Proyectos de Inversión para el Desarrollo Rural (Rural Development Investment Projects).

PNR: Partido Nacional Revolucionario (National Revolutionary Party).

Pozol: Local drink made with water and corn paste.

PRD: Partido de la Revolución Democrática (Party of the Democratic Revolution).

PRI: Partido Revolucionario Institucional (Institutional Revolutionary Party).

PROCAMPO: State subsidy to small agricultural growers for the production of basic grains.

PRONASOL: Programa Nacional de Solidaridad (National Solidarity Program).

Publicador: Publisher; a Jehovah's Witnesses preacher.

SEP: Secretaría de Educación Pública (Ministry of Education).

SSS: Sociedades de Solidaridad Social (Social Solidarity Societies).

STI: Sindicato de Trabajadores Indígenas (Indigenous Workers Union).

TCO: Trabajo Común Organizado (Organized Communal Work).

TLC: Tratado de Libre Comercio. The name used in Mexico for NAFTA.

Tzolkin: Ritual Maya calendar.

UCIRI: Unión de Comunidades Indígenas de la Región del Istmo (Union of Indigenous Communities of the Istmo Region).

UNHCR: United Nations High Commissioner for Refugees.

BIBLIOGRAPHY

Acevedo, Marina
1992   "Margaritas: Una experiencia de frontera." Master's thesis, Instituto José María Luis Mora, Mexico City.

Aguirre Beltrán, Gonzalo
1967   *Regiones de refugio.* Mexico City: Ed. Instituto Indigenista Interamericano.
1970   *El proceso de aculturación y el cambio sociocultural en México.* Mexico City: Ed. Comunidad, Instituto de Ciencias Sociales, Universidad Iberoamericana.
[1953] 1981   *Formas de gobierno indígena.* Mexico City: Serie Clásicos de la Antropología INI.

Alvarez Béjar, Alejandro
1992   "Industrial Restructuring and the Role of Mexican Labor in NAFTA." *UC Davis Law Review* 27:897–915.

Alvarez Garín, Raúl
1998   *La estela de Tlatelolco: Una reconstrucción histórica del movimiento estudiantil del 68.* Mexico City: Ed. Grijalbo.

Anderson, Benedict
1983   *Imagined Communities: Reflection on the Origin and Spread of Nationalism.* London: Verso.

Anguiano, Arturo
1975   *El estado y la política obrera del cardenismo.* Mexico City: Ed. Era.

ANIPA
1996   Proyecto de Iniciativa de Decreto para la Creación de Regiones Autónomas Presentado en la V Asamblea Nacional. April 29–May 1, 1996, Chilapa, Guerrero.

Annis, Sheldon
1988   *God and Production in a Guatemalan Town.* Austin: University of Texas Press.

Anzaldúa, Gloria
1987   *Borderlands/La Frontera: The New Mestiza.* San Francisco: Spinsters/Aunt Lute.
Aramoni, Dolores
1992   *Los refugios de lo sagrado: Religiosidad, conflicto y resistencia entre los zoques de Chiapas.* Serie Regiones. Mexico City: CONACULTA.
Arizpe, Lourdes, Fernanda Paz, and Margarita Velázquez
1993   *Cultura y cambio global: Percepciones sociales sobre la deforestación en la selva Lacandona.* Mexico City: Centro Regional de Investigaciones Multidisciplinarias/UNAM/Grupo Editorial Miguel Angel Porrúa.
Barth, Fredrik
1969   *Ethnic Groups and Boundaries.* Boston: Little, Brown.
Bartolomé, Miguel Alberto, and Alicia Barabas
1996   *La Pluralidad en peligro: Procesos de transfiguración y extinción cultural en México.* Mexico City: Colección de Regiones de México INAH-INI.
Bartra, Armando
1985   *Los herederos de Zapata.* Mexico City: Ed. Era.
Basave Benítez, Agustín
1992   *México mestizo: Análisis del nacionalismo mexicano en torno a la mestizofilia de Andrés Molina Enríquez.* Mexico City: Fondo de Cultura Económica.
Bastian, Jean-Pierre
1983   *Protestantismo y sociedad en México.* Mexico City: Casa Unida de Publicaciones.
1989   "Para una aproximación teórica al fenómeno religioso protestante en América Latina." *Cristianismo y Sociedad* 23(85):61–69.
1990   "La mutation des Protestantismes Latino-Américains: Une perspective socio-historique." Paper presented at the seminar Religion and Society CIESAS-Sureste, San Cristóbal de las Casas, Chiapas.
Beckford, James
1975   *The Trumpet of Prophecy: A Sociological Study of Jehovah's Witnesses.* London: Basil Blackwell.
Benjamin, Thomas
1990   *El camino a Leviatán: Chiapas y el estado mexicano 1891–1947.* Trans. Sara Sefchovich. Mexico City: CONACULTA.
1995   *Chiapas tierra rica, pueblo pobre.* Trans. Ramón Vera Herrera. Mexico City: Ed. Grijalbo.
Bentley, Carter
1987   "Ethnicity and Practice." *Comparative Studies in Society and History* 29(1):24–55.
Berzley, Williams, Cheryl English, and William French, eds.
1994   *Rituals of Rule, Rituals of Resistance: Public Celebrations and Popular Culture in Mexico.* Wilmington, Del.: Scholarly Resources.
Bonfil Batalla, Guillermo, ed.
1981   *Utopia y revolución: El pensamiento político contemporáneo de los indios en América Latina.* Mexico City: Nueva Imagen.
1987   *México profundo.* Mexico City: SEP-CIESAS.
Bottings, Heather, and Gary Bottings
1984   *The Orwellian World of Jehovah's Witnesses.* Toronto: University of Toronto Press.

Bourdieu, Pierre
1971   "Genèse et structures du champ religieux." *Revue Française de Sociologie* (Paris) 12:15–40.
1977   *Outline of a Theory of Practice.* Trans. Richard Nice. Cambridge: Cambridge University Press.
Bruce, Robert, and Carlos Robles
1969   "La lengua de Huehuetán (Waliwi)." *Anales del Instituto Nacional de Antropología e Historia* 1(49):115–122.
Burguete Cal y Mayor, Aracely, ed.
1999   *México: Experiencias de autonomía indígena.* Copenhagen: IWGIA-CECADEPI-RAP.
Bustamante, Jorge A.
1992   "Identidad y cultura nacional desde la perspectiva de la Frontera Norte." In *Decadencia y auge de las identidades,* ed. José Manuel Valenzuela Arce, 91–118. Tijuana: El Colegio de la Frontera Norte.
Campbell, Howard
1994   *Zapotec Renaissance: Ethnic Politics and Cultural Revivalism in Southern Mexico.* Albuquerque: University of New Mexico Press.
Cárdenas, Lázaro
1940   "Discurso en Pátzcuaro, Michoacán." Ms. INI Archives.
Casaus Arzú, Martha
1992   *Guatemala: Linaje y racismo.* Guatemala: Ed. FLACSO.
CCI Mazapa de Madero
1994   Informe sexenal (1988–1994) Centro Coordinador Indigenista Mam-Mochó-Cakchiquel. Mazapa de Madero: INI.
Ce-Acatl
1996   "Los primeros acuerdos de Sacam Ch'en." *Ce-Acatl Revista de la Cultura del Anáhuac* 78–79 (March–April):9–60.
Centro de Derechos Humanos "Fray Bartolomé de las Casas"
1996   *Ni paz, ni justicia: Informe general y amplio acerca de la guerra civil que sufren los choles en la zona norte de Chiapas.* San Cristóbal de las Casas: Ed. Fray Bartolomé.
Clifford, James
1988   *The Predicament of Culture: Twentieth-Century Ethnography, Literature and Art.* Cambridge, Mass.: Harvard University Press.
Cline, Howard F.
1962   *Mexico: Revolution to Evolution (1940–1960).* London: Oxford University Press.
Cojti Cuxil, Demetrio
1991   *Configuración del pensamiento político del Pueblo Maya.* Quezaltenango: Asociación de Escritores Mayas de Guatemala.
Collier, George
1994   *Ya Basta! Land and the Zapatista Rebellion in Chiapas.* Oakland, Calif.: Food First Book.
Collier, Jane
1995a   *El derecho Zinacanteco: Procesos de disputar en un pueblo tzotzil.* Mexico City: CIESAS-UNICAH.
1995b   "Problemas teórico-metodológicos en la antropología jurídica." In *Pueblos indí-*

genas ante el Derecho, ed. Victoria Chenaut and María Teresa Sierra, 45–78. Mexico City: CIESAS-CEMCA.

Comaroff, Jean
1985   *Body of Power, Spirit of Resistance: The Culture and History of a South African People.* Chicago: University of Chicago Press.

Comaroff, John, and Jean Comaroff
1991   *Of Revelation and Revolution: Christianity, Colonialism and Consciousness in South Africa.* Chicago: University of Chicago Press.
1992   *Ethnography and the Historical Imagination.* Boulder, Colo.: Westview Press.

Comisión Nacional de Derechos Humanos
1992   "Informe sobre el problema de las expulsiones en las comunidades indígenas de los Altos de Chiapas y los derechos humanos." Mexico City: CNDH.

CONPAZ
1996   *Militarización y violencia en Chiapas.* Ed. CONPAZ. Mexico City: Producción Editorial SIPRO.

Córdova, Arnaldo
1974   *La política de masas del cardenismo.* Mexico City: Serie Popular Era.

Cornelius, Wayne, Ann L. Craig, and Jonathan Fox, eds.
1994   *Transforming State-Society Relations in Mexico: The National Solidarity Strategy.* U.S. Contemporary Perspectives Series No. 6. San Diego: Center for U.S.-Mexican Studies, University of California, San Diego.

De la Fuente, José Manuel
1952   "La onchocercosis en Chiapas." *Ateneo* 3 (January–February–March):49–70. Tuxtla Gutiérrez: ICHC.

De la Peña, Guillermo
1997   "Notas preliminares sobre la ciudadanía étnica." Paper presented at the Annual Meeting of the Latin American Studies Association, Guadalajara, Jalisco.

Denich, Dette
1995   "Of Arms, Men and Ethnic War in (Former) Yugoslavia." In *Feminism, Nationalism and Militarism*, ed. Constance R. Sutton, 32–43. Arlington, Va.: American Anthropological Association.

Dericquebourg, Regis
1977   "Les temoins de Jehovah dans le nord de la France: Implantation et expansion." *Social Compass* (Belgium) 24:71–82.

De Vos, Jan
1988   *Oro verde: La conquista de la selva Lacandona por los madereros tabasqueños 1822–1949.* Mexico City: Fondo de Cultura Económica.

Díaz Polanco, Héctor
1985   *La cuestión étnico-nacional.* Mexico City: Ed. Línea.
1997   *La rebelión Zapatista y la autonomía.* Mexico City: Siglo XXI.

Documento Diocesano
1979   "El Congreso Indígena." Ms. Diócesis de San Cristóbal de las Casas.

Dresser, Denise
1994   "Bringing the Poor Back In: National Solidarity as a Strategy of Regime Legitimation." In *Transforming State-Society Relations in Mexico: The National Solidarity*

Strategy, ed. Wayne Cornelius, Ann L. Craig, and Jonathan Fox, 143–166. U.S. Contemporary Perspectives Series No. 6. San Diego: Center for U.S.-Mexican Studies, University of California, San Diego.

Eber, Christine
1995   *Women and Alcohol in a Highland Maya Town: Water of Hope, Water of Sorrow.* Austin: University of Texas Press.

Esponda, Hugo
1986   *El presbiterianismo en Chiapas: Orígenes y desarrollo.* Mexico City: Ed. El Faro.

Fernández Galán, María Elena
1995   "Viajeros de la Sierra Madre de Chiapas." *Anuario del Instituto de Estudios Indígenas* (Tuxtla Gutiérrez):137–175.

Fernández-Souza, Jorge, Enrique Flota, and Julio Moguel
1997   "¿Quien miente sobre los acuerdos de San Andrés?" *La Jornada del Campo* (México), October 1:8.

Field, Les
1994   "Who Are the Indians: Reconceptualizing Indigenous Identity, Resistance, and the Role of Social Science in Latina America." *Latin American Research Review* 29(3):120–132.

FOCIES
1994   "Memorias del Foro Regional de Comunidades Mames y Mochós sobre Propuestas de Producción Alternativa ante la Pobreza en Chiapas." Ms. Motozintla. March 1–3.

Foladori, Guillermo
1981   *Polémica en torno a las teorías del campesinado.* Mexico City: Colección Cuicuilco ENAH/INAH.

Foley, Douglas E.
1990   *Learning Capitalist Culture: Deep in the Heart of Tejas.* Philadelphia: University of Pennsylvania Press.

Fortuny, Patricia
1995   "On the Road to Damascus: Pentecostals, Mormons and Jehovah's Witnesses in Mexico." Ph.D. dissertation, University College, London.

Foucault, Michel
1979   *Discipline and Punish: The Birth of the Prison.* Trans. A. Sheridan. New York: Vintage.

Fox, Jonathan
1993   *The Politics of Food in Mexico: State, Power and Social Mobilization.* Ithaca: Cornell University Press.
1994   "Targeting the Poorest: The Role of the National Indigenous Institute in Mexico Solidarity Program." In *Transforming State-Society Relations in Mexico: The National Solidarity Strategy*, ed. Wayne Cornelius, Ann L. Craig and Jonathan Fox, 179–216. U.S. Contemporary Perspectives Series No. 6. San Diego: Center for U.S.-Mexican Studies University of California, San Diego.

Frente Independiente de Pueblos Indios (FIPI)
1988   "Frente Independiente de Pueblos Indios." *México Indígena* (INI) 23, no. 4(July–August):10–12.

Freyermuth, Graciela
1993   *Médicos tradicionales y médicos alópatas: Un encuentro difícil en los Altos de Chiapas.*
        Tuxtla Gutiérrez: CIESAS-Sureste/ICHC/Gobierno del estado de Chiapas.
Friedlander, Judith
1975   *Being Indian in Hueyapan: A Study of Forced Identity in Contemporary Mexico.* New
        York: St. Martin's Press.
Gamio, Manuel
1917   *Forjando patria.* Mexico City: Ed. Porrua.
[1935] 1987   *Hacia un México nuevo.* Mexico City: INI.
García, Daniel
1995   *El presbiterianismo en México.* Mexico City: Ed. El Faro.
García Canclini, Néstor
1995   *Hybrid Cultures: Strategies for Entering and Leaving Modernity.* Trans. Christo-
        pher L. Chiappari and Silvia L. López. Minneapolis: University of Minnesota
        Press.
García de León, Antonio
1985   *Resistencia y utopia.* 2 vols. Mexico City: Ed. Era.
1996   "El costo de la guerra." In *Militarización y violencia en Chiapas,* ed. CONPAZ,
        51–53. Mexico City: Producción Editorial SIPRO.
García Ruíz, Jesús
1985   "Le Mames." Ms. Paris: CNRS.
Garma, Carlos
1994   "El problema de los testigos de Jehová en las escuelas mexicanas." *Nueva Antro-
        pología* 45:21–31.
Garrido, Luis Javier
[1982] 1991   *El partido de la revolución institucionalizada: La formación del nuevo estado
        en México.* Mexico City: Ed. Siglo XXI.
Garza Caligaris, Anna María, and Rosalva Aída Hernández Castillo
1998   "Encuentros y enfrentamientos de los tzotziles pedranos con el Estado mexi-
        cano: Una perspectiva histórico-antropologica para entender la violencia en
        Chenalhó." In *La otra palabra: Mujeres y violencia en Chiapas, antes y después de
        Acteal,* coord. R. Aída Hernández, 39–62. Mexico City: CIESAS/COLEM/
        CIAM.
Garza Caligaris, Ana María, and Juana María Ruíz Ortíz
1992   "Madres Solteras Indígenas." *Mesoamérica* 23:67–77.
Gilroy, Paul
1987   *"There Ain't No Black in the Union Jack": The Cultural Politics of Race and Nation.*
        London: Hutchinson.
Giménez, Gilberto
1988   *Sectas religiosas en el sureste de México.* Cuadernos de la Casa Chata No. 161.
        Mexico City: CIESAS/SEP.
Glazer, Nathan, and Daniel Moynihan
1975   *Ethnicity: Theory and Experience.* Cambridge, Mass.: Harvard University Press.
Glick-Schiller, Nina, Linda Basch, and Cristina Blanc-Szanton, eds.
1992   *Towards a Transnational Perspective on Migration: Race, Class, Ethnicity and Nation-
        alism Reconsidered.* New York: New York Academy of Science.

González Ponciano, Jorge Ramón
1991   "Frontera, ecología y soberanía nacional: La colonización de la Franja Fronteriza de Marqués de Comillas." *Anuario del Instituto Chiapaneco de Cultura* (Tuxtla Gutiérrez):54–84.

Grajales, Victorico
1933   "Informe que el C. Gobernador Victorico Grajales rinde a la XXXIV Legislatura en el 1r. Año de su Ejercicio." Tuxtla Gutiérrez: Talleres Tipográficos del Gobierno del estado.
1934   "Informe que el C. Gobernador Victorico Grajales rinde a la XXXV Legislatura en el 2do Año de su Ejercicio." Tuxtla Gutiérrez: Talleres Tipográficos del Gobierno del estado.

Greschat, Hans-Jürgen
1967   *Kitawala: Ursprung, Ausbreitung und Religion der Watch-Tower-Bewegung in Zentralafrika.* Berlin: Elwert Verlag Marburg.

Grupo de Mujeres de San Cristóbal
1994   "Memorias del Encuentro-Taller: Los derechos de las mujeres en nuestras costumbres y tradiciones." Ms. May.

Guha, Ranajit
1988   "The Prose of Counter-Insurgency." In *Selected Subaltern Studies*, ed. Ranajit Guha and Gayatri Chakravorty Spivak, 45–86. New York: Oxford University Press.

Gupta, Akhil
1993   "Blurred Boundaries: The Discourse of Corruption, The Culture of Politics, and the Imagined State." Ms. Department of Anthropology, Stanford University.

Gutelman, Michel
1980   *Capitalismo y reforma agraria en México.* Mexico City: Ed. Era.

Gutiérrez, Efraín
1937   "Informe que el C. Gobernador Ing. Efraín Gutiérrez rinde a la XXXVII Legislatura en el 1r Año de su Ejercicio." Tuxtla Gutiérrez: Talleres Tipográficos del Gobierno del estado.
1938   "Informe que el C. Gobernador Ing. Efraín Gutiérrez rinde a la XXXVII Legislatura en el 2do Año de su Ejercicio." Tuxtla Gutiérrez: Talleres Tipográficos del Gobierno del estado.
1941   "Informe que el C. Gobernador Ing. Efraín Gutiérrez rinde a la XXXVII Legislatura en el 4to Año de su Ejercicio." Tuxtla Gutiérrez: Talleres Tipográficos del Gobierno del estado.

Gutiérrez, Margarita, and Nellys Palomo
1999   "Autonomía con mirada de mujer." In *México: Experiencias de autonomía indígena*, ed. Aracely Burguete, 54–86. Copenhagen: IWGIA-CECADEPI-RAP.

Gutiérrez Alfonzo, Carlos
1996   "Después del silencio: Historia oral de los Mames de Chiapas." Honors thesis, National School of Anthropology and History, Mexico City.

Guzmán Böckler, Carlos, and Jean-Loup Herbert
1970   *Guatemala: Una interpretación histórico social.* Mexico City: Ed. Siglo XXI.

Hale, Charles
1994   *Resistance and Contradiction: Miskitu Indians and the Nicaraguan State, 1894–1987*. Stanford, Calif.: Stanford University Press.

Hall, Stuart
1981   "Notes on Deconstructing 'The Popular.'" In *People's History and Socialist Theory*, ed. Raphael Samuel, 70–97. London: Routledge and Kegan Paul.

Hamilton, Nora
1982   *The Limits of State Autonomy in Post-Revolutionary Mexico*. Princeton: Princeton University Press.

Handler, Richard, and Jocelyn Linnekin
1984   "Tradition, Genuine or Spurious." *Journal of American Folklore* 97(385):273–290.

Harvey, David
1990   *The Condition of Postmodernity: An Enquiry into the Origins of Cultural Change*. New York: Blackwell.

Harvey, Neil
1989   "Corporatist Strategies and Popular Responses in Rural México: State and Oppression in Chiapas, 1970–1988." Ph.D. dissertation, University of Essex.
1994   *Rebellion in Chiapas: Rural Reforms, Campesino Radicalism, and the Limits of Salinismo*. Transformation of Rural Mexico No. 5. San Diego: Center for U.S.-Mexican Studies, University of California, San Diego.
1996   "Redefining Citizenship: Indigenous Movements in Chiapas." Ms. Department of Government, New Mexico State University.
1998   *The Chiapas Rebellion: The Struggle for Land and Democracy*. Durham: Duke University Press.

Hawkins, John
1984   *Inverse Images: The Meaning of Culture, Ethnicity, and Family in Postcolonial Guatemala*. Albuquerque: University of New Mexico Press.

Héau de Giménez, Catherine
1994   "Historia narrada e historia vivida." In *Oralidad y cultura: La identidad, la memoria, lo estético y lo maravilloso*, ed. Jerman Argueta and Ernesto Licona, 35–44. Mexico City: Ed. CONACULTA.

Hernández Castillo, Rosalva Aída
1987   "Mecanismos de reproducción social y cultural entre los refugiados Kanjobales en Chiapas." Honors thesis, National School of Anthropology and History (ENAH), Mexico City.
1989   "Del Tzolkin a La Atalaya: Los cambios en la religiosidad en una comunidad Chuj-K'anjobal de Chiapas." *Religión y Sociedad en el Sureste de México* 2. Cuadernos de la Casa Chata No. 162. Mexico City: CIESAS/SEP/CONAFE.
1991   "Cuando el idioma regresó al ejido." *Ojarasca* 2 (November):54–55.
1992   "Entre la victimización y la resistencia étnica: Revisión crítica de la bibliografía sobre protestantismo en Chiapas." *Anuario del Instituto Chiapaneco de Cultura* (Tuxtla Gutiérrez):165–187.
1994   "Identidades colectivas en los márgenes de la nación: Cambio religioso entre los Mames de Chiapas." *Nueva Antropología* 13, no. 45(April):83–105.
1998a   "Between Hope and Despair: The Struggle of Organized Women in Chiapas

since the Zapatista Uprising." *Journal of Latin American Anthropology* 2(3):77–99.

1998b   *La otra palabra: Mujeres y violencia en Chiapas, antes y después de Acteal.* Mexico City: CIESAS/COLEM/CIAM.

Hernández Castillo, Rosalva Aída, Shannan Mattiace, and Jan Rus, eds.

N.d.   *The Indigenous People of Chiapas in the Wake of the Zapatista Rebellion.*

Hernández Castillo, Rosalva Aída, and Ronald Nigh

1998   "Global Processes and Local Identity: Indians of the Sierra Madre of Chiapas and the International Organic Market." *American Anthropologist* 100, no. 1(January):1–12.

Hernández Castillo, Rosalva Aída, and Héctor Ortíz Elizondo

1996   "Constitutional Amendments and New Imaginings of the Nation: Legal Anthropology and Gendered Perspectives on Multicultural Mexico." *Political and Legal Anthropology Review* 19(1):59–69.

Hernández Castillo, Rosalva Aída, Norma Nava Zamora, José Luis Escalona Victoria, and Carlos Flores Arenales

1992   *La Experiencia de refugio: Nuevas relaciones en la frontera sur.* Mexico City: Ed. SEP/CIESAS/UNRISD/AMDH.

Hernández Navarro, Luis

1991   "Autonomía y desarrollo: La lucha en el campo a la hora de la concertación." *Cuadernos Desarrollo de Base* 2:101–134.

1995   *Chiapas: La Guerra y la Paz.* Mexico City: Ed. ADN.

Hernández Navarro, Luis, and Fernando Célis Callejas

1994   "Solidarity and the New Campesino Movements: The Case of Coffee Production." In *Transforming State-Society Relations in Mexico: The National Solidarity Strategy,* ed. Wayne Cornelius, Ann L. Craig, and Jonathan Fox, 217–232. U.S. Contemporary Perspectives Series No. 6. San Diego: Center for U.S.-Mexican Studies, University of California, San Diego.

Hobsbawm, Eric, and Terence Ranger

1983   *The Invention of Tradition.* Cambridge: Cambridge University Press.

Hodges, Tony

[1976] 1985   *Jehovah's Witnesses in Africa.* Report No. 29. London: Minority Rights Group.

Human Rights Watch/Americas

1997   *Implausible Deniability: State Responsibility for Rural Violence in Mexico.* New York: Human Rights Watch.

Instituto Nacional Indigenista (INI)

1965   "Reacomodo de los excedentes de población de los Altos de Chiapas en Las Margaritas." Ms. San Cristóbal de las Casas, Chiapas.

1978   *INI treinte años después: Revisión crítica.* Mexico City: México Indígena INI.

1982a   *Mames y Mochós.* Mexico City: Ed. INI.

1982b   *INI: Memoria de actividades 1976–1982.* Mexico City: Ed. INI.

1992   "Fondos PRONASOL." Ms.

ISMAM

1990   "Diagnóstico de la Sociedad Cooperativa Indígenas de la Sierra Madre de Motozintla." Ms. Motozintla.

Jameson, Fredric
1989   *Documentos de cultura, documentos de barbarie.* Madrid: Ed. Paidos.
1990   *Postmodernism, or the Cultural Logic of Late Capitalism.* Durham: Duke University Press.
Joseph, Gilbert, and Daniel Nugent, eds.
1994   *Everyday Forms of State Formation: Revolution and the Negotiation of Rule in Modern Mexico.* Durham: Duke University Press.
Kaplan, William
1989   *State and Salvation: The Jehovah's Witnesses and Their Fight for Civil Rights.* Toronto: University of Toronto Press.
Kearney, Michael
1991   "Borders and Boundaries of State and Self at the End of Empire." *Journal of Historical Sociology* 4(1):52–74.
Laclau, Ernesto, and Chantal Mouffe
1985   *Hegemony and Socialist Strategy: Towards a Radical Democratic Politics.* London: Verso.
Lash, Scott, and John Urry
1994   *Economics of Signs and Space.* London: Sage.
Le Bott, Ivone
1995   *La Guerra en tierras mayas: Comunidad, violencia y modernidad en Guatemala, 1970–1992.* México D.F.: Fondo de Cultura Económica.
Leman, Johan
1979   "Jehovah's Witnesses and Immigration in Continental Western Europe." *Social Compass* (Belgium) 26:41–72.
León Portilla, Miguel
1997   "Autonomía indígena." *La Jornada,* August 8:9.
Levine, Daniel
1992   *Popular Voices in Latin American Catholicism.* Princeton: Princeton University Press.
Leyva Solano, Xochitl, and Gabriel Ascencio
1996   *Lacandonia al filo del agua.* Mexico City: CIESAS/CIHMECH/UNICAH/FCE.
Limón, Fernando
1995   "Construcción de identidades entre los cafeticultores orgánicos de Tziscao, Chiapas." Master's thesis, El Colegio de la Frontera Sur, San Cristóbal de las Casas, Chiapas.
Linnekin, Jocelyn
1983   "Defining Tradition: Variation on Hawaiian Identity." *American Ethnologist* 10: 241–252.
Lobato, Rodolfo
1979   "Qu'ixin qui'nal: La colonización Tzeltal de la selva Lacandona." Honors thesis, National School of Anthropology and History (ENAH), Mexico City.
Lomnitz-Adler, Claudio
1992   *Exits from the Labyrinth: Culture and Ideology in the Mexican National Space.* Berkeley: University of California Press.

López Paniagua, Rosalía

1980   "Investigación social sobre conocimiento de area del Centro Coordinador Mam-Mochó-Cakchiquel." Ms.

Lowenhaupt Tsing, Anna

1993   *In the Realm of the Diamond Queen: Marginality in an Out-of-the-Way Place.* Princeton: Princeton University Press.

Lyotard, Jean-François

[1984] 1993   *La condición postmoderna.* Trans. Mariano Antolín Rato. Mexico City: Ed. Iberoamericana.

Mallon, Florencia E.

1995   *Peasant and Nation: The Making of Postcolonial México and Peru.* Berkeley: University of California Press.

Martínez Peláez, Severo

1970   *La patria del criollo.* Guatemala: Ed. Universitaria.

Masse, Raymond

1978   "Les Adventistes du Septième Jour aux Antilles françaises: Anthropologie d'une espérance." *Revue Canadienne de Sociologie et d'Anthropologie* (Montreal) 15:452–465.

Mato, Daniel, ed.

1994   *Teoría y política de la construcción de identidades y diferencias en América Latina y el Caribe.* Caracas: UNESCO/Ed. Nueva Sociedad.

1995   "Complexes of Brokering and Global-Local Connections: Considerations Based on Cases in 'Latin' America." Paper presented at the Annual Meeting of the Latin American Studies Association, Washington, D.C., September 28–30.

Mattiace, Shannan L.

1998   "Peasant and Indian: Political Identity and Indian Autonomy in Chiapas, Mexico (1970–1990)." Ph.D. dissertation, University of Texas, Austin.

Medina, Andrés

1967   "Diario de Campo, rescate etnográfico de la región Mame de Chiapas para el Museo Nacional de Antropología Sierra Madre." Ms.

1973   "Notas etnográficas sobre los Mames de Chiapas." *Anales de Antropología*, no. 10. Mexico City: Instituto de Investigaciones Antropológicas, Universidad Nacional Autónoma de México.

1994   "Ricardo Pozas en la trama de la antropología mexicana." Ms.

Middlebrook, Kevin

1995   *The Paradox of Revolution: Labor, the State and Authoritarianism in Mexico.* Baltimore: Johns Hopkins University Press.

Moguel, Julio

1994   "The Mexican Left and the Social Program of Salinism." In *Transforming State-Society Relations in Mexico: The National Solidarity Strategy*, ed. Wayne Cornelius, Ann L. Craig, and Jonathan Fox, 9–38. U.S. Contemporary Perspectives Series No. 6. San Diego: Center for U.S.-Mexican Studies, University of California, San Diego.

Montemayor, Felipe

1954   "Los efectos de la oncocercosis en la población de Acacoyagua, Chiapas." Honors thesis, National School of Anthropology and History (ENAH), Mexico City.

Morales Bermúdez, Jesús
1992   "El Congreso Indígena de Chiapas: Un testimonio." *Anuario del Instituto Chiapaneco de Cultura* (Tuxtla Gutiérrez):241–371.

Morquecho, Gaspar
1992   "Los indios en un proceso de organización: La Organización Indígena de los Altos de Chiapas, ORIACH." Honors thesis, Chiapas State University (UNACH), San Cristóbal de las Casas.

Mouffe, Chantal
1996   "Democratic Politics and the Question of Identity." In *The Identity in Question*, ed. John Rajchman, 33–47. New York: Routledge.

Myhre, David
1996   "Appropriate Agricultural Credit: A Missing Piece of Agrarian Reform in Mexico." In *Reforming Mexico's Agrarian Reform*, ed. Laura Randall, 117–138. New York: M. E. Sharpe.

Navarrete, Carlos
1978   *Un reconocimiento de la Sierra Madre de Chiapas, apuntes de un Diario de Campo*. Mexico City: Ed. UNAM.

Nelson, Diane Michele
1995   "A Finger in the Wound: Ethnicity, Nation and Gender in the Body Politics of Quincentenniel Guatemala." Ph.D. dissertation, Stanford University.

Nigh, Ronald
1992   "La agricultura orgánica y el nuevo movimiento campesino en México." *Antropológicas Nueva Epoca* 3:39–50.
1994   "Cambio tecnológico y cambio político: La propuesta de la agricultura orgánica para el campo mexicano." Paper presented at the symposium Desarrollo Sustentable Base, Latin American Studies Association (LASA), Atlanta, April.
1997   "Organic Agriculture and Globalization: A Maya Associative Corporation in Chiapas, México." *Human Organization* 56, no. 4 (Winter):427–436.

Nolasco, Margarita
1985   *Café y sociedad en México*. Mexico City: Centro de Ecodesarrollo.

Nordstrom, Carolyn
1997   *A Different Kind of War Story*. Philadelphia: University of Pennsylvania Press.

Ong, Aihwa
1995   "Postcolonial Nationalism: Women and Retraditionalization in the Islamic Imaginary, Malaysia." In *Feminism, Nationalism and Militarism*, ed. Constance R. Sutton, 9–19. Arlington, Va.: American Anthropological Association.

Ovalle Fernández, Ignacio
1978   "Bases programáticas de la política indigenista: Un esquema participativo." In *INI treinte años después: Revisión crítica*, 9–21. México City: México Indígena INI.

Paniagua, Jorge, and Toledo Sonia
1989   "Panorama histórico del desarrollo socioeconómico de la Sierra Madre de Chiapas." Honors thesis, National School of Anthropology and History (ENAH), Mexico City.

Parker, Andrew, Mary Russo, Doris Sommer, and Patricia Yaeger
1992 *Nationalisms and Sexualities.* New York: Routledge.

Paz Salinas, María Fernanda
1989 "La migración a Las Margaritas: Una historia a dos voces." Honors thesis, Chiapas State University (UNACH), San Cristóbal de las Casas.

Pedrero, Gloria
1984 "El proceso de acumulación originaria en el agro Chiapaneco, Siglo XIX." In *Investigaciones recientes del area Maya San Cristóbal de las Casas.* Chiapas: XVII Mesa Redonda, Sociedad Mexicana de Antropología.

Pellicer de Brody, Olga, and Esteban Mancilla
1978 *Historia de la Revolución mexicana: El entendimiento con los Estados Unidos y la gestación del desarrollo estabilizador (1952–1960).* Mexico City: El Colegio de México.

Pellicer de Brody, Olga, and José Luis Reyna
1978 *Historia de la Revolución mexicana: El afianzamiento de la estabilidad política (1952–1960).* Mexico City: El Colegio de México.

Penton, M. James
1976 *Jehovah's Witnesses in Canada: Champions of Freedom of Speech and Worship.* Toronto: Macmillan of Canada.
1985 *Apocalypse Delayed: The Story of the Jehovah's Witnesses.* Toronto: University of Toronto Press.

Pérez, Gloria, and Scott Robinson
1983 *La misión detrás de la misión.* Mexico City: Claves Latinoamericanas, COPEC/ CECOPE/CADAL.

Pohlenz, Juan
1985 "La conformación de la frontera entre México y Guatemala: El caso de Nuevo Huixtán en la selva chiapaneca." In *La formación histórica de la Frontera Sur.* Mexico City: CIESAS-Sureste.

Ponce, Patricia
1986 *Palabra viva del Soconusco.* Mexico City: Colección Frontera SEP/Programa Cultural de las Fronteras.

Poniatowska, Elena
1971 *La noche de Tlatelolco.* Mexico City: Ed. Era.

Pozas, Ricardo
1948 *Juan Pérez Jolote: Biografía de un Tzotzil.* Mexico City: Ed. FCE.
1952a "Los Mames de la región oncocercosa del estado de Chiapas." *Anales del Instituto de Antropología e Historia* 32:252–261.
1952b "El trabajo en las plantaciones de café y el cambio sociocultural del indio." *Revista Mexicana de Estudios Antropológicos, Sociedad Mexicana de Antropología* 13(1):31–48.
1962 "Los Mames: Guión museográfico." Mexico City: INAH/SEP.
1976 *Antropología y burocracia indigenista.* Cuadernos para Trabajadores No. 1. Mexico City: Ed. Tlacuilo.

Preciado Llamas, Juan
1978 "Reflexiones teórico-metodológicas para el estudio de la colonización de Chiapas." *Economía Campesina y Capitalismo Dependiente* (UNAM), pp. 45–67.

Price, Richard
1983   *First-Time: The Historical Vision of an Afro-American People.* Baltimore: Johns Hopkins University Press.
1990   *Alabi's World.* Baltimore: Johns Hopkins University Press.

Procuraduría Agraria
1993   *Nueva legislación agraria.* Mexico City: Unidad de Comunicación Social de la Procuraduría Agraria.

Ramos Solórsano, Cristóbal
1995   "ISMAM, una organización ejemplar." *El Orbe* (Tapachula), May 28:3.

Rappaport, Joanne
1990   *The Politics of Memory: Native Historical Interpretation in the Colombian Andes.* Cambridge: Cambridge University Press.

Regino Montes, Adelfo
1997   "La reconstitución indígena." *La Jornada,* October 21:16.

Renard, Cristina
1993   *El Soconusco, una economía cafetalera.* Mexico City: Universidad Autónoma de Chapingo.
1999   *Los intersticios de la globalización: Un label (Max Havelaar) para los pequeños productores de café.* Mexico City: CEMCA/Embajada de los Países Bajos/ISMAM/CEPCO/Departamento de Sociología Rural.

Reyes Osorio, Sergio, Rodolfo Stavenhagen, and Salomón Eckstein, eds.
1979   *Estructura agraria y desarrollo agrícola en México.* Mexico City: Fondo de Cultura Económica.

Robertson, Roland
1990   "Mapping the Global Condition: Globalization as the Central Concept." *Theory, Culture and Society* 7:15–30.

Rojas, Rosa
1996   *Chiapas ¿Y las Mujeres Qué?* 2 vols. Mexico City: La Correa Feminista.

Rosaldo, Renato
1989   *Culture and Truth: The Remaking of Social Analysis.* Boston: Beacon Press.
1993   "Reimaginando comunidades nacionales." In *Decadencia y auge de las identidades,* ed. José Manuel Valenzuela Arce, 191–201. Tijuana: El Colegio de la Frontera Norte.

Rosas Kifuri, Mauricio
1978   "Investigación previa a la instalación del CCI de Mazapa de Madero." Ms. Mazapa de Madero, Chiapas.

Roseberry, William
1994   "Hegemony and the Language of Contention." In *Everyday Forms of State Formation: Revolution and the Negotiation of Rule in Modern Mexico,* ed. James C. Scott, Gilbert M. Joseph and Daniel Nugent, 355–366. Durham: Duke University Press.

Rosenbaum, Brenda
1993   *With our Heads Bowed: The Dynamics of Gender in a Maya Community.* Albany: Institute of Mesoamerican Studies, State University of New York.

Rouse, Roger
1991 "Mexican Migration and the Social Space of Post-Modernism." *Diaspora* 1(1):8–23.

Rubin, Jeffrey W.
1997 *Decentering the Regime: Ethnicity, Radicalism and Democracy in Juchitán, Mexico.* Durham: Duke University Press.

Rus, Jan
1994 "The Comunidad Revolucionaria Institucional: The Subversion of Native Government in Highland Chiapas, 1936–1968." In *Everyday Forms of State Formation: Revolution and the Negotiation of Rule in Modern Mexico,* ed. James C. Scott, Gilbert M. Joseph and Daniel Nugent, 265–300. Durham: Duke University Press.

Rus, Jan, and Robert Wasserstrom
1979 "Evangelización y control político: El ILV en México." *Revista Mexicana de Ciencias Políticas y Sociales* (Universidad Nacional Autónoma de México), no. 97.

Ruz, Mario Humberto, ed.
1986 *Los legítimos hombres: Aproximación antropológica al grupo tojolabal.* Vols. I–IV. Mexico City: Universidad Nacional Autónoma de México.
1985 *Copanaguastla en un espejo: Un pueblo Tzeltal en el Virreinato.* San Cristóbal de las Casas: Centro de Estudios Indígenas, UNACH.
1992 *Savia india, floración ladina: Apuntes para una historia de las fincas comitecas (siglos XVIII y XIX).* Serie Regiones. Mexico City: CONACULTA.

Sánchez, Roberto
1990 *Manual práctico del cultivo biológico del café orgánico.* Motozintla: ISMAM/S.O.S.

Santiago, Jorge
1980 "El Congreso Indígena." *El Caminante* (San Cristóbal de las Casas), no. 26.

Schumann, Otto
1969 "El tuzanteco y su posición dentro de la familia mayanse." *Anales del Instituto Nacional de Antropología e Historia* 49(1):139–148.

Scott, James C.
1985 *Weapons of the Weak: Everyday Forms of Peasant Resistance.* New Haven: Yale University Press.

Sholto, Cross
1977 "Social History and Millennial Movements: The Watch Tower in South Central Africa." *Social Compass* (Belgium) 24:83–95.

Sierra, Teresa
1997 "Esencialismo y autonomía: Paradojas de la reivindicaciones indígenas." *Alteridades* 7(14):131–143.

Spenser, Daniela
1988 *El partido socialista chiapaneco: Rescate y reconstrucción de su historia.* Mexico City: Ediciones de la Casa Chata CIESAS/SEP.

Stavenhagen, Rodolfo, and Diego Iturralde
1990 *Entre la ley y la costumbre: El derecho consuetudinario indígena en América Latina.* Mexico City: Instituto Indigenista Interamericano de Derechos Humanos.

Stevenson, W. C.
1967 *The Year of Doom, 1975: The Story of the Jehovah's Witnesses.* London: Hutchinson.

Stoll, David
1990 *Is Latin America Turning Protestant? The Politics of Evangelical Growth.* Berkeley: University of California Press.

Sullivan, Paul
[1989] 1991 *Conversaciones inconclusas: Mayas y extranjeros entre dos guerras.* Trans. Carlos Gardini. Barcelona: Ed. Gedisa.

Tello, Carlos
1995 *La rebelión de las Cañadas.* Mexico City: Cal y Arena.

Toledo, Victor
1994 "La vía ecológico-campesina de desarrollo: Una alternativa para la selva de Chiapas." *La Jornada del Campo* 2(23):4–6.

Ulin, Robert C.
1995 "Invention and Representation as Cultural Capital." *American Anthropologist* 97(3):519–527.

Varese, Stefano
1989 "Multiethnicity and Hegemonic Construction: Indian Plans and the Future." In *Ethnicities and Nations*, ed. Remo Guidieri, Francesco Pellizzi and Stanley J. Tambiah, 57–78. Austin: University of Texas Press.

Vargas, Lucila
1994 *Social Uses and Radio Practices: The Use of Participatory Radio by Ethnic Minorities in Mexico.* Boulder, Colo.: Westview Press.

Vasconcelos, José
[1925] 1992 *La raza cósmica: Misión de la raza iberoamericana.* Mexico City: Colección Austral ESPASA-CALPE Mexicana.

Velasco, Jesús Agustín
1979 *El desarrollo comunitario de la Sierra Madre de Chiapas.* Mexico City: Ed. UNAM.

Velasco Suárez, Manuel
1974 "Discurso del Gobernador Velasco Suárez en el Congreso Indígena de San Cristóbal." Ms. October. DESMI Archive.

Viqueira, Juan Pedro
1999 "Los peligros del Chiapas imaginario." *Letras Libres* 1, no. 1 (January):20–28.

Villafuerte, Daniel, ed.
1993 *El café en la Frontera Sur: La producción y los productores del Soconusco, Chiapas.* Serie Nuestros Pueblos. Mexico, D.F.: ICHC.

Vogt, Evon Z.
1978 *Bibliography of the Harvard Chiapas Project: The First Twenty Years, 1957–1977.* Cambridge, Mass.: Harvard University Press.

Wagley, Charles
1949 "The Social and Religious Life of a Guatemalan Village." *American Anthropologist* 51:30–48.

Waibel, Leo
1946 *La Sierra Madre de Chiapas.* Mexico City: Sociedad Mexicana de Geografía y Estadística.

Warman, Arturo
1970   "Todos Santos y todos difuntos: Crítica histórica de la Antropología Mexicana."
        In *De eso que llaman antropología mexicana*, ed. Arturo Warman, Margarita No-
        lasco, Guillermo Bonfil, Mercedes Olivera, and Enrique Valencia, 9–38. Mexico
        City: Ed. Nuestro Tiempo.
1989   "Plan de trabajo del INI (1989–1994)." Ms.
Warman, Arturo, Margarita Nolasco, Guillermo Bonfil, Mercedes Olivera, and Enrique Valencia
1970   *De eso que llaman antropología mexicana*. Mexico City: Ed. Nuestro Tiempo.
Warren, Kay B.
1992   "Transforming Memories and Histories: The Meaning of Ethnic Resurgence
        for Mayan Indians." In *Americas: New Interpretive Essays*, ed. E. Alfred Stepan,
        28–45. New York: Oxford University Press.
Wasserstrom, Robert
1989   *Clase y sociedad en el centro de Chiapas*. México City, D.F.: Ed. FCE.
Watanabe, John
1992   *Maya Saints and Soul in a Changing World*. Austin: University of Texas Press.
Watchtower Bible and Tract Society
1985   *Annual Report*. New York: Watchtower Press.
Willis, Paul E.
1981   *Learning to Labor: How Working-Class Kids Get Working-Class Jobs*. New York:
        Teachers College Press.
Wilson, Bryan
1970   *Sociología de las sectas religiosas*. Biblioteca para el Hombre Actual. Madrid: Ed.
        Guadarrama.
Wood, Davida
1995   "Feminist Perspectives on Palestinian Political Culture under Occupation." In
        Feminism, Nationalism and Militarism, ed. Constance R. Sutton, 20–31. Arling-
        ton, Va.: American Anthropological Association.
Zarate Hernández, Eduardo
1994   *Los señores de Utopia: Etnicidad política en una comunidad purepecha*. Zamora:
        CIESAS/El Colegio de Michoacán.

Archival Material

Internal Reports of the CCI Mam-Mochó-Cakchiquel (1979–1994)
Mazapa de Madero Town Hall Acts (1920–1940)
Periódicos Oficiales (State Official Journals) (1930–1950)
Siltepec Town Hall Acts (1930–1940)

Journals

Acción Indigenista (1970–1980)
Boletín Chiapas al Día, Centro de Investigaciones Económicas y Políticas de Acción Co-
        munitaria A.C. (CIEPAC) (1997–1999)
El Día (1980–1990)
Excelsior (1934)
La Jornada (1994–1995)

Resumen Informativo del Centro de Análisis e Información de Chiapas (1989–1999)
Semanario Popular (1933–1940)
El Sureste de Chiapas (1994–1995)
La Vanguardia (1934–1940)
Uno Más Uno (1980–1990)

INDEX

CPSIA information can be obtained
at www.ICGtesting.com
Printed in the USA
FFOW03n0134090917
39748FF